Surfing & Health

British Library Cataloguing in Publication Data
A catalogue record for this book is available from the British Library

Surfing & Health
Maidenhead: Meyer & Meyer Sport (UK) Ltd., 2009
ISBN 978-1-84126-263-5

© 2009 by Meyer & Meyer Sport (UK) Ltd.
Aachen, Adelaide, Auckland, Budapest, Cape Town, Graz, Indianapolis,
Maidenhead, Olten (CH), Singapore, Toronto
Member of the World
Sport Publishers' Association (WSPA)
www.w-s-p-a.org
Printed by: B.O.S.S Druck und Medien GmbH
ISBN: 978-1-84126-263-5
E-Mail: info@m-m-sports.com
www.m-m-sports.com

SURFING & HEALTH

Dr. Joel Steinman

Meyer & Meyer Sport

Dedication

To God, for the creation.

To the memory of my father, Dr. Luiz Steinman, who introduced me, with wisdom, to the art of life and medicine.

To the love and affection of my mother, who helped me jump over my first waves.

To the love of my children, Rodrigo, Gabriel, Sam and Victor, and to my wife, Ana Cristina, who enlighten and teach me.

Photos: Flavio Vidigal

Fabio Gouveia –
Fernando de Noronha Archipelago, Braz

Acknowledgements

**To my surfing patients,
who honor me by trusting me with their health.**

I thank the following for their support:

Mormaii

Association of Professional Surfers – ASP

Association of Professional Surfers – South America

International Surfing Association – ISA

Pan American Surfing Association – PASA

Brazilian Confederation of Surf – CBS

The Santa Catarina Surf Federation – Fecasurf

Joaquina Surfing Association – ASJ

Tao Pilates Institute of Sports Medicine
– www.taopilates.com.br

Photo: James Thisted

Praia das Pitangueiras
(1971)
Carbone   Dr. Joel
Neco   Steinman
Carbone

Dr. Joel Steinman

Dr. Steinman earned his medical degree from the Santa Casa College of Medical Sciences of São Paulo, Brazil in 1982. He comes from a family of doctors and has been surfing for more than 30 years.

Convinced of the beneficial effects that surfing has on health and for spirit, the author has exercised the art of medicine and surfed in various places and countries, such as Hawaii, Indonesia, Australia, Fiji, Portugal, Spain, Israel, France, Panama, Mexico, Peru, to name a few.

Dr. Steinman conducted extensive postgraduate studies in Sports Medicine in Australia, studied acupuncture in China and Spine Manipulation-Chiropraxy in Brazil. His medical degree is in pediatrics. Inspired by several fellow members of the SURFERS'S MEDICAL ASSOCIATION, Dr. Mark Renneker, Dr. Geoff Both, Dr. Simon Leslie, Prof. Brian Lowdon (in memoriam) for a number of years, he has written a medical column for Brazil's leading surf magazines, such as the former Magazine *Inside* and then Magazine *Fluir*. He is the doctor for the Santa Catarina Surf Federation and the Brazilian Confederation of Surfing and has been the Medical officer for the Brazilian World Surfing Contest (WCT) in Brazil since 2002.

He is the author of various articles about sports medicine, nutrition and meditation, and published a pioneer study on sports injuries and accidents in Brazil.

A practitioner of Pilates, qigong, yoga and natural medicine, Dr. Steinman has participated in various courses and programs concerning holistic and preventive health in various communities, including Grajagan in Indonesia and Tavarua in Fiji.

He is a member of the Surfer's Medical Association, the Brazilian Society of Sports Medicine, the Brazilian Society of Rehabilitation Medicine and the Brazilian Medical Society of Acupuncture. Dr. Steinman lives with his family in Florianópolis, on the island of Santa Catarina, where he surfs and directs the TAO PILATES Institute of Sports Medicine that offers top a quality medical and health team for "sportspeople." TAO PILATES Institute offers quality courses and workshops in Brazil and Europe for health professionals on Pilates for Medical Rehabilitation and Training, Spinal Manipulation and Meditation.

Contents

INTRODUCTION

Surfers have been blazing the trail of adventure in true pioneering spirit for nearly 100 years. Ever since legendary Hawaiian waterman Duke Kahanamoku gifted surfing to the world, generation after generation has spread the seeds of surfing to every coastline on the planet. It is well documented that surfers are the modern-day Marco Polos, mapping uncharted waters, discovering exotic new breaks, interacting with ancient cultures and developing a lifestyle that is the envy of the free world.

On these expeditions of discovery, surfers have had to adapt to changing environments and develop a code of risk management that has been handed on to the next traveller through word of mouth and story. Trekking into the unknown is a time-honored rite of passage for any true surfer; the very essence of the surfing lifestyle requires a spirit of nomadic adventure. It has been more a case of trial and error that we step bravely into unknown lands and, at times, horror stories emerge from surfers in far-off lands completely unprepared to deal with reef cuts, infections, tropical disease, fin lacerations, waterborne illness, broken bones, debilitating injury, malnutrition and encounters with marine creatures.

In time-honored fashion, surfers refined travelling first aid kits and gleaned health tips and the means to avoiding tropical disease through information handed down generationally by their fellow travelling surfers. However, surfers have been crying out for a comprehensive journal that covers the entire gamut of health issues in surfing, from A to Z.

It is with great pleasure that I present *Surfing & Health* by Joel Steinman. For many years, Joel has compiled information and techniques from both his personal travels and experiences, as well as from a research of best practices in many areas of health and from all corners of the world. From all that living data, Joel has created what is no less than an encyclopedia of health, all related to surfing and with the objective of not only being educational but to promote a state of health and well-being as one enjoys the surfing experience.

Surfing & Health is a wonderful contribution by a truly inspirational surfer.

Wayne Rabbit Bartholomew
1978 World Surfing Champion
President ASP International

PREFACE

Some basic medical concepts apply to all sports. But the further we plunge into the field, the more we find that each sport has its own characteristics.

Surfing, as a sport of mass appeal, is a recent phenomenon and the advantages and dangers of its practice have never before been considered in such depth.

Santa Catarina, in southern Brazil, is a perfect place to surf, where numerous events, including those on the WCT and WQS circuits, attract the world's best surfers and an enormous number of fans.

It is here that Dr. Joel Steinman, who is also an excellent surfer, has attended to and treated countless surf-related injuries. This experience makes him an authority in the field.

This book is an indispensable guide for athletes, especially those who travel to distant locales with little medical support. But it is also for doctors who want to better understand this marvelous, yet sometimes dangerous, world of surf.

Dr. Marco Aurélio Rayundo
Doctor and owner of Mormaii, a pioneering company in the development of surf in Brazil

SURFING & HEALTH

Carlos Burle
Jaws – Hawaii

Photo: Sebastian Rojas

INTRODUCTION

Surfing is a millenary sport. It was born in Polynesia, set root in Hawaii and grew and spread throughout California. It has crossed the oceans and is now practiced on all of the world's beaches where there are good waves.

Surfing purifies the body, mind and spirit.

In Brazil, after many years of marginalization and social discrimination surfing has been taken up by people of all economic classes and professions, and has become recognized as a definitively healthy sport, which places the surfer in deep and direct contact with nature.

The magic of the sport and the search for the perfect wave transform the surfer into a happy, traveling dreamer!

The sound of the waves is the surfer's mantra and the waves themselves are like temples. Each surfer has his or her own Mecca. For many, it would be the Indonesian Archipelago. Its more than 13,000 islands bathed by the Indian Ocean is one of these locations that join the magic, surprise, malaria and countless tubes and dream waves on beaches such as Gland, Nias, West Java, West Sunbawa, the Mentawai Islands and a dozen crests never surfed before.

The paradise islands of the North Pacific are home to the history and legend of the constant, powerful and dangerous waves of Hawaii's north shore, with Pipeline, Sunset and the giant waves of Waiamea and Jaws.

The South Pacific has infinite crystal tubes on the islands of Fiji and Tahitia, where, at the peak of Teahupoo, are found some of the world's most dangerous waves.

Australia also has tremendous opportunity for surf, with consistently great waves. The island continent receives swells from the Indian and Pacific Oceans. The hundreds of waves in the land of the kangaroo and aborigines include: Bell's Beach, Margareth River, Kirra, Burleigh Heads, Angorie, Black Rock, Ulladula, Red Bluff, Turtles, Gnaraloo, Maldives, Ilhas Reuniao and Mauricius Island. They are the dreams of surfers in the Indian Ocean.

The icy waves of Alaska, Greenland, Ireland, and England are not very popular, but they and the somewhat warmer peaks of the French Coast at Hossegor, Biarritz and Lacanau, also offer good times, as does the Spanish coast at Mundaka, and the Portuguese beaches at Peniche, Ericeira and Alagarve.

Although they are not frequent, waves are surfed and worshiped in Israel and during the Italian winter on the coast of Sardenha.

The consistent surf in Morocco, Madeira and the Canary Islands stir the North Atlantic.

The little explored east coast of Africa and the famous peaks of Durban and Jeffrey's Bay to the south represent the opportunities for African surf.

On the Asian coast there are New Guinea, the Philippines and Japan.

The coast of California lives and breathes the culture and business of surf from the mountainous and icy waves of the Mavericks to the north, to the traditional and popular peaks at Santa Cruz, Santa Barbara and San Diego.

In Central America, the fun is found at the Mexican beaches of Baja California, Rio Nexpa and Puerto Escondido, and in the tropical surf in El Salvador, Costa Rica, Panama, and the Carribean islands of Puerto Rico, Barbados and other beaches.

South America takes the spotlight with the surf in the Galápagos and Montanita in Ecuador, with the consistent Peruvian waves at the peaks of Pacasmayo, Chicama and Punta Hermosa and is revealed in the icy waves of Chile, from Iquiqui to the north until Punta de Lobos to the south.

Opportunities for surf in Brazil range from the unique and fantastic river waves of the pororoca in the Amazon region to the recently discovered Tahiatian style waves at Lobos Island in Torres, Rio Grande do Sul. They include the surf paradise of Fernando de Noronha, the waves of the Northeast, the peaks in Rio de Janeiro and São Paulo, and the 400 km of the Santa Catarina coast with the consistent waves at Imbituba, Praia da Silveira, Praia da Rosa, Campeche, Praia Mole and Joaquina.

This book was written to help the soul surfer or the competitive surfer to realize his or her dream of surfing this infinity of the world's waves. In an in-depth and practical manner, it provides the latest information and essential techniques needed to remain healthy, giving emphasis to physical conditioning, disposition, nutrition and knowledge about prevention and treatment of sports injuries and health risks. In addition to being a serious manual of Sports Medicine, it is also a source of inspiration for a more healthy life and a search for equilibrium of body, mind and spirit.

Good surfing!

AN IMPORTANT MESSAGE

Warning

This book is not meant to be a substitute for professional medical care, but as a supplement for those who want to better understand their health problem.

Before utilizing any type of treatment, always consult your doctor.

Advances in medical science are rapid and some of the information contained in this book about medication and treatment may be subject to change.

Surf and Health!

A sport like surfing should be practiced in good health.
Surf inspires health.
Health is a blessing.
A healthy body, mind and spirit, the health of good food and of the waves.
Our health,
The health of Planet Earth,
The health of the Universe,
The health of the Eternal,
God bless everyone!
Good surfing!

Dr. Joel Steinman

SURFING & HEALTH

Guerry Lopes

The living legend
of world surf calmly surfs a tube

Guerry Lopes

Chapter 1

Master and Senior Surfers
Surfing – The Elixir of Long life

Surfing provides curing energy. It is a sport capable of prolonging and improving quality of life.

This book is for surfers of all ages, shapes, genders and colors. But we will begin by looking at the primary health issues of those surfers whose memories go back before boards had keels and webcams monitored the waves.

Older surfers have significant differences in body composition, aerobic capacity and muscle strength than younger ones. Nevertheless, surfers with many years of regular training have much less decline in these areas than those who do not exercise or participate in sports. Many master surfers have played sports throughout their lives and are strong and flexible, with excellent cardiopulmonary capacity relative to their untrained peers.

Maximum heart rate and, subsequently, cardiac output decrease with age. Blood pressure also increases as blood vessels become less supple and respiratory capacity decreases due to the decreased elasticity of the lungs, chest wall, and pulmonary vasculature. Muscles and bones become weaker, and connective tissue loses flexibility and becomes more susceptible to injury.

Afonso Freitas, 76. He is considered the oldest surfer in Brazil. He is the author of the book Health in Our Hands.

Neuronal atrophy (aging of the nerves) may impair motor response, body awareness, balance, thirst, and thermo-regulation. Fat-free mass typically decreases and body fat increases. Women experience a redistribution of body fat with menopause.

Many of these changes are significantly attenuated by regular surfing combined with exercise that includes aerobic, strength, and flexibility training.

It is important for the weekend surfer to complement surfing with other aerobic sports, such as swimming, cycling, jogging, rowing, or dance, in order to achieve ideal cardiovascular protection. This is the principle of cross training, which is based on the idea that no one sport is complete.

One of the most common diseases related to aging is arteriosclerosis, or the deposit of fats on arterial walls. It begins early, in babies, and progresses with age. There is truth to the saying: "The age of a person is determined by the age of his or her arteries." The more fat on the arterial walls, the greater the difficulty blood will have in reaching the different portions of the body, in particular the heart and the brain, leading to premature aging.

Illustration 1: Increased fat deposits on arterial walls increase the risk of heart attack and stroke.

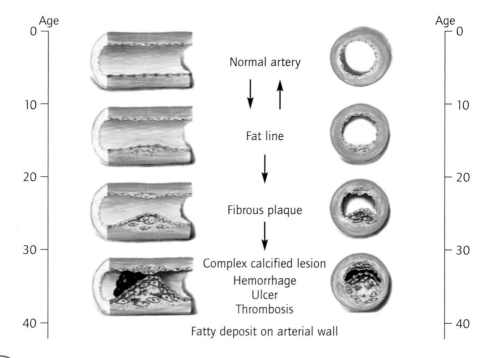

Age
0
Normal artery
10
Fat line
20
Fibrous plaque
30
Complex calcified lesion
Hemorrhage
Ulcer
Thrombosis
40
Fatty deposit on arterial wall

Age
0
10
20
30
40

Arteriosclerosis, also known as chronic degenerative disease, is a leading cause of death. It is most severe among people 50 and older, when heart attack and stroke are most frequent.

With an increasing number of surfers over 50, the prevention of fatty deposits in the arteries is essential so that those who love the waves can continue to surf.

The principal risk factors for the deposit of fat on arterial walls are:

1. Cigarette smoking

2. A sedentary lifestyle

3. High blood pressure

4. Diabetes

5. High levels of cholesterol in the blood

6. Stress

7. Family history of cardiovascular disease

A Healthy Lifestyle is Essential for Prevention

Modern medicine has confirmed that it is possible to reduce the amount of fatty plaque on arterial walls by adopting a lifestyle that most surfers know well and which should include

1. Surfing, lots of surfing

2. Eating natural, whole foods low in salt and sugar, plenty of fruits, vegetables, whole cereals and lean, white meats

3. The control of stress through relaxation programs, such as yoga, pilates, meditation, qigong, etc.

4. Maintaining total cholesterol levels below 200mg/dl of blood after 20 years of age

The Therapeutic Effects of Surfing

Surfing regularly, in addition to reducing sedentary habits, combats obesity and diabetes, and reduces cholesterol, triglycerides, uric acid and blood sugar levels. It also helps to reduce high blood pressure and functions as a natural tranquilizer (except when there's a crowd!). It even decreases the desire for alcohol and cigarettes.

Nevertheless, for an aerobic exercise such as surfing to have a protective effect on the body, it should be practiced under the following conditions:

1. 3-5 times a week
2. For at least 1 hour
3. At an intensity of 65-90% of maximum cardiac frequency, or in other words, surf dynamically

Ari Ciampolini, 74, father of 5 surfers (in memoriam). He built his first board in the 1960s in Guarujá, São Paulo, a hollow plywood plank, with straight edges and no keels.

Surfing and Your Heart and Lungs

In a regular surfing session, a surfer spends 40-50% of the time paddling, 35-40% waiting for a wave and 5-10% surfing.

The average heart rate, during 60 minutes of surfing, is about 135 beats per minute (depending on the individual and the wave conditions). This characterizes surfing as an aerobic sport, which means it's good for your heart.

Aerobic Capacity

Aerobic capacity is the ability of the body to assimilate and distribute oxygen to the muscles. Among men and women, maximum aerobic capacity, known as VO_2 max, (see Chap. 25) typically decreases approximately 10% per decade after age 30. This decrease can be attenuated by surfing.

One study found no change in VO$_2$ max over 10 years in a group that trained 3 hours per week at 86% of VO$_2$ max. Another study found that age-related loss of aerobic capacity was reduced by up to 50% in men who pursued regular endurance training.

The peak heart rate declines about 0.75 beats per minute per year. However, with training, aerobic capacity can increase in both older men and women.

Morongo, a Brazilian medical doctor and Mormaii owner enjoying Brazilian power in the early 70s.

What Happens to the Heart While Surfing?

Because of their training – and at times genetic composition – athletes, particularly those in endurance sports, have hearts that beat more efficiently and thus fewer times per minute than average people. A low heart rate, of about 70 beats per minute or fewer at rest, normally indicates good health and response to training.

Surfing increases the heart's efficiency. The heart rate during surfing is a good parameter by which to measure your aerobic endurance.

The peak heart rate declines about 0.75 beats per minute per year. However, with training, aerobic capacity can increase in older surfers.

How to Calculate the Ideal Heart Rate for Your Aerobic Training Response

To calculate your ideal heart rate during training, use the following formula:

maximum heart rate = 220 – age.

Your heart rate when training should be between 65-80% of your maximum cardiac frequency.

For example, if you are 18 years old, your maximum heart rate should be 202 beats per minute. Thus you should exercise at an intensity where your heart rate is between 121 and 161 beats per minutes, or that is, you should be slightly winded, but still capable of speaking. See the table below to assist your calculation.

Table 1. Maximum Heart rate and zone of aerobic training by age

Age	Maximum Heart Rate	85% of the Maximum heart rate for athletes	recommended zone of 65-80%
20	200	170	130-160
25	195	166	127-156
30	190	162	124-154
35	185	157	120-148
40	180	153	117-144
45	175	149	114-140
50	170	145	111-136
55	165	140	107-132
60	160	136	104-128
65 or more	150	128	98-120

How to Monitor Your Heart Rate

You can monitor your heart rate during training by using a "Polar" monitor strapped with a belt around your chest that sends signals to a special meter that serves as a receiver. These devices usually do not work in the water but offer excellent monitoring during training on land.

If you do not have this type of device, take your pulse manually by lightly placing the index and middle fingers on the wrist or throat, as in the photos below. Count the number of beats in 15 seconds and multiply by 4 to obtain the number of beats per minute.

How to count your heartbeats

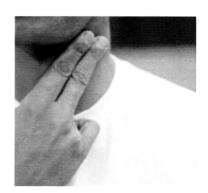

When Should I Calculate My Heart Rate?

Normally, the best moments to take your pulse are

1. In the sixth minute of training (running, bicycling or swimming)
2. In surfing, soon after paddling to the peak or after having surfed a wave
3. When waking up, still in bed, check your pulse at rest

If your pulse at rest is between 50-70 beats per minute this may indicate that surfing is increasing your aerobic capacity by reducing the heart rate at rest. This is good, your heart is working more efficiently!

Training Safety

Preliminary medical evaluation

Attention: If you are older than 30 and decide to begin surfing, running, cycling, or any other sports, you should have a complete medical examination before you begin. This check-up is especially important if you have a family history of heart disease or have been sedentary for a long time, have high blood pressure, diabetes, are overweight, smoke, suffer from stress, tiredness, anxiety, insomnia or have total cholesterol above 200mg/dl of blood. The medical examination will help identify surfing's effect on medication and other possible side effects. It will check for chronic diseases, osteoarthritis and other musculoskeletal risk factors. A treadmill electrocardiography ("stress") test is a basic way to screen for cardiovascular disease and test aerobic fitness.

CAUTIONS

Surfing, as any sport, should be individually modified to allow safe participation by senior athletes with:

- Medical problems requiring multiple medications
- Controlled heart arrhythmias
- Blood pressure problems
- Exercise-induced asthma
- Respiratory infection
- Musculoskeletal injury

Surfing regularly decreases the risk of death from cardiovascular disease. Nonetheless, there is an increased risk of acute cardiovascular problems during or after strenuous exercise, so senior athletes should "cool-down" after each wave and surf session with a light swim or similar activity.

Life guard stations and emergency medical teams should strongly consider having an on-site automated external defibrillator (AED) at master and senior events for basic life support.

Muscle Strength and Size

Functional muscle strength, including "core muscles," are essential for surfing performance and to prevent injuries (see Chapter 24).

With aging, the decline of muscle size parallels the decline of muscle strength. A progressive decrease in muscle size begins in young adulthood. It occurs relatively slowly until about 60 years of age, when the rate of decrease increases.

Functional muscle strength among senior athletes can be positively affected by surfing and a strength and core training program, even those in their 90s.

Morongo, Mormaii pioneer. His healthy lifestyle and positive attitude have not changed at 60 plus years of age.

With surfing, the strength increase is proportionately greater than the increase in muscle size.

It is important to remember that as we age, the years of accumulated microtrauma increases the incidence of tendinosis (tendon degeneration). In addition, senior athletes probably have slower healing, a slower metabolic rate and less effective circulation of oxygen and nutrients. They are therefore at greater risk of injuries, such as strained and sprained tendons.

Although their physiological responses to exercise programs may be slower and less pronounced than in younger athletes, a well-planned training program is often remarkably effective for seniors in decreasing musculoskeletal pain, improving performance and generally improving health and well-being.

The Pleasure of Endorphins

Linked to the pleasure of being in contact with the forces of nature, the aerobic component of surfing stimulates the production of endorphins and other chemical substances in the brain that reduce stress and offer a sense of well-being and positive mood changes.

World-famous U.S. surfer and medical doctor, Dorian Paskowitz, has remained active into his 80s. His basic philosophy of life is a total commitment to health.

Older surfers include:

1. John H. "Doc" Ball was the oldest American surfer when he passed away at the age of 94 in December 2001. He continued to surf throughout his final years. He was also one of the best surfer photographers ever!

2. LeRoy "Granny" Grannis, 83, was a surfer for 67 years. He was Doc Ball's best friend.

3. Woody Brown is 91 and lives in Maui, Hawaii.

4. Anona Napoleon, a 60-year-old-native Hawaiian, has surfed for 50 years.

5. Fred Van Dyke, 73, is a pioneer of big surfing waves. He wrote the classic surfing book, *Thirty Years of Surfing the World's Biggest Waves.*

6. Rabbit Kekai is 81, a waterman and a world-class big wave surfer. He is considered the principal protégé of Duke Kahanamoku, the "Ambassador of Hawaiian Surfing and of the Aloha Spirit."

In addition to surfing and exercise, good health requires a healthy diet, rest, a good night's sleep, leisure and a positive mental attitude.

Scientific studies are indicating that a safe and intelligent hormone replacement therapy is a great strategy to keep muscle strength, general health and performance.

To continue surfing until the end of your life, do not confuse the absence of disease with health. Regular exercise and check-ups are important.

Each day that we consciously seek true health is a day in search of life. If we give up this quest, we allow disease to take over.

Morongo and his athletes!

Morongo in Hawaii

Kelly Slater

9-times World Champion first rode on a surfboard when he was a kid near his home in Cocoa Beach, Florida

Photo: James Thisted

Chapter 2

The Ideal Age to Begin Surfing

The first waves leave a positive impression on the spirit of a young surfer.

Surfing helps the social integration of children and teenagers and stimulates ecological concern. It raises their awareness of the importance of physical, mental and spiritual health.

In locations with strong surf cultures, such as Hawaii, the United States in general, Australia and Brazil, you can find surfers riding the waves with their grandchildren, clear proof that surfing is a sport that can be enjoyed for a lifetime.

While surfing can be practiced into one's 80s, what is the ideal age to introduce children to surfing?

If one of the parents is a surfer, a baby may ride that first wave by its first birthday, and in extreme cases, while still in the womb.

The first wave

Photo: Flavio Vidigal

From 1 to 6 – The first wave

From 1 to 6 years of age, physical activity should be fun and stimulate the development of physical and mental abilities needed in daily activities. These activities should help children develop their aptitude and courage and use their wonderful free time to burn energy.

First board at the swimming pool

Healthy children must be comfortable in the water and know how to swim well in order to surf. Swimming is one of the healthiest sporting activities and can begin at six months.

Playing on the beach, building sand castles, contact with the waves and perhaps paddling a small float are the first steps of the young surfer from 3 to 5 years old.

At this early age, it is recommended that parents use a long board for a child to ride his or her first waves. Its breadth and flotation make it easier to push in the water thus allowing the child to quickly stand up and feel the emotion of the first wave.

Family incentive

From 6 to 12

From 6 to 12 children should begin lessons to acquire experience and contact with various sports.

Children should be introduced to a range of sports, such as swimming, gymnastics, soccer, tennis, tae-kwon-do, basketball, track and field, skating, cycling and, of course, surfing. Each child's physical abilities should be respected and participation should be encouraged without pressure.

Fortunately, there are many surfing schools that can help children to train and play safely.

Children who choose to participate in organized surfing competitions should be advised to engage in a variety of activities that they enjoy and delay sport specialization until adolescence.

However, in sports such as gymnastics, diving, figure skating, and more recently even surfing, children often specialize at a very early age to gain command of the required skills.

We recommend that young surfers participate in other activities to get all the benefits from a cross-training program.

Kids playing near the Mormaii Training Center: "Aragua", Praia Mole, Florianopolis Brazil

Training Response

Strength training may make a critical difference in preventing injuries for those children who specialize in surfing at an early age. Strength training is particularly important for the child who has previously been relatively inactive and then begins intensive sporting activity.

All of the musculoskeletal structures —the bones, musculotendinous units, and ligaments — must gradually and progressively adapt by gaining strength and size to support the demands placed on the child's body. Increased strength occurs mainly from neuromuscular adaptation, and there is little hypertrophy of the skeletal muscle. A strength-training program for children must be well supervised. Many sport injuries in children can be prevented by a program that combines strength and flexibility training. In addition to improved performance, the goals of a youth strength-training program are learning safe strength training principles, improved balance and proprioception, and injury reduction.

We encourage core training exercises that use the child's own weight, such as push-ups and pull-ups, or exercises using balls to balance on, which increase challenges because of the instability.

It is best if the strength-training program is part of a conditioning program with specific phases. The components of the conditioning program should vary in intensity and volume during the year. Other components of the conditioning program typically include flexibility and aerobic and anaerobic training (see Chapter 24).

Training Safety – Exercise in heat or cold

Those who coach or provide healthy care for prepubscent children who exercise in hot or cold conditions must always be aware of how a child's response to these environments differs from that of an adult. Children have greater skin surface area relative to total body mass than adults. Therefore, they are more susceptible to developing hypothermia and hyperthermia.

A good, warm and flexible wetsuit will help to prevent hypothermia (see Chapter 16)

Young children also do not have fully mature thermal regulatory mechanisms, and the intensity and composition of their sweat is different from adults. Children often do not feel thirsty until they are quite dehydrated, so they must be encouraged to drink during exercise, long before they begin to feel thirsty. Furthermore, children proportionally generate more thermal energy than adults due to relative physiological and metabolic inefficiency.

Their gait mechanics are not yet mature, so they typically expend more energy for a given amount of surfing, compared with adults. The best treatment for illness or injury caused or exacerbated by the heat is prevention. Adequate hydration is key.

The Benefits and Risks of Surfing – Injury patterns

Surfing encourages a comprehensive development of a child's growing body, increasing aerobic capacity and motor control. The objective in this period of life is to make a child a complete athlete, and not a precocious surfer, because despite good flexibility, muscular strength, power, concentration and stamina for prolonged activity still need to be developed. Despite the overall benefits, the risk of muscular imbalance, which can cause chronic back problems in the near future, is critical to consider, and a progressive core training program must be initiated as soon as possible to develop trunk stability (see below).

Unilateral sports, such as soccer, tennis and volleyball stimulate asymmetrical development; that is one side of the body becomes more developed than the other. This may lead to postural imbalance and musculoskeletal problems. In these sports, compensatory and muscular equilibrium exercises are important for the treatment and prevention of these alterations.

In tennis, for example, the fact that a child uses only one arm to play over years of training and competition can lead to a discrepancy in the size and length of one arm in relation to the other, with disproportional development of the musculature and loss of elasticity and flexibility. In grave cases, this can cause accelerated degeneration of the joints and deformation of the spinal column.

Prepubescent children have more joint laxity and often more musculotendinous flexibility than adolescents and adults. They rarely sustain musculotendinous strains. However, patellar tendon and Achilles tendon pain are not unusual among jumping athletes (who may have both problems) or

Tennis player – Bruno Rosa

kicking athletes (who often strain the patellar tendon). The weakest link in this age group is most often the growth plate rather than the ligament.

The physis (growth plate) can be three to five times weaker than adjacent connective tissue structures, depending on the rate and phase of growth.

Fractures of the growth plates can be difficult or impossible to recognize on simple x-rays, so a careful clinical examination is needed to rule out these diagnoses before allowing a return to surfing and to provide appropriate immobilization until healing is complete. Surfing injury rates increase with age throughout childhood. Increasing specialization in surfing at a younger age seems to be related to increased injury rates, particularly from overuse injuries, among prepubescent athletes. Greater volume and intensity of training appears to increase the risk of injury among children and adolescents.

Photo: James Thisted

Young Cayman surfing. Surfing is a fun and complete sport that encourages symmetrical and total growth of a child's body.

From 12 to 15 Growth and Development

From 12 to 15 years of age, a child enters puberty and experiences an explosion of sexual and growth hormones. There is a significant increase in muscular mass, height and weight.

While boys gain muscle mass due to the effects of testosterone, girls gain both lean body mass, as well as fat. As a consequence, from ages 6 to 18, the "average" (50th percentile by age) boy increases his body fat percentage from 10% to 13% while the average girl increases hers from 14% to 25%. Athletic adolescent males typically have 5% to 12% body fat while most athletic adolescent females have 16% to 18%.

But bones grow relatively faster than muscles and tendons. This "mismatch" is particularly notable with muscles that cross 2 joints, such as the hamstrings, rectus femoris, iliotibial band, and gastrocnemius, significantly reducing the flexibility of the adolescent and leading to an increase in sports injuries. Stretching should be stimulated regularly.

Another important factor to be considered by adolescents is concerning decreased strength of growth plates and adjacent bone at periods of fastest growth (near peak height velocity) and the risk of increased injury.

Injury patterns

The mechanism of avulsion injury is typical among teenage surfers. It is most often a sudden violent muscular contraction, during a surfing maneuver or a wipe out followed by a movement like a leg split.

The youth may have pre-existing pain in the region of the apophysis (the special area in the bone where a tendon is attached) from repetitive or chronic injury before the avulsion injury occurs.

Treatment includes determining and removing the cause of the injury (tight muscle, biomechanical abnormality, incorrect technique (too much intensity or repetition for the tissues to adapt), active rest, and appropriate rehabilitation. In addition to traction injuries to apophyseal growth plates, repetitive stress may also injure a growth plate that is responsible for longitudinal growth.

Adolescents must also pay attention to weight control for psychosocial reasons, as well as avoid substance experimentation and abuse.

At this age, it is important to develop a team spirit through group participation, broaden respect for sports and their rules, team members and competitors, and learn to work towards a goal.

Brazilian WCT star Neco Padaratz, who was around 12 years old, receiving an award from Edson "Ledo" Ronchi and Morongo.

The importance of surfing should be emphasized in schools as a type of physical education for children of this age who can participate in tag-team type competitions.

Many amateur and professional surfers began to surf at 12 to 15 years old. A fun board or a mini-Malibu fascilitate learning, but small boards are most common.

Neco Padaratz, a Brazilian surfer who has spent many years on the WTC

Photo: Flavio Vidigal

circuit, began to play with a Styrofoam board at the age of 8 and had his first surfboard at 10.

Surfing encourages respect for the ocean and its forces, an awareness of the need for good eating habits and good physical health. Getting up before the sun with friends to be the first to surf at the peak, and the first surf trips are great experiences for a young surfer.

Surfing integrates teenagers with their community and awakens and strengthens their social and ecological awareness.

When to Begin Competing?

Between 12 and 15, a surfer can begin to specialize. Training will build cardiovascular endurance, muscular strength, speed, elasticity and flexibility, motor coordination and quick reflexes.

Talent hunter Netão and his pupils at the Mormaii Training Center, Aragua

Photo: Flavio Vidigal

ISA-World Surfing Games Parade, International Surfing Association

ISA, Games-Surfing Champions-Masters

It is in this phase that participation in championships should be encouraged. **Fábio Gouveia was world amateur champion at about 18 years old.**

Ian Gouveia, son of Fabio

Photo: James Thisted

Brazilian surfing team. World Junior Championship, ISA Games, France, 2008

Mormaii Training Center, Aragua, Praia Mole, Florianópolis – Santa Catarina, Brazil

Age of Initiation, Peak and Conclusion of Competitive Sport Life

The table below presents a comparison between the initiation, peak and conclusion of participation in different competitive sports and illustrates certain characteristics and particularities of each sport, including surfing.

Table 1. Sport, initiation, peak and concluding age.

Competitive sport	Initiation	Peak	End of participation
Swimming	6-8	18-20	24
Olympic gymnastics	6	14-16	18-20
Volleyball/Handball/Long jump	12	24	30-34
Judo	8-12	24-26	30
Indoor Soccer	12-14	24-26	30
Outdoor Soccer	12-14	24-26	30-34
Tennis/Fencing	12-14	26-28	30-32
Long distance track	15	30	36-40
Surfing	6-10	25-28	30-36

Note: The ages in this table are averages and not absolute. There may be variations and exceptions.

Like Olympic gymnastics, competitive surfing has had increasingly younger initiation ages, with the youngest beginning at about 5. Nevertheless, the average starting age is 6 to 10.

A surfer reaches peak performance at about 25 to 28. This is about the average age in terms of peak performance for psycho-motor, mental and technical development. A competitive surfer's career usually concludes at around age 30 to 36.

Kelly Slater competed for his 9th world surfing title at age of 36. Layne Beacheley, 36, seven-time ASP Women's World Champion, has been on the tour for 18 years now!

In Olympic gymnastics, the peak age is about **14 to 16, and a career ends at about 18 to 20**. It is clear that surfing has one of the earliest initiation and latest termination ages among all sports. In other words, it can be enjoyed in good health for the longest amount of time.

There are obviously individual variations among surfers and athletes of other sports.

Risks of Surfing and Their Prevention

Despite the many physical and psychological benefits that surfing offers to the development of children and teenagers, the long hours of competitive practice can cause attrition to the spinal column in the region of the intervertebral discs, in addition to premature aging of bone structure (see Chapter 6).

The most common postural imbalance problems found in young surfers include:

- tension and tightness of the back muscular chain
- increased cervical and lumbar lordosis
- anterior pelvic tilt
- weak abdominals and core muscles

The Posterior Muscle Chain

Excessive stress on the lower back caused by surfing initially leads to a progressive muscular imbalance characterized by a swayback or lordosis posture (see Chapter 6). This is caused by tension in the lumbar and rear thigh muscles that become shortened and weak, while the abdominal muscles, if they are not well developed, become even weaker (especially the lower ones). If this muscular imbalance is not corrected, excessive pressure is transmitted to the intervertebral discs and can cause compression of these shock absorbers, leading to disc dehydration and degeneration, and possibly even herniated discs. The pressure may also affect the joint cartilage, causing degeneration and arthrosis.

This condition is frequently aggravated among athletes who do not stretch and among teenagers who have rapid bone growth and whose muscles and tendons do not accompany this growth. The repeated movements that rotate and compress the backbone progressively strain the region.

It is therefore essential to correct this muscular imbalance to prevent back pain. I recommend a core training program based on the Pilates method in order to correct the muscle imbalance and develop trunk stabilization, coordination and motor control. It will also help prevent the most common surf injuries.

Long hours exposed to the sun during a surfer's life is a risk factor that must be considered. The regular use of sun protection to prevent premature aging and skin cancer is of extreme importance (see Chapter 17).

For children who are beginning to surf: Never surf alone, always have someone on the beach to supervise, avoid crowds, and respect the order of priority on the waves.

Gabriel Steinman taking his first steps on a board

Great sport for socializing: Rodrigo Steinman and friends getting ready

Young, talented surfer

Ícaro Ronchi
Wave host

Chapter 3

Surfing Injuries and Accidents

The most common surfing accidents and injuries, and their prevention

Surfing is comparatively safer than most sports, so parents can let their children practice with few worries.

Surfing is one of the most complete sports. It combines aerobic and anaerobic activity of moderate to high intensity.

The risk of collision comes principally from the contact of the surfer with his own board, another surfer or with the sea bottom (sand, rock or coral).

Surfing requires a high level of neuromuscular ability and involves movements of the upper and lower limbs, the abdomen and the spinal column.

Photo: Flavio Vidigal

Some people associate surfing with danger because it is practiced in the ocean, which at times can be hostile, and surfers are exposed to wind, sun, rain, cold, different types of ocean bottoms, wave size, tidal variations, currents, sharks and other elements.

Yet surfing has a much lower risk of accidents than other so-called extreme sports, such as skateboarding, windsurfing, kitesurfing, parachuting, hang gliding, paragliding, rollerblading and snow skiing.

Skateboarding

A number of studies conducted in the United States compared injuries related to surfing and other sports, and found that in a single year, there was a tremendous difference between the rate of injuries in surfing, 9,900, compared to 38,000 in squash, 137,900 in skateboarding and nearly 1,370,900 in American football.

The reality is that traditional amateur and recreational surfing is safe. Despite the growing popularity of surfing and changes in board design that have made them faster, allowing surfers to perform powerful maneuvers, there has not been a significant increase in the rate of injuries in the past 15 years. However, there have been changes in the types of injuries.

A study conducted in Victoria, Australia by Brian Lowdon in 2005 found less than one injury per surfer per year (0.26 injuries/surfer/year) – an injury rate that has been quite stable over the past 6 years.

In a study I conducted in collaboration with the Sports Center of the Federal University at Santa Catarina, Brazil (2003), the rate of injuries that prevented an athlete from surfing for one or more days or that required medical attention was 2.5 per 1,000 surfing days, which is even less than that found in Australian studies conducted by professor and surfer Brian Lowdon (1983), which found 3.5 injuries of moderate to grave severity for every 1,000 days of recreational surfing and 4.0 injuries per 1,000 surfing days for professional surfers.

In a study conducted among competitive surfers in 2007, Andrew Nathanson found 6.6 acute surfing injuries per 1,000 hours of competitive surfing and 2.9 injuries per surfer per 1,000 heats. The risk of injury is more than double in large waves.

The injury rate in moderate waves is much lower than that found in parachuting, soccer, rugby kitesurfing and snow skiing as seen in Table 1.

Table 1. Rate of moderate to serious injuries in different sports

Sport	Injuries per 1,000 days of training or play
Parachuting	65.6
Soccer	10-35
Rugby	55
Kitesurfing	7.0
Snow skiing	6.0

Research among U.S. student athletes revealed that wrestling and volleyball are among the sports with the highest rates of serious injuries as shown in Table 2, which indicates the number of injuries per 100 athletes, during a year, in different sports.

Table 2. Indicates the number of injuries per 100 athletes, during a year, in different sports.

Wrestling	38.2 %
Volleyball	29.9 %
Gymnastics	20.6 %
Basketball	19.2 %
Soccer	13.8 %
Track and Field	7.2 %
Swimming	5.4 %
Fencing	4.7 %

Changes in Surfboards and Their Relationship With Injuries

Changes in board design since their initiation in Polynesia have changed the type of injuries found in surfing. The weight of the first boards made them difficult to maneuver and most surf injuries in the first half of the 20th century were related to bangs from the boards and being dunked by waves.

Sketch at the Bishop Museum in Hawaii titled: Surf Swimming by Sandwich Island. *Many legends and songs tell of the spectacular achievements of male and female surfers.*

Hawaiian surfer in the late 19th century

The beach boys of Waikiki, including the ambassador of surfing, Duke Kanhanamoku
Photo:
Herb Wetencamp

Members of the Palo Verde Surf Club, the first California club
Photo: Dr. Jack Ball

In this photo of Snow Maclister, the danger is focused on the neck region
New Castle. 1928.

Wally Froiseth was one of the first to modify the format of the tails in order to prevent slipping

In the 1940s, most boards were still flat and made of solid wood, they were 6 to 10-feet long, heavy and thick, with a flat bottom and slightly rounded edges. They were known as "basic redwoods." Injuries were caused by boards hitting the body and head.
Photo: Dr. Jack Ball

The first balsa boards were thinner, had narrower tails and a "V" carved on the bottom that allowed the surfer to establish a good angle with the wave and expand the space for the surfer to move. Mickey Munhoz with the "balsa redwood" board San Onofre style.
Photo: Jeff Divine

Bob Simmons and Joe Quigg introduced fiberglass. Historic surfboard collection of Rennie Yater.

The ability to ride tubes increased with the mono-keels, which provided greater board stability. They allowed new maneuvers but also new possibilities for accidents from lips and wipe outs.

Since the late 1950s, the era of the Malibus and the changes in boards caused by the use of polyurethane blocks allowed surfers to explore new limits.

Over the last 30 years, boards have become smaller and lighter. They have evolved from one to two to three to four keels.

Surfing maneuvers have evolved with boards keels.

The breakthrough of three fins or thrusters – developed by Simon Anderson – allowed fantastic board stability.

Board design changes have created surprising hydrodynamic flow, allowing surfers greater flexibility and more radical movements, markedly changing the repertoire, speed and power of maneuvers and turns. This has increased the risk of serious, traumatic injuries to the head, shoulders, knees and spinal column and the appearance of chronic over-use injuries. The nature of injuries in surfing, in addition to being directly related to the personality of each surfer, result from the changes in surfboard design.

Photo: Flavio Vidigal

TWIN FINS –
(four-time champion)
Mark Richards' generation

Photo: Flavio Vidigal

The Surfboards of the '70s

Shaper creativity and hydrodynamics stimulated the evolution of surfboards
Shapers M.Dio; Mark Jakola and Avelino Bastos.

M. Giorgi – Indonesia

Photo: Sebastian Rojas

Three Fins (thruster) created by Simon Anderson in the 1980s, changed surfboards' stability and became the most popular

The adventurous spirit and courage of the big riders who search for large waves (at Marvericks, Todos os Santos, Jaws, Teahoopo, etc), which are more powerful and dangerous, and the growing practice of tow-in surfing, have led to more serious wounds and traumas.

Romeu Bruno
in Jaws

Surfers and Injuries

Many severe traumatic injuries are caused by the collision of a surfer with the surfboard, with another surfer or with the sea bottom (sand, rock or coral). The most common injuries (see Table 3) are cuts (44%) and bruises (16.9%) followed by muscle and ligament injuries (15.5%), jellyfish stings (8.9%) and broken bones (2.5%). Injuries involving eyes and ears are common. Fortunately, catastrophic injures involving the spinal column and the head or drownings are not frequent, as shown in the table below. Older surfers, more experienced surfers, and those surfing large waves have a higher relative risk for significant injury.

Nathanson's study among competitive surfers in the United States and Taylor's Australian study had confirmed an overall low rate of surfing injuries similar to our Brazilian study.

Taylor's found that lacerations account for 42% of all acute injuries, contusions 13% and sprains and strains 12%. However, he found a higher incidence of fracture (8%) and head and neck injuries (37%).

Andrew Nathanson's study of competitive surfers found more sprains (39%), lacerations (30%) and dislocations or fractures (11%,). This is related to the high performance powerful and acrobatic maneuvers used by competitive surfers.

Table 3. Incidence of injury by type

Type of injury	Brazilian study percentage	American study percentage	Australian study percentage
Cuts	44	30	46.4
Bruises	16.9	14 (bruise +abrasion)	
Muscle-ligament injuries- sprains/strains	15.5	39	28.6
Fractures	2.5	11(fracture and dislocation)	8.9
Dislocations	3.2		10.7
Perforated ear drum	0.5		
Jellyfish stings	8.9		
Ear infections	3.5		
Acute gastroenteritis	0.3		
Hypothermia	0.3		
Herniated discs	0.8		
Drownings	0.8		

In contrast, studies of recreational surfers have consistently found that lacerations, predominantly to the head and lower extremities, are most common.

The observed injury rate at professional contests was 8.7 per 1,000 surfer heats, as compared with 2.7 per 1,000 surfer heats at amateur contests. But the professional contests were, on average, held in larger surf, more often over a hard bottom, and longer in duration.

Most injuries take place when the surfer is riding a wave (62%). A smaller number of injuries occur from board recoil (9%), paddling (7%), getting in or out of the water (6%), or while duck diving (6%) (see Table 4).

Table 4. Moment of injury

Injuries are most common to the lower limbs, head and upper limbs. (Table 5)

Table 5. Injuries to different parts of the body

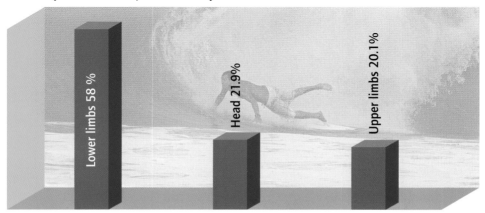

Similar results were found in the U.S. and Australian studies.

Nathanson found that the most frequently injured body parts were the lower limbs (45.8%) and the head and face (26.2%). Taylor found that 37% of acute injuries were to the lower limbs and 37% to the head and neck.

Cuts and bruises were most common to the feet, arms and legs (see Table 6).

Table 6. Incidence of cuts and scrapes to different parts of the body.

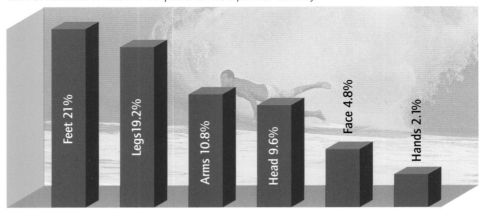

Feet 21%   Legs 19.2%   Arms 10.8%   Head 9.6%   Face 4.8%   Hands 2.1%

Bruises are more common to the legs, arms and head (see Table 7).

Table 7. Incidence of bruises to different parts of the body

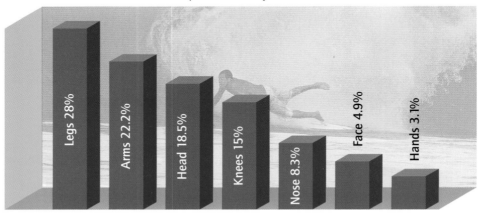

Legs 28%   Arms 22.2%   Head 18.5%   Knees 15%   Nose 8.3%   Face 4.9%   Hands 3.1%

Muscular sprains are most common to the groin. They most often occur when an athlete's foot slips during a maneuver or when a surfer is hit by a strong lip, which causes an extreme and abrupt stretch of the thigh's abductor muscle. The lumbar region is affected in 23.4% of the injuries as a result of intense and explosive rotations to the spinal column while surfing (see Table 8).

Table 8. Incidence of muscular strains to different body parts

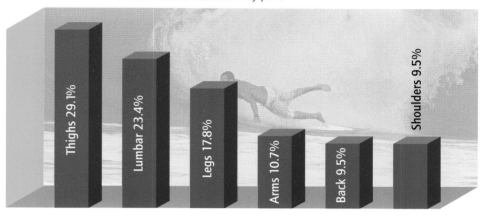

Photo: Sebastian Rojas

Injuries to the ligaments more frequently occur at the knees, ankles and shoulders and are most common in tubes, drops, snaps and floaters (see Table 9).

Table 9. Incidence of ligament injuries to different body parts

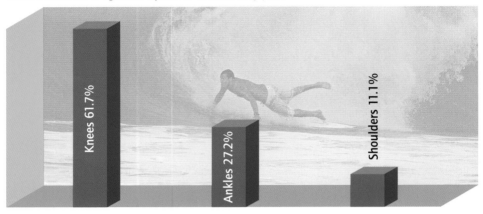

Eye injuries may occur, and can be serious. Fortunately they are less common when nose guards are used on the boards to cover the pointy board tip.

Wipe out

Fractures represent a small portion of injuries among amateur and recreational surfers (2.5%), however, the incidence increases among competitive surfers – among whom they account for 8.5%. They most often affect the lower limbs (58%), with the leg (tibia) and ankles most commonly affected (20%). But they can also affect the back, nose, arms, feet and teeth.

Dislocations (3.2% of all injuries) were most common to the shoulders and more frequent among competitive surfers (among whom they account for 10.7% of injuries).

"Surfer's rib" is an isolated fracture of the first rib, which is usually caused by the execution of a lay back.

Fortunately, it is not common for injuries and accidents to threaten a surfer's life.

It is estimated that grave traumas that require hospitalization occur in one of every 175,000 days surfed. Although they are not frequent, fractured necks and backs can be caused by collisions with a sand or coral bank and can leave an athlete paraplegic or tetraplegic. Fractures, vertebral compression and herniated discs are common after trauma and are more frequent when surfing large and heavy waves.

Grave multiple trauma to the head, multiple fractures, ruptured spleens, and injury to the axiliar artery are not commom. However they can occur – and cause death – but usually this occurs among experienced surfers, who are surfing large waves. This occurred with Tahitan surfer Briece Tacerca, who was killed by the lip of a wave at Teahupoo in 2000.

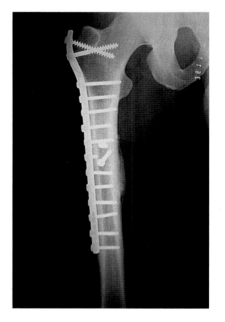

Fractured femurs are not common in surfers but may occur. This X-ray shows a fractured femur caused by a wipe out of a healthy 25-year-old surfer. It required surgery to place a plate and screw

Teahupoo, Tahiti, some of the world's most dangerous waves

SURFING & HEALTH

Photo: Flavio Vidigal

Approximately eleven surfers have died while surfing the Pipeline over the past 10 years and there have been hundreds of serious injuries. Head trauma, with contusion and lacerations are quite common.

To mention a few injuries: Tamayo Perry received 50 stitches in his scalp and Australian Steve Clements came close to drowning. The Tahitian-born Malik Joyeux, a Teahupoo specialist, drowned at Pipeline, most likely due to a head contusion, caused by a blow from the lip.

Head Injury

These kinds of accidents at Tahiti, Pipeline and other spots have raised discussions about the use of a helmet when surfing peaks with dangerous banks. In 2000, Neco Padaratz was probably saved by his helmet when he struck the reef at Teahupoo.

Photo: Flavio Vidigal

Neco Padaratz in Teahupoo

Although head injury accounts for a considerable proportion of total injuries when surfing, very few surfers wear protective headgear.

There has been a heated debate about the use of helmets, but there is no doubt that they can save lives in certain situations. They help avoid cuts and bruises to the head and reduce the intensity of contusions and the possibility of a "knock out" that can lead to drowning.

Many surfers argue that the phenomenon of deceleration, known as whiplash to the head and neck, caused by using a helmet during a wipe out, is not a threat.

Nevertheless, because of the potential risk of death from head wounds, surfers should consider the use of protective headgear, especially when surfing near stone or coral reefs. In addition to a helmet, a surfer should try to protect oneself from the board during a fall by getting into a fetal position.

When using a helmet, be careful when "duck diving" and keep your forehead close to the board, because waves can fill the helmet with water and force the head back.

Some characteristic surfing injuries include:

- Drownings, which may occur among unprepared or poorly trained surfers.

- Jellyfish stings were responsible for 8.9% of injuries. They usually affect the upper limbs.

- Perforated ear drums can be caused by direct trauma to the ear drum when hitting the water during a wipe out.

- Skin injuries, such as rashes or irritations, due to friction of the chest and abdomen with paraffin are frequent in the summer and spring. Irritations to the neck and underarms are also frequent due to friction of the skin with wetsuits.

Some injuries are crowd related

- Injuries caused by lightning can occur while surfing. Do not surf when there is lightning nearby.

- Shark attacks are less frequent than injuries caused by lightning. But be careful in areas known to have sharks (see Chapter 17).

Wipe out

Causes of Injuries

As shown in Table 10, most injuries are caused by a direct blow from your own board during a wipe out or when performing surfing maneuvers.

Table 10. Most frequent causes of surf injuries

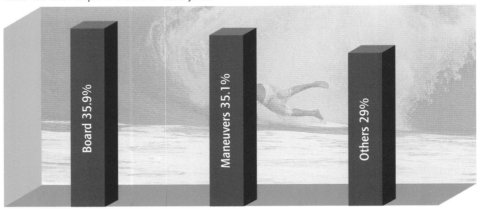

Board 35.9% Maneuvers 35.1% Others 29%

American and Australian studies found the percentage of injuries caused by a surfer's own board to be even higher than Brazilian studies.

According to the Nathanson study, 55% of injuries resulted from contact with a surfer's own board, 12% from another surfer's board, and 17% from the sea floor. In his U.S. study, Taylor found most injuries were caused by blows from a surfboard or clashes with another surfer (45.2%) or hitting the sea floor (17.9%).

Keels: Most cuts and bruises are caused by wipe outs

Most cuts and bruises continue to be caused by wipe outs followed by contact with the board (35.9%). The keel, which is hit in 42.7% of the cases, followed by the nose (11.9%) and the tail (10.1%) are the main culprits for injuries (see Table 11).

Table 11. Part of the board responsible for injury

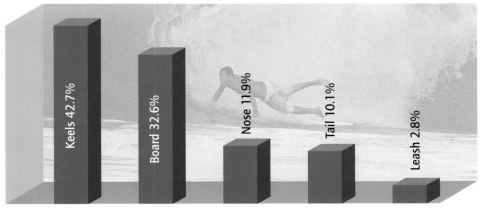

Keels 42.7% Board 32.6% Nose 11.9% Tail 10.1% Leash 2.8%

The tubes are among the moves that cause the most injuries

Photo: Flavio Vidigal

The tube, the "top turn," the floater and the aerial are among the moves that cause the most injuries (see Table 12).

Table 12. Moves that cause the most injuries

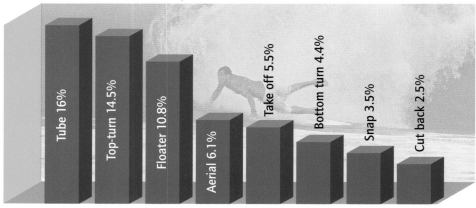

Tube 16%

Top-turn 14.5%

Floater 10.8%

Aerial 6.1%

Take off 5.5%

Bottom turn 4.4%

Snap 3.5%

Cut back 2.5%

Floater

Photo: Flavio Vidigal

The floater is one of the moves most commonly associated with fractures and serious ligament injures to the ankle

Time Between Injury and Medical Attention

Just 42.3% of injured surfers seek immediate medical attention following injury; 33% continue to surf after an injury and 64.1% within 14 days after the accident. Nearly 8% are hospitalized and nearly 38% of all surfers lose more than a day of work or school due to injury.

Time of Inactivity Caused by Injuries

In more than half of surfing injuries, the athlete returns to the waves in 7 days, demonstrating that most injuries are not grave. Injuries responsible for more than 30 days off the board include fractures (42.8%), sprains and torn ligaments (28%), dislocations (27.5%) and herniated discs. (see Table 13).

Table 13. Time away from surfing

Less than 7 days – 54.2%
7 to 14 days 20.8%
14 to 30 days 14.8%
More than 30 days – 10.2%

Photo: Flavio Vidigal

Transporting an injured surfer

67

According to our study in Brazil, most accidents take place in waves of two meters or less (56.1%) (Table 14), on sand banks (89.6%) and in water with comfortable temperature (59%) in the spring and fall (Table 14)

Most of the accidents take place in water up to 1 meter deep (36%).

Table 14. Wave height in surfing injuries

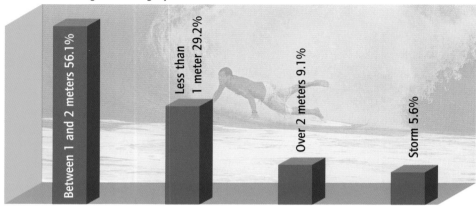

Sun (see Chapter 17)

Despite campaigns to raise awareness about the danger of skin cancer, more than half of all surfers continue to surf between 10 a.m. and 3 p.m. and are thus exposed to the damaging effects of the sun. Preventive measures should reinforce the importance of using sun protection, Lycra shirts, and avoiding surfing in the hours with the greatest exposure to ultraviolet light.

Older surfers should have their skin frequently evaluated to allow early detection of any pre-malignant blemishes.

Body areas of high risk that are not frequently examined include the top of the ears, the back and the rear of the legs.

Lightning

Statistically, the probability of being hit by lightning (and dying) is 30%-40% greater than being attacked by a shark. Stay out of the water during lightning storms.

Chronic Injuries

Although most injuries are traumatic, it is very common for surfers to suffer chronic muscular-skeletal microtrauma from repetitive stress. This usually involves the back, neck, shoulders and knees (Table 15).

Table 15. Regions of the body where overuse injuries are most common

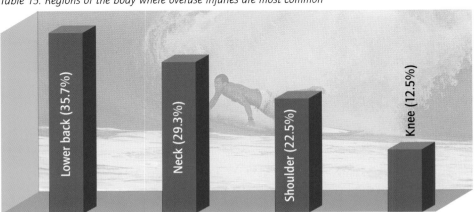

Lower back (35.7%) Neck (29.3%) Shoulder (22.5%) Knee (12.5%)

Nearly 45% of all surfers with some type of chronic injury seek medical treatment. Two percent are hospitalized and 34% lose a day of work or school. Frequent complaints of lower back pain among surfers leads us to believe that degenerative disc disease may be a common problem among surfers.

Some biomechanical characteristics of surfing are associated with overuse injuries and are mainly related to strains on the body's center of gravity.

These include:

1. The hyperextension of the back and neck while paddling leads to muscular imbalance by changing the center of gravity. This position is probably related to premature degeneration of spinal structures (disc and cartilage aging).

Paddling position

Photo: Sebastian Rojas

2. Duck diving – hyperextension of the back and neck increase muscular imbalance.

Duck diving

Photo: Sebastian Rojas

3. Repeated paddling movements can strain the muscles and tendons of the shoulders and elbows, especially on boards with very low floatation.

4. The repeated compression and rotation of the intervertebral discs of the upper and lower back during maneuvers can lead to dehydration, degeneration and hernias of the intervertebral discs.

Photo: F. Chagas

Compression and rotation of the intervertebral discs of the upper and lower back during maneuvers

5. The common squatting surfing posture leads to imbalance in the pelvic region and strains the thigh and hip flexors (iliopsoas muscle).

6. The frequent flexed-hip position associated with crouched position of the knees, while hips and knees are pointed inwards can strain the internal hip and knee structures.

Aerial

71

Lesions Caused by the Elements

Exostosis (bone growth) in the ear canal was the principal chronic lesion caused by exposure to the elements, while otitis (see Chapter Ear Problems) inflammation and infection and sinusitis were the most common infections.

Pinguecula and Pterygium is the most common chronic lesion of the eyes. It involves the thickening of the connective tissue of the conjunctiva, over the cornea, caused by irritation from sun, water and wind (see Chapter 14).

Other chronic problems commonly found among surfers include:

1. Chronic rhitinis.
2. *Surfer's knots*, or surfer's knees, which involves the growth of connective tissue in the patella region of the knees due to repeated duck diving.

   They can also occur in the dorsal region of the feet, mainly among longboard surfers who are accustomed to paddling while kneeling.
3. Surfer neuropathy is caused by the compression of the fibular nerve. It also occurs among longboarders who paddle while kneeling, which can cause weakness and tingling in the ankles.

Summary of Recommendations to Prevent of Surfing Injuries

The following precautions should be adopted by surfers to increase their safety in the ocean:

1. Use a proper wetsuit to prevent hypothermia.
2. Use a nose guard on your board.
3. Use less pointy tails and keels and opt for rubberized materials – to reduce the impact of the board on the surfer.
4. Use a professional leash (from a reliable brand), of the correct size to avoid losing your board.
5. Use a leash of adequate size to avoid collision with the board.
6. Use adequate sun protection.
7. Know the places that you surf, including the depth, the tides and the currents. Make a habit of watching the ocean and series before surfing.
8. Don't surf alone.
9. Stay away from surfers while paddling.
10. Be careful of the board after falling off the wave; it is the main cause of accidents.
11. Do not use drugs while surfing.
12. Study basic first aid procedures (especially important on surf trips).

Broken board

Photo: Tony Fleury – Revista Fluir

Transport of injured surfer (neck immobilization)

Education about the prevention of surfing accidents should be introduced in surfing schools and better promoted by surfing magazines.

Nose guard

Prevention of Chronic Injuries

As mentioned above, overuse injuries among surfers most commonly affect the neck, backbone, shoulders and less often the elbows and knees. Fortunately, the human body has a great capacity to respond to physical stress, due to adaptations in muscles, tendons and bones, which become stronger and more resistant.

Nevertheless, if the microtrauma and stress applied exceeds the body's ability to adapt, the excessive load will cause microscopic injuries that can cause inflammation; this is the body's natural response. Signs of inflammation include swelling, warmth, redness, pain and progressive loss of movement.

There are 4 stages of overuse injuries:

1. Discomfort that appears while warming up.

2. Discomfort that disappears during warm-up but reappears at the end of the activity.

3. Discomfort that gets worse and aggravated during the activity.

4. Persistent pain and discomfort.

The earlier you recognize and begin medical treatment for a repetitive stress injury caused by sport, the shorter the rehabilitation time. By permitting an injury to reach stage two or three can result in, in addition to greater recovery time, an inability to train and compete.

The principal measures for treating repetitive stress injuries are:

1. Remove the cause of pain (this can mean having to stop surfing). Rest often works miracles.

2. Consult your doctor. He or she will conduct a diagnosis and recommend anti-inflammatory measures through medication, ice, acupuncture and physical therapy.

3. Listen to your body and follow a detailed rehabilitation program. Slowly increase recuperative exercise and don't rush your return. Remember, the greatest cause of sports accidents are poorly rehabilitated injuries. Allow complete recovery before returning to surf, and progressively increase the training load. Pain is a warning sign and requires explanation and attention.

Preventive measures include a muscular re-balancing strategy, that includes a deep core training program (involving abdominals, pelvic floor muscles, pelvic trochanteric muscles and spinal muscles).

We recomend Pilates (see Chapter 24).

Focus on body stability, flexibility strength and coordination. It is important to warm up and stretch before and after surfing.

Although the impact with the water protects against fractures, there is a risk of fractures to the cervical vertebrae and lower back when surfing shallow banks. It is important to be aware of the danger of falling off the board and colliding with shallow sand banks or rocks. Learn falling techniques used in judo and other martial arts. Be familiar with basic care for proper transport in case of back injuries (see Chapter 30).

Summary

The relatively low incidence of injury and the fact that in more than half (54.02%) of all surfing injuries result in time away from the sport that is not more than seven days, demonstrates the safety of surfing and the low risk of becoming incapacitated by surfing. Nevertheless, surfing giant waves is dangerous and can lead to grave and complex injury and trauma.

The power and speed generated by waves surfed by tow-in considerably increases the risk of serious injuries that are not common in paddle-in surf.

Big waves
Romeu Bruno

Caused by falls of greater impact, these injuries can affect the surfer in either large or small waves. Considerable experience, physical training, confidence and total determination is necessary.

SURFING & HEALTH

Keels are the main causes
of cuts and lacerations

Chapter 4

Cuts and Lacerations

Prevention is fundamental. Your risk of injury can be reduced with the use of nose guards, keels with rubbers borders, a helmet, boots and wetsuits.

Cuts and lacerations are the most common injuries to surfers. They occur in nearly 44% of accidents and are usually caused by the surfboard. They mainly affect the feet (17.7% of the time), the legs (8.7%), the head (7.9%) arms (7.7%), and the face 3.6%. Keels are the main villains, causing 55.2% of these injuries, followed by the tail (11.9%). Coral is frequently involved in these accidents, principally during tropical surf trips.

Fortunately, most of these injuries are not serious, and the surfer can be back on the board in less than a week.

Foot laceration

What to Do?

When a laceration occurs, two crucial questions always arise: Are stiches needed? What should be done to get back to surfing as soon as possible?

Follow the instructions below:

1. Evaluate the size and depth of the laceration. Deep cuts longer than an inch usually require stitches. Smaller and superficial wounds can be treated by pressing the sides of the wound together, using an adhesive bandage. Cuts that are not stitched generally take longer to heal and often leave larger scars.

2. If there is bleeding, the first step is to stop the hemorrhage by applying firm, direct pressure on top of or slightly above the wound for 5 minutes or less. To do so, use gauze and apply enough firm pressure to staunch the bleeding while avoiding excessive pressure.

M. Giorgi

Photo: Sebastian Rojas

Always go to the emergency room:

- If lacerations involve damage to vascular tissue, nerves, or tendons
- Facial lacerations requiring cosmetic repair
- For lacerations of the palm with any signs of infection
- If there is a sign of infection
- If foreign bodies remain after cleaning
- For glass-related injuries
- For complex lacerations

Photo: Levy Paiva

Doctor attending a wounded surfer on the beach

78

Take special care of wounds caused by corals and reefs

The proteins of living organisms found in corals can cause skin infections. Careful cleaning is essential. The use of antibiotics is often advisable in the case of suspected infection. See a doctor.

The living organisms found in corals

How should I clean a laceration before closure?

1. Cleaning the wound

The golden rule for treating lacerations is to eliminate the risk of infection or contamination.

All superficial and deep cuts should be brushed and irrigated (using a clean tooth brush) with saline solution or running water and soap and rinsed with lots and lots of *clean* water.

Cleansing the wound is essential for removing foreign bodies, such as sand, pieces of board and coral, as well as for the prevention of infections. Cuts that are not carefully cleaned are frequently infected by bacteria, such as staphylococus *aureus* and streptacocus or others, which commonly inhabit the skin.

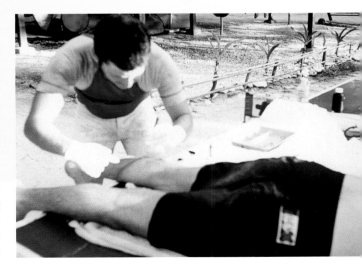

The presence of a doctor on a surfari allows fast, safe suturing and a quick return to surfing. The author stitching a leg in Grajagan, Indonesia

Disinfect the skin around the wound with an antiseptic, such as povidone iodine solution.

Adhesive strip bandages should be used to close wounds 1-2 inches or less when there are no risk factors for infection, the wound edges are easily brought together without leaving any dead space and the wound is not subject to excessive flexing, tension, or dampness.

Rook point – Hawaii

Adhesive strip bandages are not adequate if any risk factors for infection are present. **Stay out of the water for a few days to allow proper healing and avied infection.**

In cases of simple and superficial cuts, the use of a waterproof bandage may allow a return to surfing in the intial phases of healing.

Do not allow the wound to be exposed to the sun and after surfing, wash with lots of clean water. Apply a fresh bandage daily after surfing, cleanse with saline solution and soap, apply liquid anti-septic, such as "povidone," and cover with gauze. Change the gauze daily. You can also use topical antibiotic creams, such as "neomicin."

2. Wounds that need stitches (deep lacerations 3 to 5 cm)

• If a laceration needs stitches, they should be made in the first 6-12 hours in a hospital or first aid station. Nevertheless, certain large cuts can be stitched up to one week after the accident. Sutures allow low-tension apposition of the wound edges and proper healing.

Scalp wounds tend to bleed considerably and need immediate attention. Facial cuts should be stitched to avoid ugly scars.

The deepest cuts can damage tendons, muscles, bones, nerves and veins.

Looks are not deceiving:
A cut tendon looks like a cut cord
A cut muscle looks like raw beef
A cut nerve looks like crushed spaghetti

- Apply a bandage after closing the laceration.
- Dress with a low-adherence, absorbent, perforated dressing with an adhesive border. These are also available with a plastic film covering to protect the dressings from getting wet.
- Take paracetamol or ibuprofen for pain.
- Keep the wound dry. Waterproof dressings accept some moisture, such as a shower. Non-waterproof dressings must be protected from moisture at all times.
- Complications caused by poorly cared for wounds include secondary bacterial infections that can place a surfer's health in risk.
- Seek medical attention if you develop symptoms or signs of infection (increasing pain, redness, swelling spreading from the laceration, fever or general malaise).

You should immediately see a doctor and probably need oral antibiotics such as amoxicillin, penicillin and tetracycline;

3. Prevention of tetanus is done through an anti-tetanus booster vaccine every 5 years. If you are not sure when you had your last vaccination, a new dose should be taken. A fully immunized person will have had a primary course of three vaccines followed by two boosters spaced 10 years apart.

If you have planned a surfari for beaches where there are no doctors or anyone prepared to conduct a simple suture, speak with your doctor and organize a basic training to learn how to execute a basic suture. Do not forget to prepare the first aid kit (see Appendix I).

While any surfer can learn to stitch a wound, it is not recommended to risk stitching tendons, muscles and nerves. The procedure requires considerable knowledge of anatomy, in addition to clean tools, and must be conducted in a sterile surgical environment.

What to Do After Closing a Laceration

- If symptoms and signs of infection develop after closure of the laceration, see a doctor. You probably need antibiotics.
- Remove sutures after 3–5 days on the head, 10–14 days over joints, and 7–10 days for other areas.
- Surfers with lacerations closed with adhesive strips must remove these themselves after 3–5 days for head wounds and 7–10 days for wounds in other areas.

Dressings should be removed at the same time as sutures or adhesive strips. Low-adherence absorbent dressings should be replaced if the exudate has significantly wet the dressing.

SURFING & HEALTH

Wipe out

Photo: James Thisted

Chapter 5

Head Injuries

Bangs and cuts to the head represent 15% of surfing accidents. Trauma to the head is dangerous and may result in contusion, bleeding and swelling of the brain.

Direct impact to the head from a surfboard, a shallow beach break (sand bar), coral or stone may cause a brain injury from acceleration and/or deceleration of the head or neck.

Beach Assessment

If the surfer has any decreased level of awareness following an impact to the head, a head injury should be suspected. A progressive declining level of awareness, confusion, seizure, or breathing irregularity may suggest a rapidly progressing head injury.

Acute trauma to the head should be taken seriously. The athlete should be stabilized and immediately transferred to a hospital (see Chapter 32).

The athlete should be transported with cervical spine immobilization and air passages cleared, especially if there is a depressed level of consciousness.

A magnetic resonance image (MRI) is required for diagnosis and appropriate treatment.

Head cuts and lacerations often require stitches (see Chapter 4).

Concussions

Beach assessment

A concussion is defined as an alteration in mental status due to head trauma that may or may not cause loss of consciousness.

A concussion is characterized by immediate and transitory damage to neurological functions and can be manifest in different ways, such as alterations in consciousness and mental state, headache, visual disturbances and dizziness, nausea, and/or blurred vision (among other symptoms), which are generally classified according to the size and gravity of the neurological wound. Symptoms may appear immediately after the injury or take several minutes to develop.

In the most serious injuries, known as third degree, there is loss of consciousness, which creates a risk of drowning.

Due to the risk of a "second impact syndrome" that may be cumulative in nature, the return to surfing following a concussion should be considered only when there is complete neurological recovery and tests show that the athlete has returned to pre-injury levels of function.

Concussion Classification

First-degree concussion
In this case there is no loss of consciousness, however, there may be some mental confusion. After the trauma, the victim should remain under observation for 20 minutes. If there is no alteration in memory, vomiting, headache or other symptoms, there can be an immediate return to the surf.

Second-degree concussion
There is no loss of consciousness, but there is mental confusion such as a loss of memory or dizziness. Surfing should be interrupted (competition or training) and the surfer should remain under medical observation for 6-12 hours. Frequent re-evaluations on the days after the injury are advisable. The victim can usually go back to surfing after a week.

Third-degree concussion
In this situation there is a loss of consciousness for a variable period, which creates a risk of drowning. The athlete may be unconscious for a few minutes or a few hours. Cardio-pulmonary resuscitation (CPR), should be started and then transport (properly immobilized) the victim to the closest hospital for neurological evaluation and complementary exams (computerized tomography or magnetic resonance). If the results are normal, the victim can usually go home, although should be observed over night (for the level of consciousness and response to verbal stimuli and

Surfer with a helmet

pain). Surfing should only be allowed after two full weeks without symptoms.
Persistent alterations in consciousness, in mental state and abnormalities in the neurological exam require immediate evaluation from a neurosurgeon.

Studies show that athletes who suffer a mild concussion have a four-times greater risk of having a second concussion while surfing. For this reason, it is very important that the victim suspend training and competition until there is total and complete neurological recovery. (see Table 1).

A victim who recovers consciousness and then becomes unconscious again is in imminent danger.

All victims found unconscious because of a head injury should be properly transported to a hospital due to the risk of brain damage and/or a possible spinal cord injury.

Following are the guidelines of the American Academy of Neurology about return to activity after a concussion:

Table 1. Concussion – American Academy of Neurology (AAN) Guidelines, 1997

	1st concussion	2nd concussion	3rd concussion
First-degree Without loss of consciousness, Confusion –duration less than 15 minutes	Can return to surfing if there are no symptoms for 15 min.	Can return to surfing in 1 week. If there are no symptoms for at least one week.	End of season
Second-degree Confusion- lasting over 15 minutes. Without loss of consciousness	Can return to surfing one week after end of symptoms.	At least 2 weeks without surfing. Can then surf again if there are no symptoms for at least a week, if not, consider ending the season.	End of season
Third-degree Any loss of consciousness	At least 2 weeks rest.	1 month	End of season. Only return to surfing in the next season if there are no symptoms

The duration in each square suggests how long an athlete should avoid activities. The number of episodes is calculated as the number of concussions during the present season. A season is generally considered a period of six months.

Should a Helmet be Used While Surfing?

Few surfers use a helmet.

Nevertheless, it is common to hear surfers say "the helmet saved my life," or surfers who found their helmet scratched and chipped (see Chapter 3).

Common sense recommends the use of a helmet when surfing shallow breaks.

Pipeline
CJ Hobgood

Photo: James Thisted

Fabio Gouveia
Fernando de Noronha Archipelago

Photo: James Thisted

Chapter 6

Neck Problems

Although traumatic injuries to the neck region are serious, they are fortunately not frequent in surfing.

A lthough not common, acute trauma to the neck should be taken seriously. Chronic neck pains are among the most common in surfers.

Acute Trauma Involving the Neck

Fractures and dislocations to the cervical region are usually caused by a wipe out. Neck injuries are usually caused when the head hits the water or the ocean floor causing an axial load to the cervical spine and a forceful flexion or extension of the head with or without rotation.

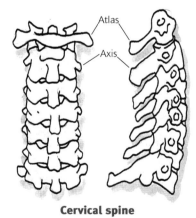

Atlas

Axis

Cervical spine

Wipe outs often cause neck and head injuries

The trauma can occur when large and heavy waves break on deep water or powerful waves break on a shallow sand, stone or coral bottoms.

These injuries are potentially serious because they can cause contusions of the spinal cord and injury to the surrounding nerve roots causing temporary or permanent paralysis of the four limbs.

All trauma involving the head and cervical region should be treated with care since it may be associated with a life-threatening airway obstruction (see Chapter 31).

In the event of a serious head and/or neck injury, the initial response should always be as follows:

1. Identify the injury
2. Stabilize the athlete
3. Transport the athlete for definitive treatment

Correct and careful transportation of the victim is essential to survival (see Chapter 32) .

Traumatic wounds to the spine are more frequent in motorcycling, hang gliding, paragliding, football, skateboarding and diving into pools, rivers or the sea without knowing the depth of the water and colliding with the bottom with the head generally inclined forward.

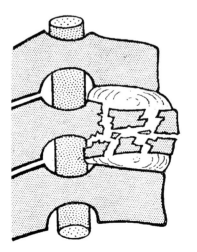

Diagnosis

A computer tomography (CT) scan or magnetic resonance imaging (MRI) of the head and neck may be required to confirm and define any fracture and identify potential injury to the brain, spinal cord or nerves.

Vertebral fracture can injure the spinal cord and nerves.

Treatment

Neck fractures may require immobilization or surgery, if the stability of the neck is compromised and there is risk of injury to the spinal cord. A neurosurgeon or orthopedic surgeon should advise treatment.

Acute Cervical Hernia

Warning:

Wipe outs on large, strong waves can cause whiplash injuries from the sudden jerking of the head. This trauma can lead to an acute cervical hernia. The symptoms usually include cervical pain radiating to the arm. Diagnosis is confirmed by magnetic resonance imaging. This condition usually requires surgical treatment.

For this reason, any persistent neck pain following a wipe out should be carefully investigated.

This magnetic resonance image (MRI) (see illustration) shows a large hernia of the cervical disc (C4/C5) of a Brazilian surfer as a result of a wipe out from the lip of a wave at Sunset Beach in Hawaii. He was treated there for neck pain for more than 40 days with massage and physical therapy but continued to feel tingling along the arm without improvement. The correct diagnosis was eventually made and surgical treatment included the substitution of the disc by a titanium prosthesis. The result was excellent and the athlete is surfing again.

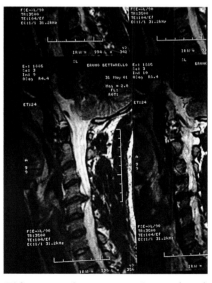

This magnetic resonance image (MRI) shows a large hernia of a surfer's cervical disc (C4/C5) caused by a wipe out triggered by the lip of a wave at Sunset Beach, Hawaii

Chronic Neck Pain

Chronic neck pain affects nearly 30% of all surfers and is – along with lower back pain – one of the most common complaints made by surfers.

The leading causes of biomechanical neck problems include muscle and postural imbalance aggravated by:

1. The paddling position

During paddling, which accounts for about 50% of a surf session, the neck is held in a hyperextended position, which is arched up and toward the back, with the shoulders raised and in constant movement.

This rowing posture requires constant contraction of the muscles at the back of the neck and of the upper, middle and lower back (trapezius and scalenus muscles). This causes tension and muscular shortening that leads to pain and discomfort.

Kelly Slater paddling

2. Duck diving

This is an essential movement. For every 10 waves surfed, the surfer executes about 30 – 50 duck dives. The duck diving biomechanics include:

1. Paddling position facing the upcoming wave.
2. Pushing the surfboard below the wave by projecting the body down and forward, generally with the spine arched and one of the knees and a hip flexed and the other extended.
3. It continues with a forceful hyperextension (a backwards movement) of the entire back (from the neck to the lower back) towards the surface of the water.
4. The movement is completed by a return to paddling.

These repeated and abrupt movements of the backbone aggravate the tension, pain and muscular contraction caused by the paddling position, causing excess pressure on the small cervical joints.

Andrea Lopes duck diving   Photo: A. Junior

3. Maneuvers

Common maneuvers, such as the roundhouse cut-back, extreme snaps, tail slashes, floaters, 360s, etc., cause repeated and intense and extreme rotations in the most mobile area of the neck, between the first and second vertebrae, and between the fifth, sixth and seventh cervical vertebrae, leading to repeated microtraumas that can cause even greater pressure on the cervical structures.

Neco Padaratz

4. Poor 'Core Muscle Control; Poor Body Alignment and Posture; Poor Flexibility

Surfing can lead to muscular tension in the neck. This increases pressure on the intervertebral discs and can cause inflammation of the neck joints.

Over years of surfing, if chronic tension, poor alignment, poor vertebral body adjustment and inflammation are not corrected, they can cause progressive disc and cartilage degeneration (ostheo discarthrosis).

In others words, surfing can cause dehydration of the vertebral discs, reducing the natural cushioning of the spine. This creates a condition favorable to cervical disc hernias. This situation is also aggravated by a lack of stretching, improper posture while sleeping, watching television, working on the computer or driving.

Symptoms

Persistent pain and tension in the neck and back usually occur after a surf session. They may require a few days to improve, but they worsen after each additional surfing session. The athlete's condition will deteriorate and pain will appear during rest. Constant feeling of a neck sprain and headache are also common.

You must see a doctor!

Careful medical examination may reveal numerous painful points along the neck and upper spine. Movement in the region is restricted, and there may be pain and tingling, which radiate to one or both arms.
Our experience shows that despite pain, the surfer will continue to ride the waves. This aggravates the injury from repetitive microtraumas, increasing muscle imbalance, poor posture, and reducing the range of movements of the spinal muscles.

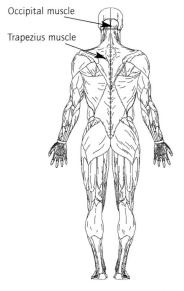

Occipital muscle

Trapezius muscle

Upper back muscles

What to do?

A precise medical diagnosis is essential. This includes, in addition to a postural and orthopedic evaluation, a neurological examination and often an X-ray of the spine. In persistent cases that are difficult to treat, an MRI is necessary.

Diagnosis

Disk-disease may take the form of a degenerative disc, disc bulge, or an actual herniated disc (see Chapter 7).

As mentioned above, an athlete with degenerative disc disease generally has nonspecific complaints of back-pain. The range of motion may be limited and accompanied by pain and muscle spasms.

Disc bulges (and disc degeneration or even disc herniation) can be found in many asymptomatic surfers.

Tears of the disc's annulus fibrosus can lead to acute back pain.

Actual disc herniation can lead to nerve root compression with ensuing radiating pain, numbness, and weakness. Acute disc herniations are rarely a source of back-pain in surfers. Disc herniation pain is typically aggravated by flexions and even by coughing, sneezing, or sitting.

Treatment

This depends on the medical diagnosis but usually consists of four phases, which range from rest to a return to surfing. The guidance is the same as for the lower back (see Chapter 6).

First phase

In the most critical phase, it is best to keep away from the surf. Disc problems usually do not require surgery, but a period of rest from vigorous physical activity (not necessarily bed-rest). Warm compresses and anti-inflammatory medication should be routine. A neck brace, a support for resting and immobilizing the neck muscles, is generally recommended for one to two weeks.

Physical therapy should begin with ultrasound, electric stimulation and deep warming techniques.

Acupuncture has been quite successful in removing sensitive and painful muscle points along the spine.

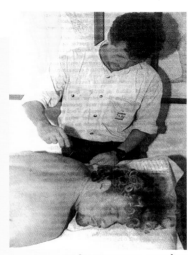

Acupuncture session

Generally, 90% of athletes with disc problems improve over 12 weeks.

If nerve compression (known as radiculopathy) persists, epidural steroids may be warranted.

Only if symptoms continue despite these interventions should surgery be contemplated. Surgery is only performed for refractory pain (over 6 to 12 weeks) or progressive neurologic deficit.

Second phase

Light manipulation with chiropractic techniques including plenty of traction help to readapt the pressure within the joints, through better vertebral juxtaposition, and should be conducted after an X-ray.

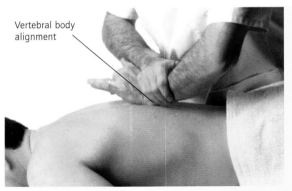

Vertebral body alignment

Chiropractic maneuver

As pain subsides, the neck can be mobilized as long as there is no pain. It is very important in this phase to conduct hydrotherapy in a heated pool. Excellent results have been obtained with aquatic exercise to stabilize the cervical, thoracic and pelvic region, which include stretching and strengthening the muscles.

Third Phase

In this phase, complete and free movement should return to the entire spine. We recommend treatments that include global postural reeducation, increasing body awareness, control and integration to reestablish muscular skeletal balance, such as Alexander techniques or Feldenkrais exercises. The exercises should progress to total core control through Pilates with an appropriate level of challenge. Manual therapy, including massage using Chinese (tui na) or Japanese (shiatsu) techniques, rolfing, do-in, or trigger points will certainly help relax muscles and relieve pain.

To avoid repeated neck movements, swim with a snorkel to keep the spine in a neutral position. When possible, return to aerobic exercises, such as cycling and running.

Fourth Phase

You must be pain free, with complete range of motion in the spine and proper control of core stabilizer muscles, before you go back to surfing.

This phase should maintain the stretching and strengthening exercises of the neck and scapula region seeking muscular reequilibrium and prevention of new injuries.

Swimming, freestyle, should be returned to with care.

The good news is that with postural reeducation and muscular rebalancing exercises (Pilates), 90% of surfers with disc injuries return to surfing in 4 – 12 weeks.

If a nerve-path-compression (radiculopathy) due to disc hernia persists, epidural steroids may be warranted. There is new research indicating the benefits of ozone injections in these cases.

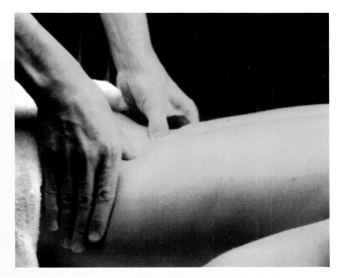

Massage should be part of a surfer's care for spinal column muscles

Only if symptoms continue despite these interventions should surgery be contemplated. Surgery is only performed for refractory pain (over 6 to 12 weeks) or progressive neurologic deficit syndrome.

Warning:

When returning to the waves, try to use a board that offers greater buoyancy. While paddling, reduce the angle of the neck and head back and up.

Neck Rehabilitation Exercises

All of the exercises should be conducted within a range of movement that is in harmony with breathing and does not cause pain. They are generally begun after the second phase of treatment. The challenge should be progressive, always within the "pain-free zone" and based on the core-muscle stability program (see Chapter 24).

Exercise 1

Lying flat, imagine your back being lengthened, while you lower your shoulders. Be aware of the alignment of the pelvis, trunk and scapular region. Use the "breathing wave pattern" described below to activate the pelvic floor, buttocks, abdomen and spinal muscles and stabilize the "core." You can do this exercise on the Feldenkrais roll.

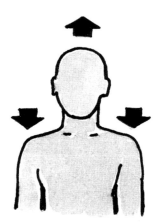

Progress with this exercise to a sitting or standing position.

Here is the correct way to conduct the breathing wave pattern or breathing stabilization sequence, also known as lateral thoracic breathing:

1. Lie flat, with your head and cervical region in a neutral position (maintaining the natural curves of your spine). You may use a pillow if necessary.

2. Keep the back and pelvic bone in a neutral position, as well.

3. Keep the hips and knees flexed and aligned.

4. Place the arms along the body.

5. Breathe in and out – the spine must remain in this neutral position.

6. Exhale, lowering your chest, using your rib cage muscles. Contract your abdominal and pelvic floor muscles.

7. Breathe in, keeping the chest down and the abdominal and pelvic floor muscles activated.

8. Do not put tension in the neck while breathing.

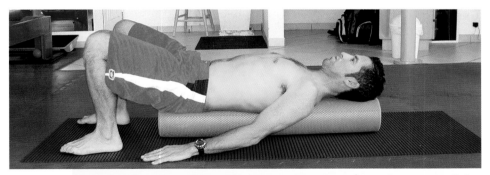

Fabio Gouveia – Tao Pilates Institute of Sports Medicine

Exercise 2

Lie flat, use the breathing wave pattern. Exhale and bend your neck to the left and comfortably place your ear on your shoulder, stretching your neck muscles. Keep breathing. To stretch even more, lower the opposite shoulder. Return to the initial position and repeat the stretch on the opposite side. Hold the

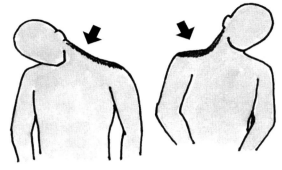

stretch for 30 seconds. As the pain decreases with time, increase the range of motion. Always keep your core muscles (abdominals, pelvic floor, buttocks and spinal muscles) stable while breathing. Progress with the exercise to sitting, sitting on a balance ball and standing positions.

**Everaldo Pato Teixeira –
Tao Pilates Institute of Sports Medicine**

99

Exercise 3

Stretch the neck to the front, trying to place the chin on your chest. Hold for 30 seconds. As your condition improves, progressively increase the stretch:

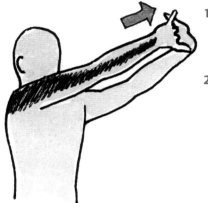

1. Place the hand over your head and press down.

2. While standing, interlace your fingers in front or your body, pressing the palms of your hands away from your body. Place the shoulders forward while attempting to touch the chin to your chest. Hold the stretch for 30 seconds and relax.

Exercise 4

Lie flat; use the breathing wave pattern. Breathe out, lengthen your neck and turn the head to either side, trying to place your chin on the shoulders.

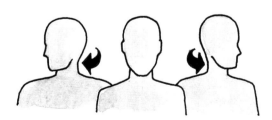

Hold the stretch for 30 seconds. Breathe and do the exercise on the other side. Repeat a few times. Progress the exercise to a sitting and standing position. Keep breathing.

Exercise 5

Lie flat; use the breathing wave pattern. Exhale, lengthen your neck, and twist the head to both sides in a semicircular motion. Avoid backward movement. Progress the exercise to sitting, then standing positions. Keep breathing.

Exercise 6

Lie flat; use the breathing wave pattern. Exhale, lengthen your neck. Inhale deeply and raise and roll the shoulders to the front and up. Exhale, letting the shoulders return naturally to their normal position. Repeat 10 times on both sides.

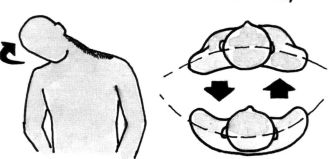

Alternately try to cross your elbows, moving the right arm to the left and vice versa, feeling the stretch on the upper back. Repeat 10 times.

Exercise 7

Begin strengthening the front of the neck with isometric contractions, without moving the neck.

To do so, cup one of the hands over the forehead, lightly forcing the head forward. Maintain the contraction for 10 seconds and repeat 10 times. Then, lying down on your belly, press the head down. Hold for 10 seconds and repeat 10 times.

Always activate your core muscles.

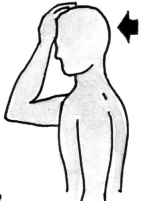

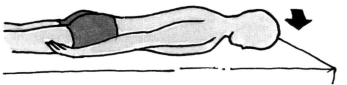

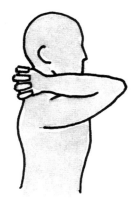

Exercise 8

To strengthen the back of the neck, standing or sitting, cross your fingers behind the neck, slowing forcing the head back, while holding the neck with the hands. Hold the contraction for 10 seconds and repeat 10 times. Then, lying down, press the head down, forcing the chin down. Hold for 10 seconds and repeat 10 times.

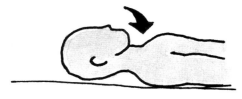

Exercise 9

To strengthen the side of the neck, repeat exercise 8, placing your hand on the side of the head and forcing the movement to the opposite side. Repeat the exercise on the other side.

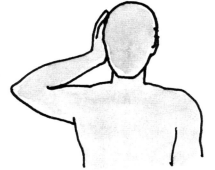

Exercise 10

To strengthen all your spinal muscles, initiate prone exercise with core breathing stability muscles.

You can do the exercise on a Feldenkrais Roll or balance ball.

Exercise 11

As soon you recover your basic core stability, begin a roll-up exercise. Progress slowly.

Using a balance ball is a good idea. Progress to mat and Feldenkrais Roll exercise. Correct your posture, when going to sleep, at work, watching television, driving etc., (see Chapter 7).

Pipeline Hawaii

Photo: Sebastian Rojas

M. Giorgi

Chapter 7

Back Pain

Back pain is among the most common complaints among surfers. It affects three of every 10 athletes.

Acute Trauma to the Lower Back or Lumbar Region

Fractures, contusions and muscles sprains of the lower and upper back are generally caused by wipe outs and the consequent shock of the spinal column against the water when surfing large and powerful waves, or falls on shallow sand, rock or coral bottoms. As with injuries to the spinal column in the cervical region presented in Chapter 6, back problems can result in permanent or temporary paralysis of the legs. Thus, any trauma involving the upper or lower back should be treated with great care. The transportation of the victim should be considered essential for survival (see Chapter 32).

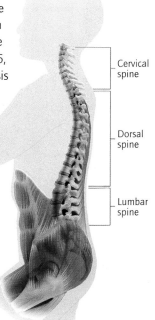

Cervical spine

Dorsal spine

Lumbar spine

Vertebral spine

Wipe out

Chronic Lower Back Pain

Photo: James Thisted

2007 world champion Mick Fanning

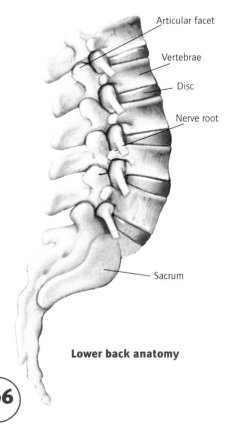

Articular facet

Vertebrae

Disc

Nerve root

Sacrum

Lower back anatomy

Chronic lower back pains are among the most common complaints of surfers, affecting three of every 10 athletes. We calculate that a dedicated surfer, who conducts 5-8 maneuvers per wave, surfing 50 waves per day, 6 days a week, will conduct 6,000-9,200 maneuvers per month that involve the rotation and or compression of the lower back and vertebral discs.

It is believed that 90% of surfers will have some type of back problem during their lives that requires medical attention. The good news is that most improve within 4-12 weeks and go back to surfing. But the problem can be chronic if not cared for. Among famous surfers, the difficulty that three-time world champion Mark Richards has with his back is well known. Surfing for more than 20 years, without any type of stretching or specific training, Richards now has lower back pain that has restricted his surfing.

Causes

The main biomechanical causes are related to the demands that surf places on the body, in particular the lumbar region.

1. Paddling position

Hours of paddling with the spine in a hyper-extended position (arched backwards from the neck to the lumbar region) causes muscle tightening, tension and pain.

Photo: Sebastian Rojas

The spinal column while paddling

2. Maneuvers

The explosive and repeated rotation and compression of the spine during such maneuvers as bottom turns, snaps, cutbacks, lay backs and tubes and the impact from floaters and aerials strain the lumbar region, including its nerves, muscles, ligaments, intervertebral discs, joints, articular capsules, and bones.

B. Rodrigues – Explosive maneuver involving spinal rotation

Photo: Sebastian Rojas

107

3. Duck diving (see description of the maneuver in Chapter 6)

The pain and muscular contractions caused by this movement can affect both sides of the lumbar region and usually serve as a defense mechanism to protect and immobilize the spine. The pain often radiates to one or both of the legs and is known as sciatic pain. It can be accompanied by the tingling or numbness of a certain region of the thigh and leg.

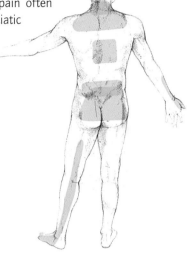

Photo: Sebastian Rojas

Duck Diving

Most common locations of back pain

Typical Posture of a Surfer

The most common anatomy (anatomical condition) found in adult surfers includes:

1. Tension and shortening of the muscular chain of the upper and lower back

2. Hyper cervical and lumbar lordosis

3. Elevation and blockage of the upper thorax (upper thoracic respiration)

4. Tension on and shortening of the hip flexor muscles (iliopsoas and quadriceps)

5. Imbalanced hip muscles due to usual stance (goal or regular foot)

6. *Genu varum* – arched knees

7. Pronated foot (flat foot)

The typical surfer from 6-12 years old tends toward an accentuated hyperlordosis of the cervical and lumbar region and shortening of the muscular chain of the lower back.

The Muscle Chain of the Lower Back

Cervical curvature

Thoracic curvature

Lumbar curvature

The excessive stress on the lower back caused by surfing initially leads to a progressive muscular imbalance characterized by a swayback or lordosis posture. This is caused by tension of lumbar and rear thigh muscles that become shortened and weak, while the abdominal muscles, if they are not well developed, become even weaker and over extended (especially the lower ones). In case this muscular imbalance is not corrected, the excessive pressure over the years is transmitted to the intervertebral discs and can cause compression of these shock absorbers and even herniated discs. The pressure may affect the joints, causing degeneration and arthrosis.

Anatomy of vertebral spine

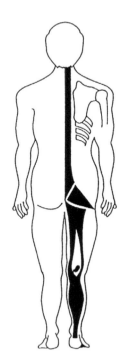

109

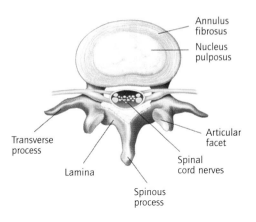

Annulus fibrosus

Nucleus pulposus

Articular facet

Transverse process

Spinal cord nerves

Lamina

Spinous process

This condition is frequently aggravated among those athletes who do not stretch and among teenagers with rapid bone growth, whose muscles and tendons do not accompany this growth. Repeated movements that rotate and compress the backbone progressively strain the region. It is therefore essential to correct this muscular imbalance in order to prevent lower back pain.

Anatomy of a vertebral segment

The Imbalanced Hip Muscle

Surfers usually have imbalanced hip muscles due to their usual stance, which is a predisposing factor for lower back, pelvic and hip problems and injuries. Goofy foot surfers have more control and strength on their left hip and leg (back leg) and regular foot surfers on their right hip and leg.

This imbalance musculard control on the hips is transmitted to the pelvic bones and therefore to the lower back during surfing. It is essential to restore muscular balance of the hip muscles using lunge exercises in order to prevent lower back problems.

What's the Diagnosis?

In cases of sharp or chronic lumbar pain, a doctor's consultation is necessary for a detailed evaluation. Special attention must be given to the evaluation of the posture, any limitations to movement, the degree of stretching, the muscle strength and the vitality and sensibility of the lumbar nerves. Pre-existing postural or orthopedic problems generally wind up becoming complicated by surfing and should be corrected.

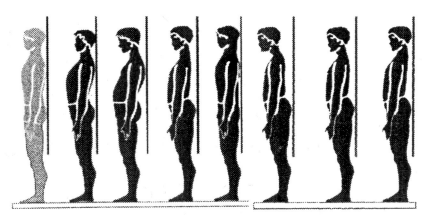

Profile of the most frequent postural alterations

Whenever necessary, an X-ray of the spine or even an MRI helps in the diagnosis and planning of treatment. The most common problems include:

1. Muscular contraction and sprain

2. Torn ligaments

3. Facet syndrome (cartilage injury)

4. A slipped or herniated disc

5. Small fractures of the vertebral joints, known as spondylosis (inflamed vertebrae)

Spondylolisthesis

6. Spondylolisthesis – the forward displacement of a vertebra.

7. In older surfers, we find arthrosis (cartilage degeneraion), a degenerative disc disease and, more rarely, stenosis of the vertebral channel.

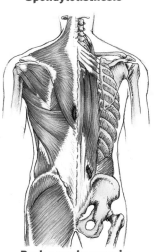

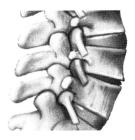

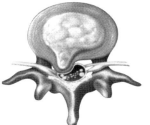

Disc degeneration   **Disc hernia**   **Back muscles sprain and distension**

111

Herniated Disc

The intervertebral disc functions like a shock absorber located between the vertebrae. It is composed of a gel around a fibrous ring (like a rubber band), as shown in the illustration below.

Powerful and explosive maneuvers that involve the rotation and compression of the disc can generate sufficient force to cause a disc protrusion (stage A) or in a more advanced stage, a slipped or herniated disc (stage B) that can then compress the nerve structures around them and cause considerable pain. The disc can also suffer an extrusion (stage C) and even slip outside of the channel (stage D).

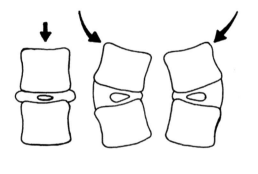

The intervertebral disc is flattened during the vertical compression and in the movements from front to back

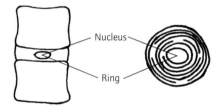

Nucleus

Ring

Anatomy of vertebral disc

A. Protrusion: the intervertebral disc. The gelatinous portion begins to move to the sides.

B. Prolapse: the movement of the content of the disc increases.

C. Extrusion: the contents of the disc breaks the fibrous ring that surrounds it and can compress the nerve root.

D. Sequestration: the contents of the disc seep out.

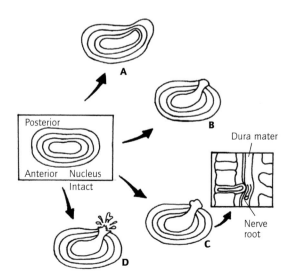

Posterior

Anterior   Nucleus
Intact

Dura mater

Nerve root

Magnetic resonance image of the lumbar region showing a herniated disc

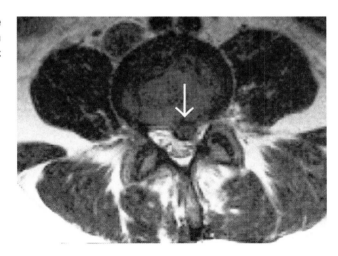

A significant percentage of the population has herniated discs with no symptoms

Emergency

In the event of sharp lower back pain not related to a trauma or fall when one's back is literally paralyzed, it is best to rest. Find a comfortable position. This may include: lying on one's back with a pillow under the knees or lying on your side with the knees and hip bent and with a pillow under the knees (fetal position). Do not let anyone manipulate your spine. Ask for help and wait for an ambulance or medical transport.

Treatment

In more than 95% of all cases treatment is rest followed by the same regimen given for the cervical column (Chapter 6). Surgical treatment should be carefully specified and reserved for cases in which the pain is difficult to control or when there are signs of compression of the nerve root or the medulla.

Rehabilitation from lower back pain involves four phases, which range from rest to a return to surfing. A gradual transition should be made from one phase to another, with constant care to avoid pain during movement.

Respect the speed of your body's recuperation. Learn to listen to your body. Do not force an early return. The leading cause of sports injuries are poorly recovered injuries.

In most cases, you will be ready to return to surfing in 4-12 weeks.

First phase

The initial medical recommendation includes, in addition to rest, the use of anti-inflammatory medication, corticosteroid injections and muscle relaxants in combination with hot compresses.

Acupuncture is often used and has shown excellent results and a shortening of recovery time. Physical therapy is also recommended.

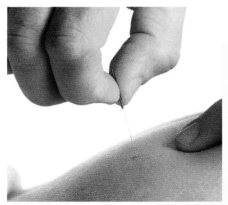

Acupuncture session

Second phase

As soon as the pain subsides, after a rest period of 7-14 days, light stretching exercises on the ground should begin, as well as exercises in the water. Manual therapy with plenty of traction is essential.

Pilates, core training should be started.

Teco Padaratz ready to undertake a session of hyrdotherapy using an aqua jogger

Among the advantages of aquatic rehabilitation is the reduction of the force of gravity, which allows the beginning of walking and other exercises that should not be done on land because in the water there is less load and the risk of microtrauma is highly reduced.

Gradually introduce swimming (preferably the backstroke) and progress with floor exercises. Some patients benefit from chiropractic sessions, which, must only be conducted after an X-ray evaluation.

It is very important to synchronize your mind and posture. Observe the position of your body during your daily activities: at work, while watching TV, driving, sitting, surfing, etc.

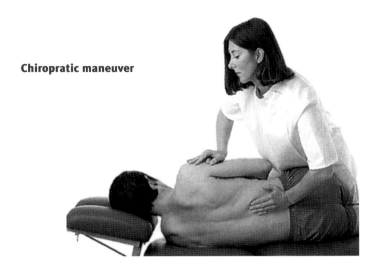

Chiropratic maneuver

Third Phase

As with the neck, during this phase, complete pain-free movement is restored to the entire back. Treatment programs are frequently indicated that include postural reeducation through biofeedback, Global Postural Reeducation (GPR) or Alexander Technique, which seek to reestablish muscular-skeletal equilibrium (see the suggestions below about GPR positions). Surfers who have previous experience with yoga should return to their practice, initially avoiding any position that reproduces the movements of paddling and maneuvers. Remember that no exercise should produce pain or discomfort. This is a basic principle of rehabilitation. That is, explore the exercises in a range of movement that does not cause pain.

To avoid repetitive movements of the neck, use a snorkel when swimming. This allows swimming without constant rotation of the neck and keeps the spine in a neutral position. Return to aerobic activities, such as cycling and running, when they can be executed without pain.

Body control and awareness are principal tools. To improve them, undertake exercises that use an imaginary thread that passes through the middle of the head and leaves the body between the legs. Whenever the thread is inclined, you should readjust it, repositioning your various body segments (see Exercise 10).

A progressive, pain-free, Pilates core training program is essential.

The surfer has to master breathing strategies to control each of his vertebrae, controlling all the deepest spine muscle, abdominal and pelvic floor muscles.

Prone exercises on the ball are very important for back strength and stability!

Pilates will help improve stretching, strength, balance and coordination (see Chapter 24). Most surfers' back problems come from imbalance in the muscles used for paddling. You must master core stability for paddling.

Go slowly, always maintain control.

Lie prone with ball under chest/abdomen, legs hip-width apart, pelvis in neutral. Place your center of gravity on the ball.

Master the breathing wave technique to have your core provide total trunk stability.

Exhale and extend your trunk with your arms outstretched in front of you. Maintain your alignment, avoid lower back and neck compression! Keep your shoulder blades down!

Inhale, exhale and return to the rest position.

Repeat 8 to 12 times.

Fourth phase – Maintenance – Return to Surfing

Return to surfing gradually. Relaxing massage, including do-in, shiatsu, tui na or foot reflexology are good options to eliminate tension and muscular contraction after the sessions. If you have frequent lower back pain and continue to surf, it is recommended that after medical evaluation, you conduct muscular rebalancing exercises that include Pilates (Chapter 24) in addition to swimming, stretching the lower back muscles and the back portion of the thighs and strengthening of the abdominal muscles.

It is often necessary to go back to surfing with a longer, larger and thicker board. With greater buoyancy, your rowing will be easier, which will reduce stress on the lumbar region. It also encourages rail-to-rail surfing, which reduces rotation and lower back twists in maneuvers. Try to paddle with the legs crossed (one over the other), to provide greater protection for your back.

Avoid surfing in the morning, because your spine is less flexible. The late afternoon is the best time and after a good stretch. Avoid surfing immediately after long car trips.

Manual therapy – massage is essential for a surfer's back

Surfing After Herniated Disk Surgery

Three to six months of rehabilitation are generally necessary before returning to surfing after herniated-disc surgery. As soon as your doctor permits, begin hydrotherapy, running in a deep pool and swimming. Keep as healthy and active as possible. Remember that no movement or activity should cause pain. Follow these suggestions.

Tips:

1. Observe the correct manner of getting up from a lying down position, especially in the initial phases of recuperation. Turn your legs and then raise your trunk.

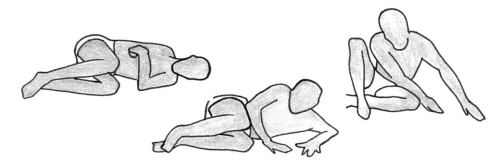

2. On long car trips, make frequent stops for stretching. Use a small pillow or rolled towel to support the lower back region on the seat of the car, which should alleviate lordosis (forward curvature of the lower spinal column).

117

3. Put your wetsuit on while lying down (raising the knees to the chest). This can help avoid pain.

4. Specific exercises should be included for this problem and based on a postural evaluation. In any case, improve your posture during your daily activities, while standing, sitting, lying down or working. The best posture is that which places the lowest amount of stress on the spine. Keep your weight in a healthy range.

5. If you work sitting down, stretch frequently and avoid crossing your legs.

6. Stretching on a bar is an excellent technique.

7. Use an orthopedic mattress with suitable support and density for your weight.

8. Try to sleep on your back with a pillow under the knees or on your side with a pillow between your legs.

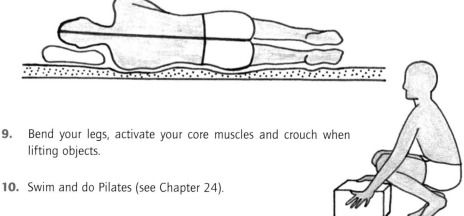

9. Bend your legs, activate your core muscles and crouch when lifting objects.

10. Swim and do Pilates (see Chapter 24).

11. Sit ups (at least 500 per day with your knees bent and your feet on the floor).

12. Always stretch before and after surfing.

13. Keep a core training program all year round.

14. Develop a good weight-training program, using light weights and lots of repetitions.

Rehabilitation Exercises
(Always Initiate with Your Breathing Wave)

Exercise 1

Lying flat, imagine your back being lengthened, while you lower your shoulders. Be aware of the alignment of the pelvis, trunk and scapular region. Use the "breathing wave pattern" described below to activate the pelvic floor, buttocks, abdomen and spinal muscles and stabilize the "core."

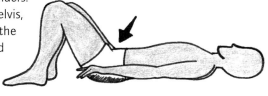

You can do this exercise on the Feldenkrais roll.

Progress with this exercise to a sitting or standing position.

Here is the correct way to conduct the breathing wave pattern or breathing stabilization sequence, also known as lateral thoracic breathing:

1. Lie flat, with your head and cervical region in a neutral position (maintaining the natural curves of your spine). You may use a pillow if necessary.

2. Keep the back and pelvic bone in a neutral position, as well.

3. Keep the hips and knees flexed and aligned.

4. Place the arms along the body.

5. Breathe in and out – the spine must remain in this neutral position.

6. Exhale, lowering your chest, using your rib cage muscles. Contract your abdominal and pelvic floor muscles.

7. Breathe in, keeping the chest down and the abdominal and pelvic floor muscles activated.

8. Do not put tension in the neck while breathing.

Exercise 2

Lie on your back on the floor and pull the left leg toward the chest. Keep the other leg stretched out without forcing it. Repeat the same exercise for the right leg. Hold the stretch for 30 seconds. Repeat the exercise a few times.

Exercise 3

Rolling like a ball

From a sitting position, bend your hips and knees with feet off the ground. Place the ball over your knees. Keep your back in a C position. Be careful to not lift your shoulders or flex your neck too much.

While inhaling, roll back, while exhaling, roll up. Maintain the distance between your chest and knees. Do not touch the floor with your head or feet.

Repeat a few times.

Exercise 4

Cat

While supported on your hands and knees, slowly arch the back, while lowering the head like a stretching cat. Then reverse the arch, raising the head and forming a U shape with the spine. Hold for 10-15 seconds in each position, breathing in or out with each movement. Repeat 5 times.

Always keep your core muscles activated.

Exercise 5

Lie on your stomach and place a pillow under the abdomen, contracting and relaxing your core muscles. Repeat 10 times, holding each contraction for 10 seconds.

Exercise 6

Sit down over your folded legs and stretch your arms to the front. Keep your arms and back stretched for 30 seconds.

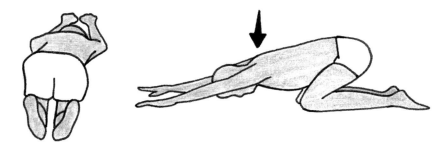

Exercise 7

Lie on your back and use a towel or belt to help stretch the hamstring muscle at the rear of your leg. First wrap a towel or belt around the point of your foot and pull on it to lengthen the calf. Then, place it around the heel. Hold it while completely extending the leg for 30 seconds.

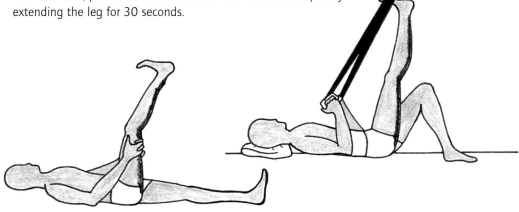

Exercise 8

Initiate the strengthening of the abdominal and trunk muscles. Always control the movement. Keep the hips and knees folded and the backbone in contact with the floor. Do not flex your neck or upper back. Roll up the neck and the upper back 15-20 degrees. Begin with 5 series of 10, holding the contraction for 5-10 seconds. Return one vertebra per vertebra. You can use a Feldenkrais roll for challenge.

Everaldo "Pato" Teixeira – core training using Feldenkrais roll and flex ring

Exercise 9

As soon as the pain is gone, begin stretching with rotation of the trunk. Hold for 30 seconds.

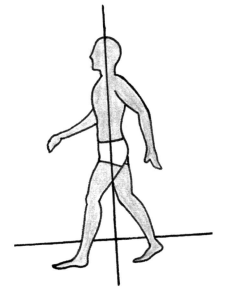

Exercise 10

Exercise good posture. Walk as erectly as possible. To do so, imagine a thread pulling your body up. Imagine that this thread runs from your head and leaves between your legs. Relax the shoulders and keep the imaginary thread perpendicular to the ground.

Exercise 11

Lift an object from a table or shelf without bending forward.
Use your core muscles.

Exercise 12

When sitting, do not cross your legs. Keep your back
straight. The ideal chair should have the same height as
your knee, and a depth equal to the length of the thigh
and the back with a maximum inclination of 100 degrees.

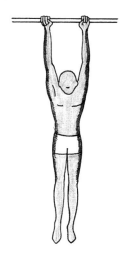

Exercise 13

Hang from a bar.

Exercise 14

Carefully begin strengthening
the back muscles. On your hands
and knees, simultaneously
stretch one arm and the opposite
leg. Begin with 3 series of 10.

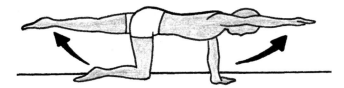

Pool Rehabilitation

Exercise 1

Begin by walking in the pool, to the front, backwards and to the sides. As you improve, introduce resistance with the use of gloves or walking while holding a flat board in front of you. If there is no pain, you can begin walking in deep water (deep walking). Maintain good posture.

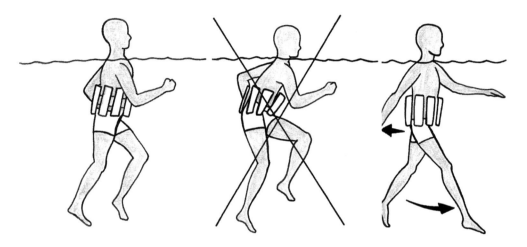

Exercise 2-3

Progressively begin abdominal exercises while standing, correcting the pelvis position. Standing with your back against the wall and feet separated to the distance of the shoulders, contract the abdominal muscles while keeping your back against the pool wall. Progress with the contraction of the abdominal muscles, flexing the knees and supporting yourself along the edge of the pool (15/34).

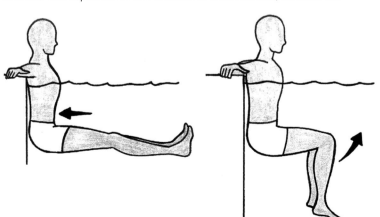

Exercise 4

Lying down, supported by a cervical collar and a back vest (aqua jogger), keep the abdomen slightly contracted while opening the arms and kicking the legs.

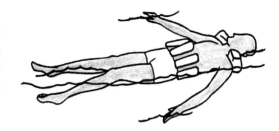

Exercise 5

With your head in the water and the use of a snorkel, begin flexing the knees in the direction of the chest. Then alternate moving the arms, progressing to moving the arms and legs simultaneously, Always use a lumbar flotation vest. As you progress, begin swimming with the vest until removing it. Then, when possible, remove the snorkel and swim the crawl and backstroke, which are basic exercises for the back.

Exercise 6

Begin hip flexion exercises and progress with hip flexion and knees extension. (core training-leg series).

Exercise 7

Progress with the trunk rotation. Advance to running in the water (deep run) and swimming. Stretch and relax.

Below are some suggestions for active global stretching exercises for the back muscle chain.

Based on techniques of Global Postural Reeducation, these exercises should be conducted with the supervision of a rehabilitation team.

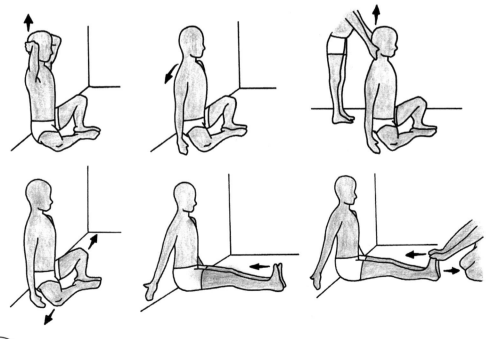

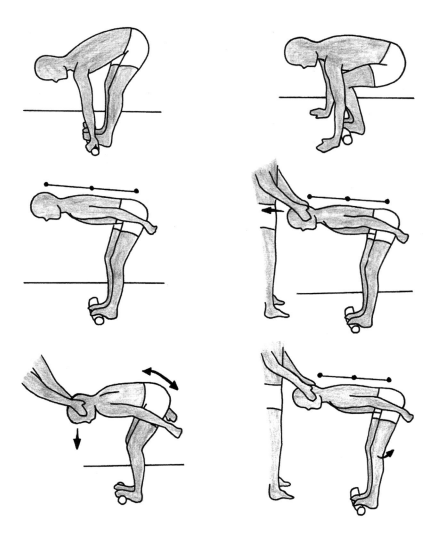

Continue your core training – see Pilates for Surfers in Chapter 24.

Pato: Bosu core training

SURFING & HEALTH

Fabio Gouveia
Fernando de Noronha Archipelago

Chapter 8

Shoulder Problems

Shoulder pain is a very common complaint among surfers. It affects nearly 30% of amateur athletes and an even higher percentage of professionals.

Acute Trauma to the Shoulders

Although they are not frequent, severe injuries to the shoulders do occur in surfing. Fractures are generally caused by whacks from surfboards during wipe outs. Acute injuries to the shoulder include fractures of the clavicle, humerus, or scapula; acromioclavicular (AC) and sternoclavicular (SC) separations; and shoulder subluxations and dislocations. Occasionally an athlete will sustain a ruptured tendon or muscle tear.

You must see a doctor

Explosive maneuver

Photo: Marcelo Preto

Fractures

Beach Assessment

The athlete has severe pain following a wipe out. Generally the traumatic force was on the point of the shoulder or caused an axial load (direct blow) to the humerus when hitting the water, surfboard or ocean bottom. Severe local tenderness indicates a likely fracture. The injured limb should be supported with a sling and ice applied to the injured region until X-rays or a tomography are conducted and the specific diagnosis confirmed.

Treatment

Shoulder fractures may require surgery to ensure anatomic reduction in the dominant shoulder.

Most cases of clavicle fractures nearly always heal well by using a sling or figure-eight brace for comfort. Some do require surgery.

Scapula fractures are usually high-energy injuries and usually take place on powerful waves, like Teahupoo and Pipeline. CJ Hobgood had a scapular fracture following a wipe out at Teahupoo. Most scapular fractures can be, treated by immobilization in a soft dressing, such as a sling and bandage. Check for associated injuries to the ribs, lung, and heart.

Rehabilitation

Once the fracture has healed – normally about 60 to 90 days following injury – strength, range of motion and proprioception must be restored before returning to surf. A typical training progression includes early passive motion, followed by active motion and a muscular strengthening program. Advanced exercises for shoulder control and stabilization are mandatory.

Shoulder Dislocation

Beach Assessment

Shoulder dislocation generally occurs following a wipe out when the arm is forced into extreme external rotation and abduction after a clash with the water, surfboard or a sand bottom.

To avoid further pain, the surfer should secure the arm (in external rotation and adducted, if possible). The athlete often feels the shoulder pop out of the joint and there is obvious deformity.

On rare occasions (when the person has suffered recurrent dislocations and conducted this procedure), the shoulder can be put back in place by the surfer and some athletes have returned to surf competition minutes after such subluxations or dislocations. However, you must have experience to do this without creating further damage.

More than 90% of traumatic shoulder dislocations occur in the forward direction.

This may injure the axillary nerve, causing decreased sensation and deltoid muscle weakness. If possible, an X-ray should be made before executing any reduction (replacement) maneuvers, particularly in young surfers, due the risk of associated fracture.

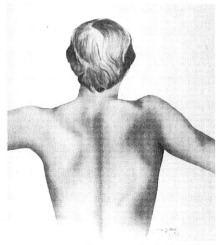

Asymmetrical shoulders following dislocation

Treatment

It is possible for the shoulder to be put back in place at the beach by someone with proper training. This should be done as soon and as smoothly as possible. However, good muscle relaxation (often requiring medication) is usually needed for reduction, which should also be performed by someone with proper training. The possibility of a fracture must also be ruled out by an X-ray and a doctor should conduct a complete orthopedic evaluation.

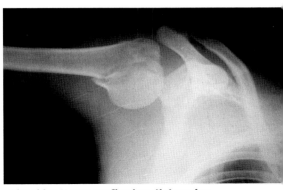

Shoulder X-ray confirming dislocation

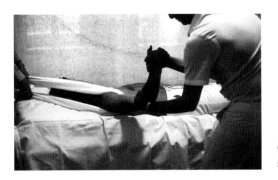

One of the maneuvers to put a shoulder back in place

Treatment of dislocations is controversial.

After a first anterior glenohumeral* dislocation, up to 90 % of competitive athletes will suffer repeated dislocations if there is no surgical correction. For this reason, for first-time dislocations, we recommend conservative treatment with 4 to 6 weeks of rest in a sling and bandage, followed by therapy to restore motion, strength and stability and to eliminate multidirectional laxity.

Depending on the athlete's situation, however, surgical repair, usually arthroscopic, should be considered. Recurrent dislocations are can be stabilized by open or arthroscopic surgery.

Rehabilitation

Whether treated non-surgically or surgically, in general, three to four months of rehabilitation are required to achieve pre-injury status. In all cases, attention is paid to restoring strength, stability, full range of motion and perfect control before a return to surfing. Surfers with shoulder dislocations treated non-operatively may return to their sport after the pain subsides and full range of motion and strength are restored.

Following surgical repair, four months is usually needed before returning to the waves to achieve adequate healing, strength, and proprioception.

WARNING
All shoulder dislocations should be X-rayed to confirm reduction and to check for fractures of the articular surface of the head of the humerus (found after severe and recurring shoulder dislocations) which is known as a Hill-Sachs injury.

Bankarts injury is an injury to the lip of the glenoidal capsule (internal shoulder structure). It is caused by an impact when the arm is bent, in abduction, and rotated outwards. The injury increases vulnerabilty to shoulder dislocations. It is often difficult to diagnosis, requiring an arthro-magnetic resonance image. It may require surgery.

---

*   The glenoid labrum is a special internal structure responsible for shoulder stability. It is a type of fibrocartilage that can be torn during dislocation or subluxation. It is usually treated with conservative therapy through exercise. However, if this fails, surgical stabilization should be considered. This can be performed openly or arthroscopically and the labrum should be repaired at the same time.

Shoulder Separations

Beach assessment

Shoulder separations, known clinically as acromioclavicular and anterior sternoclavicular separation, are usually caused by a fall directly on the point of the shoulder. This is not frequent among surfers, although it is common among snow boarders. The severity of pain is related to the severity of the injury. Athletes are usually unable to continue surfing. Local tenderness and deformity (in more severe injuries) provide the likely diagnosis. If examination on the beach reveals a posterior sternoclavicular separation, emergency cardiopulmonary evaluation and treatment are required. If the injury is a typical acromioclavicular or an anterior sternoclavicular separation, a sling will provide comfort until a full assessment is completed.

Diagnosis

You must see a doctor

A specific X-ray or tomography must be conducted to confirm the diagnosis, and special attention should be given to young surfers.

Treatment

Acromioclavicular separations are usually treated without surgery.

Rehabilitation

An acromiodavicular separation can be rehabilitated with general shoulder strengthening as soon as pain allows. Generally, post-operative treatment for acromiodavicular requires 4 to 6 weeks of healing before motion and strengthening exercises can be started. Whether treated non-surgically or surgically, three to four months of rehabilitation is usually required to return to pre-injury status.

Explosive maneuver

Photo: Levy Paiva

133

Acute Muscle/Tendon Rupture

Beach Assessment

Sudden severe pain in the region of a muscle following a forceful contraction – usually as the muscle is actually lengthening – suggests muscle or tendon rupture. Strength is immediately markedly decreased and there is local pain and swelling, with rapid muscle spasms. Ice and an elastic compressive wrap can decrease symptoms on the beach.

You must see a doctor

Diagnosis

Muscle or tendon rupture to the pectoralis major, long head biceps, subscapularis, and other rotator cuff muscles can occur. Palpation along both sides of the muscle tendon can help confirm suspicions of a complete tear. Muscle weakness is another symptom. physical examination will identify most of these ruptures. Magnetic resonance imaging (MRI) or ultrasound can confirm the diagnosis.

Treatment

For all of these injuries, except those to the long head biceps tendon, surgical repair is necessary. A rupture of the long head biceps tendon is frequently degenerative, and it is difficult to achieve satisfactory repair. The resulting weakness has not been found to be significant.

Rehabilitation

After surgical muscle or tendon repair, passive motion is begun immediately followed by active motion, for 6 weeks post-operatively. Strength training can also be started at 6 weeks after surgery.

Repetitive Stress Injuries

In addition to surfing, sports such as tennis, volleyball, swimming and those that involve throwing are among those that place excessive stress upon and injure the shoulder.

Shoulder movement in tennis

Shoulder movement in volleyball

Shoulder movement in swimming

135

To better understand the excessive stress that surfing can place on the shoulders, an understanding of shoulder anatomy is essential.

The shoulder is formed by the scapula, clavicle, and the humerus (See Illustrations 1 and 2). The shoulder is an extremely complex joint, capable of moving in all directions. Its stability is provided by the rotator cuff, which is composed of four muscles and their tendons, as shown in the illustrations below (the supraspinatus, infraspinatus, the teres minor and the subscapularis). They provide stability and allow adequate movement of the shoulder during paddling to catch a wave.

Shoulder anatomy

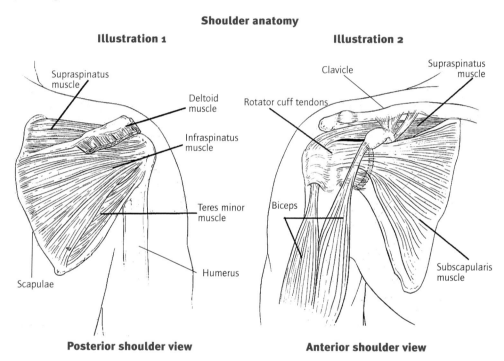

Illustration 1

Supraspinatus muscle
Deltoid muscle
Infraspinatus muscle
Teres minor muscle
Humerus
Scapulae

Posterior shoulder view

Illustration 2

Clavicle
Supraspinatus muscle
Rotator cuff tendons
Biceps
Subscapularis muscle

Anterior shoulder view

Recurring Pain in the Shoulders and the Impact Syndrome

Shoulder pain is a very common complaint among surfers. It affects nearly 30% of amateur athletes and an even higher percentage of professionals.

The principal cause is repeated paddling. To prevent this pain, it is important to know how the shoulders work while you are looking for a wave.

Unlike swimming, where the average distance traveled in a training session is 1,500–2,000 meters for recreational athletes and between 4,000 and 8,000 meters for those who compete (in two sessions per day; 2 hours per session; 5 days a week), in surfing it is not known exactly how many strokes are taken or the distance traveled by a surfer in a typical 2-hour surfing session.

It is estimated that the number of paddling strokes in surfing easily exceeds 2,000 in a two-hour surf session, especially if the athlete is riding one wave after another and the swell is heavy, making the surfer fight the current.

The stress on the shoulders increases even more if you have to paddle quickly and intensely, and use explosive effort to catch a wave, or during a sequence of maneuvers in which the shoulders are used to stabilize the body.

It is natural for shoulders to be tired after surfing and after three to four swells, they will need rest. If another swell begins to roll, there will not be time for recovery and if overuse occurs, there can be microtraumas to the tendons, beginning an impact syndrome and leading to tendonitis in the rotator cuff (see Illustration 3).

Illustration 3

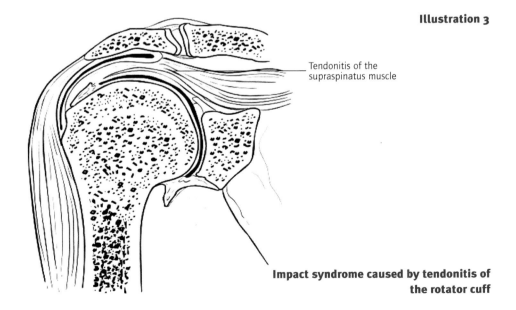

Tendonitis of the
supraspinatus muscle

**Impact syndrome caused by tendonitis of
the rotator cuff**

Paddling in Surf

Paddling in surf differs somewhat from the strokes used in swimming because the trunk and the neck are raised and lifted towards the back (in hyperextension) and the body is supported on the board.

Paddling consists of four phases:

First phase

Illustration 4

The phase of entrance, when the arm reaches in front of the head and begins to enter the water.

Second phase

The initial movement of pulling the hand and arm through the water.

Illustration 5

Third phase

The continuous phase of pulling the hand and arm through the water.

Fourth phase

The recovery phase, when the arm returns to the initial position to begin another cycle.

Paddling

Swimmer's Shoulder (Surfer's Shoulder)

Diagnosis

"Swimmer's shoulder" is an anterior problem, caused by overdevelopment of the pectoralis major and anterior deltoid muscles.

Frequently, there is decreased internal rotation and a tight posterior capsule. Prolonged imbalances and abnormal motions of swimmer's shoulder can lead to instability and shoulder (labral) degeneration. Associated biceps tendinitis occurs frequently.

Muscle Imbalance

An imbalance between the front muscles (internal rotators) and those behind the arm (external rotators), generated by repeated paddling can cause mechanical irritation and decrease the flow of blood to the rotator cuff tendons, principally in the phase when the hand enters the water (Illustration 4) and in the first half of the paddling phase (Illustration 5) when the arm is stretched to the front (flexed), to the side (abduction) and rotated inward.

This position forces the humeral head too far forward or upward and can impinge upon the acromion or coracoacromial ligaments through the rotator cuff. The resulting friction can lead to bursitis, tendinitis, tendonosis and tears.

Strong pectoralis major and anterior deltoid muscles are frequently associated with decreased internal rotation and a tight posterior capsule. Prolonged imbalances and abnormal motions by surfers' shoulders can lead to instability and degeneration. Associated tendinitis of the biceps is common.

It is very important to discover the cause of muscle imbalance.

In addition to paddling, some structural abnormalities in the shoulder can cause an impact syndrome. Among the most common, which should be confirmed with X-rays, are the anatomic changes to the shape of the acromion, which can become curved (type II) or hooked (type III). These anatomical changes can decrease the space where the rotator cuff tendons move.

The impact syndrome can be aggravated by explosive movements of the shoulder during maneuvers.

Diagnosis

The acute phase of the injury is characterized by tendon inflammation, while chronic injuries can show signs of degeneration, known as tendinosis, which can lead to calcium deposits and a partial or total tearing of the rotator cuff tendons. These chronic injuries are usually caused by poorly healed injuries in situations where the injured surfer continued to train despite the pain.

In the first phases, the pain comes at the beginning of surfing and improves as the muscles warm up. Without treatment, the pain will worsen, making training difficult. Then comes nocturnal pain and difficulty sleeping on the side affected. The pains are located on the front and side of the shoulder (see Illustration 6) and are aggravated when the arm is raised to the front and the side, usually between 60 and 100 degrees.

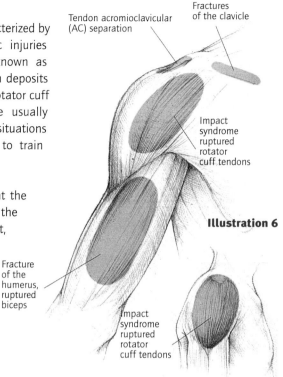

Tendon acromioclavicular (AC) separation

Fractures of the clavicle

Impact syndrome ruptured rotator cuff tendons

Illustration 6

Fracture of the humerus, ruptured biceps

Impact syndrome ruptured rotator cuff tendons

Painful areas on the shoulder and possible diagnosis

See your doctor and begin treatment at the first symtoms.

The first examination includes a detailed analysis of posture, range of movement, degree of stretching, muscular strength and the stability of the arms, in addition to specific tests that confirm the diagnosis.

It is often necessary to study the relationship of the shoulder bones with an X-ray and observe the tendons, muscles and bursa in detail through ultrasound and an MRI.

Postural evaluation allows visualizing the effects of surfing on the body. It was explained how the paddling position shortens the entire muscle chain along the back (in Chapter 7).

Paddling also shortens the upper and front muscles of the shoulder and upper arm, and can lead to an impact syndrom (Illustration 7).

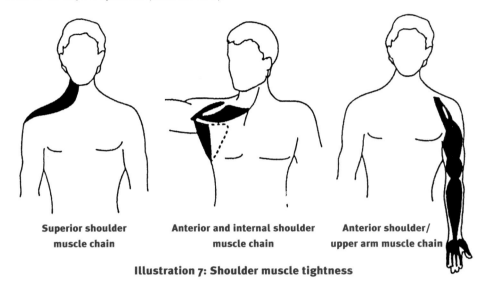

| Superior shoulder muscle chain | Anterior and internal shoulder muscle chain | Anterior shoulder/ upper arm muscle chain |

Illustration 7: Shoulder muscle tightness

Treatment and Rehabilitation for Rotator Cuff Injuries

The treatment should be taken seriously and begin as soon as possible. Rehabilitation takes 6-12 weeks. Some athletes, however, go back to training too soon, complicating the healing and recovery process. In some cases, complete rehabilitation takes one year.

Remember that the principal cause of sports injuries is a poorly rehabilitated injury.

Wipe outs risk shoulder injuries

Photo: James Thisted

141

First Phase

The rehabilitation of the shoulder begins with rest. It is necessary to rest the arm for a few days. In some serious cases, when the pain is very intense, it is common to immobilize the arm with a sling.

The use of oral anti-inflammatory medication is recommended for one to two weeks. Massages with ice for nearly 20 minutes, three to four times a day are essential. Excellent results are achieved with the use of acupuncture.

Acupuncture

Recent studies have confirmed that sports mesotherapy is an excellent option. This is a French technique in which a mixture of diluted medications are administered intradermally in small doses (Illustration 8).

The treatment also involves physical therapy with laser, ultrasound, electric stimulation and other methods.

Second Phase – Recovery of the Range of Movement

As soon as the pain subsides, begin a progressive program of exercises on the ground and in the water. Treatment of impingement (pressure from the scapula on the rotator cuff) first requires rotator cuff and scapular strengthening and balance.

This should include mobilization exercises and stretching of the shoulder, in particular abduction and outward rotation, in an arc of movement that does not cause pain.

Early mobility in the water is the first stage of reinforcing the shoulder muscles.

Ice massages should be continued after the exercises.

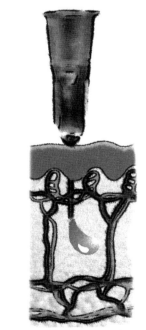

**Illustration 8:
Mesotherapy injection technique**

142

Third Phase – Muscular Rebalancing and Proprioception

Since impingement is classically caused by relatively weak rotator cuff muscles, strengthening the subscapularis, supraspinatus, infraspinatus, and teres minor is mandatory. Frequently, the scapular stabilizers including the rhomboids, trapezius, levator scapulae and the serratus anterior must be strengthened as well. These muscles must be strengthened in non-operative treatment of shoulder instability as well as following operative glenohumeral repairs. The strengthening program should include the entire muscle chain involved in the movement, particularly the trunk muscles where the scapulae are placed.

ATTENTION:
Always keep your core muscles stabilizing your trunk!

Use a progressive load (resistance) in movement through the use of stretch cords (flexiband) and free weights (see the exercises below).

In this phase of rehabilitation, the exercises for fine adjustment between the brain and shoulder called proprioception exercises are very important (exercises 13-14). They relate to control of the shoulder at all points of motion.

Restoration of muscle balance and endurance are fundamental principles of rehabilitation. In the shoulder, this refers to balance between the rotator cuff and the major muscles and between internal and external rotators. Any imbalance can lead to excessive motion and instability.

In this phase, it is important to maintain cardiovascular training through cycling and ergometrics.

Fourth Phase – Return to Surfing

Return to surfing when you can conduct all the shoulder movements without pain. Begin with light training and try to use a board with greater buoyancy, which makes paddling and the biomechanics of the arm easier.

Progress to the realization of strengthening and proprioception exercises that simulate surfing without risk of reinjury. It is important to work both arms due to the effect known as cross training, which means when the healthy arm is trained for strength and endurance, an increase of strength and neuromuscular activity also will occur on the injured side. If there is pain, reduce the load and massage with ice.

Ideally, the shoulder (including the core and scapulothoracic region) should have a full, pain-free range of motion with balanced strength and endurance and normal proprioception.

In reality, if the shoulder is relatively well balanced and pain-free and if extreme or painful motions (e.g. external rotation) can be restricted, the athlete can return to surfing.

Photo: Sebastian Rojas

Gabriela Leite

Exercises for Rehabilitation of Rotator Cuff Injuries

Exercise 1: Mobilization

Pendulum movement. Bend forward. Gently move the arm front to back for one minute, rest and move it from side to side for one minute; rest and then rotate clockwise and counterclockwise for one minute. Progressively widen the swing of the pendulum.

Shane Hering

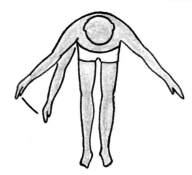

Exercise 2: Mobilization with Weight

With the improvement of symptoms, begin exercises with 1/2 kg weights and gradually increase. Exercises should not cause pain.

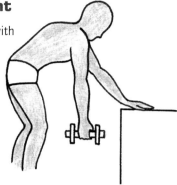

Exercise 3: Mobilization with Flexing and Abduction

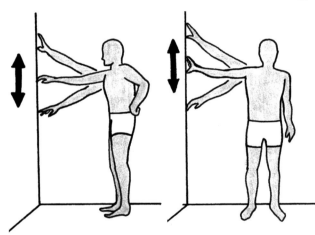

Let your fingers climb the wall. Face the wall with your elbow extended, walking your fingers up the wall as high as they can go (without pain). Keep your shoulders relaxed. Do not raise them. Repeat the exercise standing perpendicular to the wall. Repeat 10 times.

Exercise 4: Mobilization

Standing or sitting, place your hands on your shoulders. Try to bring your elbows together, forming two arcs inward and then outward. Repeat 10 times for both sides.

Exercise 5: External Rotation

Begin without weights. With the elbow close to the body, move the shoulder outward. With the improvement of your symptoms, progressively raise the elbow. At the right time and with guidance, begin the same exercise with an elastic band.

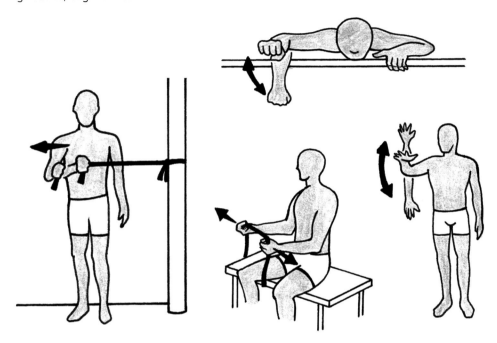

Exercise 6: Isometric Contraction of the Scapular Muscles

With the trunk stabilized, interlace your hands behind your head and force the elbows back, bring the scapulas together. Hold this position for 10 seconds and repeat 10 times.

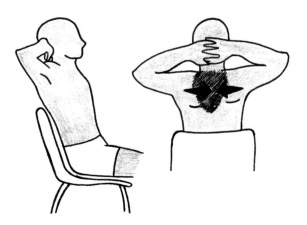

Exercise 7: Strengthening the Scapular Stabilizer Muscles

These are exercises to strengthen the back of the arm (trapezius and scapular stabilizers). Begin without weights. With hands at your waist, raise them toward the chest. When ready, begin using an elastic band passed under your feet and held with your hands. Begin with three series of 10 repetitions. Gradually increase to 30-40 repetitions.

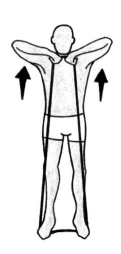

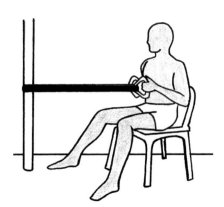

Exercise 8: Strengthening the Scapular Muscles

With the arms and hands extended in front of the body, bring the hands toward the chest. As strength returns, begin using an elastic band. Sitting, pull the band, bringing the elbows toward the body. Begin with 3 series of 10 repetitions. Gradually increase to 30 or 40 repetitions.

Exercise 9: Strengthening the Scapular Muscles

Raise the arms and bend the elbows. When ready, begin using an elastic band. Begin with three series of 10 repetitions. Gradually increase to 30-40 repetitions.

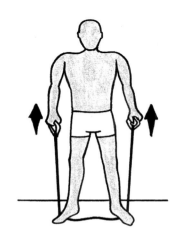

Exercise 10: Strengthening the Deltoid Muscles

Laterally lift the arm to the height of the shoulder, with the thumb pointing toward the ground. Imagine that you are emptying a can. Begin with three series of 10 and gradually increase to 30-40 repetitions. Do **not** go over 90 degrees.

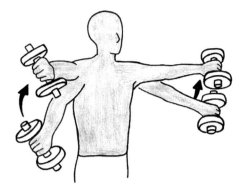

Exercise 11: Strengthening of the Abductors and Supraspinatus

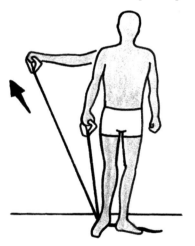

Place an elastic band under the foot. Begin with the arm at your side. Raise it in a diagonal motion until your arm is parallel to the ground. Begin with 3 series of 10 and gradually increase to 30 or 40 repetitions.

Exercise 12: Proprioception and support

Begin supporting both arms on a table as shown in the illustration. Shift support from one arm to the other.

Exercise 13: Proprioception With and Without a Ball

Support your arm on a wall as shown in the illustration. Slowly move your arm up and down, frontward and backward. When you are ready, support your hand on a ball and conduct the same exercise.

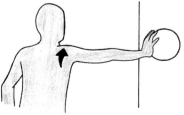 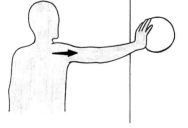

Exercises in the Water

All of the exercises presented previously can be conducted in the water.

Exercise 1: Mobilization

Begin mobilizing the arm forwards and backwards, while walking.

Exercise 2: Shoulder Movements Using a Stick and Neck Support

Exercise 3: External Rotation Mobilizations with the Use of a Cervical Collar

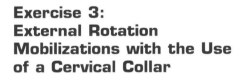

Exercise 4: Aquatic Weight Exercises

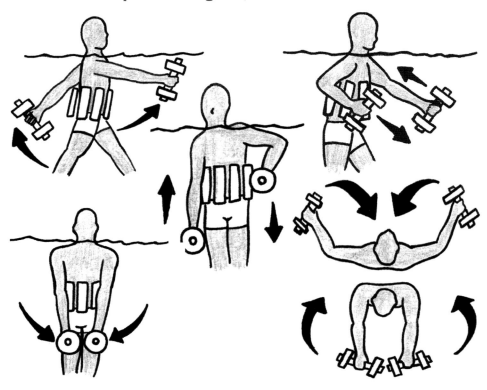

Exercise 5: Stretching

Hold each stretch for 30 seconds with coordinated breathing.

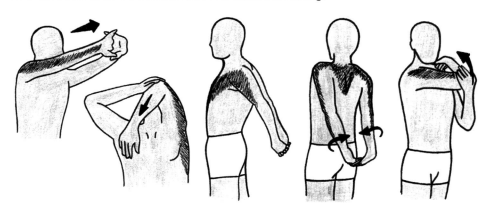

Prevention

This is the best way to keep surfing:

1. Correct your paddling technique. Avoid extending the arms too far to the sides when paddling. They should rotate and plunge deeply alongside the edge of the board. Warm-up and stretch the arms slowly and carefully to the full extent of movements before and after surfing.

2. Conduct muscular reinforcement and rebalancing exercises. External rotation, abduction and shoulder stabilization exercises are essentially preventive and should be used to correct muscular imbalance.

   If you feel pain, immediately leave the water, conduct careful stretching in the opposite direction of paddling and massage with ice for 20 minutes.

4. Seek medical help.

5. Do not use rubber gloves to improve paddling.

6. When falling off the board with the arms open (in a "Superman" position) keep them firm when hitting the water, so that they do not bend backward and hurt the shoulder.

Taylor Knox

Surfing maneuvers require powerful hips and knees!

Photo: James Thisted

Chapter 9

Hip and Pelvis Injuries

Powerful and competitive surfing requires tremendous hip mobility!
Core strength and stability is needed to protect the hips!

Adductor Muscles Strains

Beach assessment

Symptoms

Adductor muscle strains usually result from a sudden stretch in the adductor muscles. Typical is a split type of motion. Athletes always complain of sudden pain in the groin region.

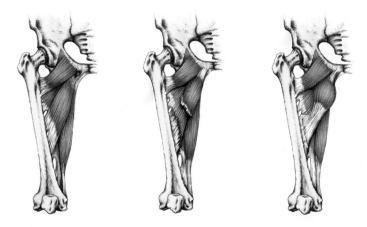

Anatomy – Adductors muscles sprain and distention

153

Classification

Muscle strains can be classified based upon their severity. A grade-1 strain is a "slight pull" without obvious tearing (it is microscopic tearing).

There is mild pain, which may prevent the surfer from continuing to surf. There is usually no significant loss of strength.

A grade-2 strain results in the tearing of some of the fibers within the substance of the muscle. There is significant pain. There may be difficulty bearing full weight on the affected leg and there is decreased strength.

A grade-3 strain is a tear of all the fibers of the muscle. There is marked pain and difficulty or inability to walk. There is significant loss of strength and a gap in the muscle injured.

Grade-1 and grade-2 strains are most common and may take a few weeks to heal, depending on the severity of the injury. An ultrasound or MRI may be helpful, especially for high-level surfers, in determining the severity of the injury and estimating the time until a return to surfing.

Grade-3 muscle strain may require surgery and a long period of rehabilitation.

The adductor longus muscle is most frequently involved. The diagnosis is suspected if there is tenderness, swelling over the adductor tendons and muscles, and hip movement causes pain. Other conditions, such as osteitis pubis, hernia, or even obturator nerve entrapment (diagnosed by an electromyogram) should be suspected in long-standing cases.

Hamstring Strain

Hamstring strains result from a sudden stretch in the hamstring musculature, usually with the hip in flexion and knee in extension.

Symptoms

Symtoms typically include spasm, swelling, and localized tenderness over the hamstrings. Mick Fanning sustained a severe hamstring injury that resulted in a complete rupture of the hamstring muscle and required immediate surgical repair.

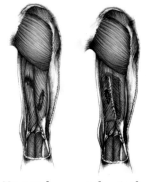

Hamstring muscle strain

Treatment of Adductor and Hamstring Strain

Treatment of adductor and hamstring strains is generally conservative with rest, ice, anti-inflammatory medication, elastic wraps (compressive bandage), and acupuncture initially followed by physical therapy modalities using ultrasound, electric stimulation, acupuncture and laser. Manual therapy and massage with anti-inflammatory analgesic cream (see Appendix 3), will help. Chiropractic manipulation may help vertebral adjustment.

Stretching exercises begin after acute symptoms resolve, followed by rehabilitative exercises in the swimming pool. Aquatic rehabilitation is required in order to keep the endurance for safe early mobilization. Rehabilitation progresses by gradual resistive exercises as symptoms decrease.

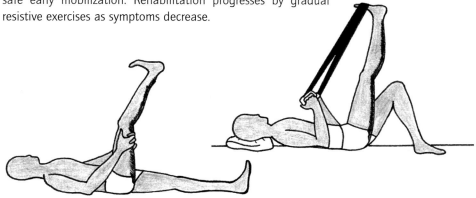

With hamstring strains in athletes, recurrence is unfortunately relatively common. Often repeated injuriy is more severe with a longer recovery time.

Emphasize dynamic strengthening exercises with the injured muscles on its full length (eccentric contraction).

Core training is important to keep pelvic and hip muscles well balanced (see Chapter 24).

Return to Surfing

The athlete may return to surf when pain-free, full-range of hip motion is regained. Stretching before activity and limiting motion of the injured muscle group with strapping or compression may help prevent injury recurrence. Running, jumping, and stairs should be avoided if they cause pain.

Snapping Hip

Snapping hip most commonly consists of snapping a tendon (the iliotibial band or the iliopsoas tendon) over a bony prominence on the femur.

Symptoms

The athlete's symptoms are usually of gradual onset and rarely require on-beach attention. Symptoms include localized tenderness of the hip. The surfer can usually reproduce the snapping symptom voluntarily.

Snapping hip often occurs with bursitis and tenosynovitis.

Surfers with a prolonged history of groin pain and painful snapping hip typically have imbalanced hip muscles with significant contractures of the hip flexors (quadriceps and iliopsoas) and hamstrings.

Heitor Alves

Photo: Sebastian Rojas

Treatment

Rest, ice, and anti-inflammatory medication help the athlete control pain. Bursitis and tendonitis can be treated by massage, ultrasound, and laser. Chiropractic manipulation may help the sacroiliac, lower back and hip alignment.

Treatment for snapping hip includes stretching any tight lower extremity muscles and improving core spinal stability by appropriate Pilates strengthening exercises.

Hip Labrum Injuries

Advances in the medical knowledge about hip injuries have highlighted the problem of a contusion or a torn acetabular labrum (a special tissue around the hip joint). In the past, these injuries would have gone undiagnosed, but now the diagnosis can be confirmed with an MRI done with contrast and arthroscopically.

The injury is not always visible on a straightforward MRI or CT scan.

Hip Labrum Contusion and Tear

Surfers usually have imbalanced hip muscles due to their usual stance, which is a predisposing factor for hip labrum injuries. Goofy foot surfers have more control and strength on their left hip and back leg and regular foot surfers on their right hip and leg.

Signs and Symptoms

The injury happens mainly on a weight-bearing, twisting hip (internal rotation) during a powerful surfing maneuver. The onset of pain is immediate and is usually located at the front of the hip joint. The pain may become diffused and difficult to pinpoint. There may be a pinching sensation when the surfer flexes the hip by bringing the knee up to the chest. There is recurrent pain during surfing maneuvers that require twisting.

Hip Labrum Contusion and Tear Treatment

Treatment includes rest, ice, anti-inflammatory medication and acupuncture, initially followed by physical therapy using ultrasound, electric stimulation, and laser. Manual therapy and massage with anti-inflammatory and analgesic cream (see Appendix 3) will help. Chiropractic manipulation may help vertebral and sacroiliac adjustment.

A significant tear in the labrum can be seen and trimmed using the arthroscope, with the whole procedure taking less than an hour.

Following surgery it is recommended to use crutches for four or five days. This is purely precautionary because of the load-bearing nature of the hip joint. Rehabilitation is continued under the supervision of a physiotherapist. Rehabilitation includes the mobilization of the hip joint to regain full range of movement. Exercises in a hydrotherapy pool are particularly effective because they allow mobilization without compression through the joint. A buoyancy belt will allow walking and running in the water without touching the bottom of the pool.

Core stability and progressive hip-muscle strengthening using resistance bands are essential. Once the operated side has normal range of motion and strength, functional exercises can be started. A return to sports is usually possible between two and three months after the operation. Many athletes find that compression shorts (warm pants) provide reassurance following hip labrum injury and surgery.

Foward lunges, side lunges and squats are very important for hip injury rehabilitation and training

Photos: Michele Cruz

158

Photo: James Thisted

Wipe outs can cause hip injuries

SURFING & HEALTH

Guilherme Tripa
Aerials can cause knee stress

Photo: Michele Cruz

Chapter 10

Common Knee Injuries

The knees are essential structures in surfing maneuvers and suffer constant stress.

Although frequent, knee injuries from surfing are usually not serious. However, radical maneuvers on powerful waves, surfing on large waves and tow-in surfing can cause serious injuries. Soccer, jiu-jitsu, skiing, volleyball and snowboarding are sports that cause more frequent and severe knee injuries. In soccer, for example, nearly 20% of all injuries involve the knees and they are often serious, in many cases requiring surgery.

The Causes

The knees are essential to surfing maneuvers and suffer constant stress. As a consequence, nearly 15% of all surfers complain of recurring knee pain, principally due to:

1. Rotation or torsion of the knees during a vertical and fast top-turn an off-the-lip or similar maneuver.

2. Compression of the knee structure, which occurs while in the typical crouching position (with the knees flexed) and takes place in finalizing floaters, snaps, lay backs, inside tubes and aerials.

M. Giorgi

Tube

Photo: Aleko Stergiou

161

3. Combinations of movements of rotation and compression of the knees during laybacks, backside tubes, roundhouse cut backs and others like surfing backwashes.

4. Core weakness, muscle imbalance and poor pelvic and lower-limb alignment.

Anatomy

To better understand the stress that surfing places on the knees, it is important to understand their anatomy.

The knee is formed by the thigh bone (fibula), the lower leg bones (tibia and femur) and by the patella that slips up and down in front of the knee. These bones are wrapped by the synovial capsule that produces synovial liquid, a type of joint lubricant.

The bones are attached to each other by ligaments, which are fibrous cords that stabilize the knees during forward and backward movements (the anterior and posterior cruciate ligaments) and lateral movements (the medial and lateral ligaments). The pressure between the thigh and lower leg bones is absorbed by the meniscus. At the surface of these bones, including that of the patella, there is cartilage that facilitates the movement of one bone over the other.

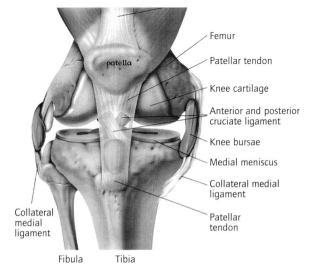

Femur
Patellar tendon
Knee cartilage
Anterior and posterior cruciate ligament
Knee bursae
Medial meniscus
Collateral medial ligament
Patellar tendon
patella
Collateral medial ligament
Fibula   Tibia

Illustration 1: Knee anatomy

Acute Surfing Injuries

In surfing, the most common serious knee injury affects the medial collateral ligament (MCL) (the inside of the knee, see Illustration 1) and, at times, the meniscus, as a consequence of compression and torsion that force the knees inward. This is common when crouching (with the knees pointed toward each other), during a tube, in snaps, when a foot slips in a maneuver or even when the lip of a wave hits a surfer's back. When the compression and torsion are severe, the anterior cruciate ligament (ACL) can be damaged.

Roni Ronaldo

Aerial

Treatment – First Aid

Beach assessment and initial treatment include:

1. Rest, ice compresses and elevation of the leg, which should be rested on a pillow.

2. Immobilize the knee with a fixed or mobile brace, depending on the injury. Walk only with support (using crutches or a cane) to avoid placing weight on the joint.

3. See a doctor immediately, especially if the knee swells rapidly (indicating possible intra-joint bleeding) or if there is instability, that is, when there is a sensation that the knee is out of place. One or two punctures are often necessary to drain the joint.

Proper treatment and rehabilitation of knee injuries depend on a precise and correct diagnosis of the injured joint. In some cases, it is necessary to rest and keep the knee immobilized for 24-72 hours for a precise diagnosis. After this period, reduction of swelling and pain allow the doctor to perform a more detailed clinical exam. X-rays and MRIs are often necessary to confirm the diagnosis.

In some cases, an arthroscopic procedure may be necessary, which involves placing a fiber optic device inside the joint. This allows both diagnosis and surgical treatment.

Injuries of the Medial Collateral Ligament

Beach assessment and initial treatment is the same as above.

Diagnosis

The injury is often caused by a surfing maneuver in which the knee suffers an "internal twist," also called a "valgus force."

These injuries can vary from a simple strain to a partial or complete tear (see Illustration 2), with rupture of the outer (extra-articular) and/or inner (deep, distal portion that is the intra-articular portion of the medial collateral ligament (MCL). An MRI is needed to confirm the diagnosis.

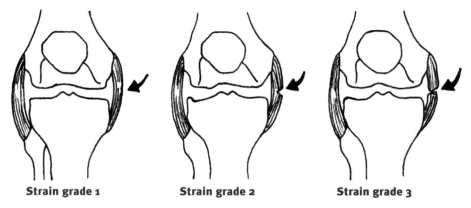

Strain grade 1   Strain grade 2   Strain grade 3

Illustration 2: Injuries of the Medial Collateral Ligament

WARNING:
Injuries to the inner fibers of the MCL may be associated with a torn meniscus that may require surgery.

Treatment and Rehabilitation

In the initial phase, the use of anti-inflammatory medication is recommended to combat pain and inflammation. This should be accompanied by rest, elevation of the joint and its immobilization with a brace with lateral metallic supports. The brace should allow the application of ice. Physical therapy is recommended with the use of electrical stimulation, ultrasound and laser. Acupuncture and intradermal injections of medications can help speed recovery.

As soon as pain subsides, begin a stretching program and mobilize the knee in a heated pool. Exercises should include close chain (with feet supported on a surface) quadriceps/hamstring strength training.

On the ground, conduct exercises without weights or impact, avoiding any movement that can cause pain.

Begin with exercises for the control and strengthening of the hip, thigh and calf muscles. It is often necessary to use a knee brace that offers a sense of protection.

Progress slowly to an "aqua jogger" or similar equipment and to swimming (with flippers when possible), which also help maintain cardiovascular conditioning. Progressively, initiate ergometric bicycling and intensify the program to strengthen the muscle.

WARNING:
An orthopedic surgeon should be consulted if a meniscus injury is suspected.

Avoid the breaststroke (because of the frog-kick motion) when swimming and avoid jumping activities for 3 to 8 weeks. Bicycling, step-ups, swimming the crawl and closed-chain strength training are good early training alternatives

Begin running between the second and third month of rehabilitation. First in a straight line, then in curves and with jumps. Gradually go back to surfing, using a brace (see rehabilitation exercises below).

Return to Surfing

This injury may require a 6 to 12 week absence from competitive activity that requires pivotal movements. Clinical follow-up should be continued until the athlete is symptom free (usually 8 to 12 weeks). If there is persistent pain or swelling, there may be an associated medial meniscus tear.

Knee brace helps lateral stabilization Photo: James Thisted

Anterior Cruciate Ligament Injuries

Injuries to the "anterior cruciate ligament" are serious and frequent in sports other than surfing (such as soccer, volleyball or jiu-jitsu). A surfer often reports having heard a "pop" at the time of injury.

The injury is often caused by performing a surfing maneuver in which the knee suffers a twist inwards and frontwards with the foot fixed on the board. The pain is severe, accompanied by internal bleeding. Walking is impossible. These injuries often leave the knee unstable, and it is common for an athlete to describe a sensation in which the knee is "giving way" in pivoting or cutting motions. There is usually swelling of the knee.

Attention: This mechanism of injury may result in complementary injuries to the Medial Collateral Ligament and the Medial Meniscus (known as the unhappy triad: MCL, ACL, and Meniscus Injuries). An MRI will help establish the correct diagnosis.

Treatment

Stop sports activities to avoid further damage to the joint, until the diagnosis is certain. An acute knee sprain should be treated immediately with a compression bandage to stop the bleeding (after clinical examination). Then begin rest, ice and copression (bandage) therapy. The athlete should use crutches and avoid placing any weight on the injured leg. Medical advice from a qualified specialist should be sought as soon as possible.

When ACL injuries are severe, the ligament cannot regenerate spontaneously and surgical reconstruction is necessary. Without treatment, the knee can become unstable, allowing it to slip forward, aggravating the injury. This viscous cycle allows degeneration of the joint. Typically there is atrophy of the quadriceps and recurrent swelling of the knee.

Partial ACL injuries can be treated with muscular reinforcement and balancing. The need for surgery, however, depends on the stability of the knee and the age and lifestyle of the athlete.

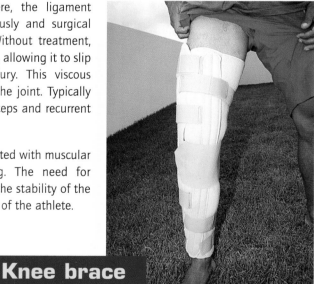

Knee brace

Weekend athletes, with a partial ACL injury, can tolerate a small degree of instability in the knee and continue to surf after a period of muscle strengthening. Functional rehabilitation exercises are essential. The use of a knee brace with metallic sides and Velcro bands that wrap the knee is recommended. It simulates the function of the wounded ligament. This creates a certain degree of confidence, but does not reduce the chance of another injury. If there is pain, increased instability and recurrent swelling, surgery must be considered.

For most active surfers, an ACL injury requires surgery. In some cases, functional non-operative rehabilitation is successful.

Surgery can be arthroscopic, using fiber optics and small incisions in the skin. A piece of tendon from the semitendonosis muscle (located on the posterior part of the thigh) or patellar tendon is often used to repair the injured ligament. Recuperation is slow, 6–8 months is required accompanied by a rigorous rehabilitation program.

Rehabilitation

Early mobilization is the standard procedure after surgical intervention (see rehabilitation exercises for knee injuries below). This is followed by 6 to 12 months of rehabilitation beginning with closed chain activities.

Maximum protection phase – up to 10 weeks should be supervised by a rehabilitation specialist. Avoid feet in straps or leg spring workouts.

As soon as possible, begin bicycling and closed-chain strength training, but avoid jumping, fast running and pivoting activities. Squatting between 60 to 90 degrees can cause stress to the ACL and should be avoided.

Return to surfing

The injury may, despite treatment, result in 6 to 12 months absence from competitive surfing. However, regular participation in modified and controlled training (running in straight lines for example) should be encouraged to avoid other negative effects of being sidelined.

We advise returning to the waves only when full range of motion and at least 90% of normal strength and endurance is recovered.

Tube

M. Giorgi

Photo: Aleko Stergiou

Meniscus Injuries

Beach assessment is the same as previously described injuries.

Although injuries to the meniscus are not common, they may occur while surfing, usually from twisting or crouching movements. At times they are associated with LCA.

The meniscus is a type of fibrous cartilage in a crescent shape located between the femur and the tibia. Its principal function is to resist compression, absorb energy and reduce the shock that the cartilage and bones can suffer during crouching and twisting movements.

Diagnosis

The most common injury is vertical and takes place on the periphery of the meniscus. In some cases, it is possible for a portion of the meniscus to be dislocated, thus impeding knee movement (bending

Different types of meniscus injuries

and extending the leg becomes difficult). There is considerable pain in movement, especially when changing direction on the board, getting out of a car, or climbing or descending stairs. It is common for the knee to swell slightly in a meniscus injury. An MRI will help the diagnosis.

Treatment and Rehabilitation

Anti-inflammatory medication may be used to decrease the inflammation and pain.

An orthopedic surgeon should be consulted for possible arthroscopic treatment. Arthroscopy should be performed if there is locking, hemarthrosis, or recurrent swelling. During arthroscopy, if the meniscus injury does not allow correction with sutures, a partial removal is conducted. Whenever possible, an attempt is made to preserve the edge of the meniscus to facilitate stability of the joint.

A rehabilitation program including core training, alignment and balance, must focus on muscle strength, range of motion, and proprioception and should be initiated as soon as possible.

Return to Surfing

Surgical arthroscopic meniscus repair, requires 6 to 12 weeks for sufficient healing before a return to surfing. Good muscular control is needed to allow safe participation in most sports (see rehabilitation exercises below).

Chronic Knee Injuries

Patellofemoral Syndrome

WARNING:

The Patellofemoral syndrome is one of the most difficult to be treated in sports because of the long rehabilitation period and the need for great patience on the part of the athlete. Surfers must be well educated about this injury.

Diagnosis

The surfer describes activity-related pain in the front of the knee. Prolonged sitting aggravates the symptoms (you'll notice while watching a movie), as well as squatting and walking downhill or downstairs. Running also increases the pain.

Pain in the front of the knee is a "working diagnosis" comprising a number of problems with similar clinical descriptions, which may include:

1. Chondromalacia patella – degeneration of patella cartilage
2. Osteoarthritis – degeneration and inflammation of the femur and tibia cartilage
3. Patella maltracking syndrome
4. Subluxated/dislocated patella
5. Meniscus injury
6. Tendonitis
7. Bursitis
8. Functional disorders, such as tight and/or weak quadriceps muscles

The key to successful management is identifying the cause of pain.
X-rays and an MRI are required and a complete analysis of muscle function (strength, muscle balance, range of motion, proprioception) and gait (predisposing factors of foot and ankle biomechanics).

The most common predisposing factors are:

1. Deformities of the thigh and leg (arched knees or knocked knees)
2. A high positioning of the patella
3. Flat feet
4. Overdevelopment of the lateral thigh muscle
5. Poor core control and strength

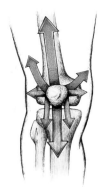

Stabilizing forces on the knee

This does not mean that all surfers with arched or knocked knees or flat feet will have painful knees. Predisposition to this problem can be hidden throughout one's life. There is usually some factor that triggers the pain, which is frequently repeated stress from non-surfing activities, such as running in deep sand, soccer, cycling, diving or other activities. Bruises to the knee can also trigger the problem. Pain becomes aggravated after repeatedly climbing or descending stairs, or in a sitting or crouching position with the knees bent. At times, there is instability in the patella, a sense that the patella is slipping out of place.

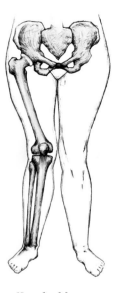

Knocked knees

Injury to the patellar cartilage is frequent among surfers 10 to 25 years old and is associated with pain while surfing maneuvers in a crouched position.

Misalignment and Instability of the Knee in Extension

ATTENTION, GIRLS!

Instability is one of the frequent causes of knee pain. It is more common among female surfers and athletes. These disturbances between the patella and the femur are the most common complaint in sport injuries. Approximately 30% of all repetitive stress injuries are related to the knee and involve the knee extension mechanism.

In some vigorous activities that involve the knees, such as jumping, running, gymnastics or ballet, the incidence can reach up to 75%.

Passive stability of the patella is provided by sound anatomy while active stability is maintained by the thigh muscles.

Photo: James Thisted

Gabriela Leite

Treatment

Treatment depends on the diagnosis.

Initial treatment involves rest, ice, anti-inflammatory medication, acupuncture and physical therapy. A knee brace often helps. Whenever possible, begin rehabilitation exercises in the water.

Exercises that aggravate the injury should be avoided, including total extension of the knee (completely extending the leg).

Orthopedic treatment seeks to minimize the anatomic deformity through the use of corrective exercises, shoe inserts, and in complex cases, surgery.

Consult an orthopedic surgeon if symptoms do not improve.

Rehabilitation

Core stability and proper control of the patella-femur is more important than pure muscular strengthening. Special attention should be given to stretching exercises. Muscular balance of the quadriceps and hamstrings and gait coordination are very important.

With an emphasis on the training of the vastus medialis obliqus muscle, progressive closed chain quadriceps training is the first line of treatment (see exercises below).

As soon as possible, begin bicycling, exercises in the water, skating.

Be careful when running and stick to soft, level ground.

Avoid prolonged sitting.

The most practical advice is: "Walk up stairs and take the elevator down." This will increase your knee protection.

Bruises and Fractures of the Chondral Bone

These injuries occur when a surfer is hit by the lip of a wave when entering or leaving a tube. The diagnosis is made with an MRI. There may be bleeding requiring drainage. Treatment includes rest and immobilization with a splint for 6-8 weeks, followed by physical therapy.

Surfer's Knee

The term surfer's knee refers to a bone protrusion that develops on the front of the knee, generally over the patella, as a result of the repeated shock of the knee with the board during countless duck dives. It is generally a bit painful to touch, and this bony callus can interfere with the knee motion if it is inflamed. Apply ice and rest for a few days.

Knee Osteoarthritis

Osteoarthritis of the knee is a leading cause of physical disability. Generally, adult and master surfers (those over 65 years old) who have knee arthritis report persistent pain, stiffness, or swelling in the knee joint on most days. Knee and hip arthritis can have a severe effect on surfing performance and the ability to walk and climb stairs.

The risk of disability from knee arthritis is as great as that from cardiovascular disease.

What causes osteoarthritis of the knee?
Knee arthritis is usually caused by repetitive trauma and poor body alignment. The cartilage becomes damaged and diminished reducing the space between the joint. This can be seen in X-rays.

The bones adapt by becoming thicker, growing outward and forming spurs. The inner knee membrane, known as the synovium, becomes inflamed and thickens, producing excessive fluid, commonly known as "water on the knee."

With time, the joint slowly changes shape as the articular cartilage wears away and the thickened bones rub against each other. Surfing becomes painful and difficult.

Keep your core strong and balanced, and you'll surf forever!

Carlos Burle at Mavericks, waves over 60 feet

Photo: Frank Quirate

Treatment

Initial treatment aims at pain management. Pain caused by knee arthritis may have different causes, depending on the individual and the stage of the disease. Thus, treatment is tailored to each individual case.

Treatment options include:

- Physical therapy, acupuncture, rehabilitation exercise, weight loss, and bracing will help in the early phases.
- Anti-inflammatory medications and/or pain killers, such as diclofenac sodium and ibuprofen, can be used but should be done so with care because of their side effects.
- Intra-articular treatments, including injections of corticosteroids or hyaluronic acid (viscosupplementation).

- Vitamin and mineral regimens including antioxidants, such as vitamins C, E and A, and minerals, such as magnesium, manganese, borum, zinc and selenium (see Appendix 3).

- Natural and complementary treatments include use of herbs with anti-inflamatory properties, such as arnica (see Appendix 3).

- Topical pain relievers based on a combination of 10% methyl salicylate, 8% menthol and camphor are widely available.

- Oral supplements with glucosamine sulfate and chondroitin sulfate may provide pain relief and stimulate cartilage nutrition. They are available without prescription at pharmacies and supermarkets.

- Surgery, including arthroscopy, osteotomy (bone shaping) and arthroplasty (joint replacement).

Rehabilitation exercise is fundamental for you to keep surfing despite osteoarthrosis of the knees.

Keep your core strong and balanced, and you'll surf forever!

Aquatic Exercises

Aquatic exercises are essential in the rehabilitation of knee injuries. Whenever possible (with your doctor's permission) begin rehabilitation in the water.

The reduced gravity, combined with the support from the water, allows for the realization of a series of exercises without causing excessive stress to the joints. In addition, the movement against the resistance to the water allows muscular improvement that is important in the initial phases of rehabilitation. You will need a floating cushion like an aqua jogger.

Begin by walking and progress to running in deep water.

Always keep your core stability muscles active.

Exercise 1:

Deep running and its variations. Running in deep water, align your body. Move your legs and arms as if you were running. You can run by raising the knees.

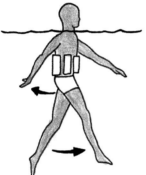

Exercise 2:

Walk in deep water with the legs and arms extended.

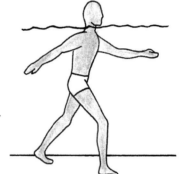

Exercise 3:

As soon as possible, begin walking on the soles of the feet.

Exercise 4:

Alternate flexing and extending the legs, as if you were running up a slope (rock climbing).

175

Exercise 5:

Conduct alternate opening and closing of the arms and alternate flexion/extension of hips and knees.

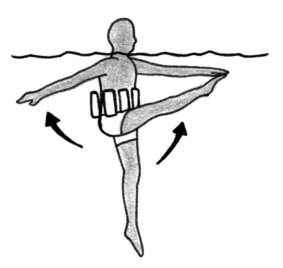

Exercise 6:

Raise a leg and touch a finger of the opposite hand. With the body vertical, keep the legs extended. Alternately raise one leg in the direction of the surface of the water and touch the opposite hand.

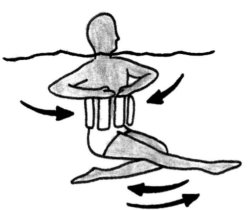

Exercise 7:

Kick sitting down: sit down with the back straight and alternately flex and extend the knees. Control the motion to avoid aggravating the injury.

Ground Exercises

Use "Breathing Wave" exercises to activate your core stability muscles. Always keep your muscles activated.

Exercise 1:

Isometric contractions of the quadriceps. Lying on your back, contract the thigh for 10 seconds and then relax. Repeat 10 times.

Exercise 2:

Pilates initial leg series. Stabilization and dissociation.

Raising the leg with the knee bent:

Lying on your back with a pillow under the knees, raise the leg and then return it to the initial position. As conditioning improves, and the movement can be executed without pain, begin weight training as follows:

Level 1: 3 sets of 10 repetitions without weight

Level 2: 3 sets of 10 repetitions with 1 kg

Level 3: 3 sets of 10 repetitions with 2.5 kg

You can use resistance training with elastic bands.

Exercise 3:

Elevation of the leg without bending the knee.

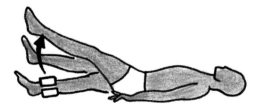

Lying on your back, raise the leg 30 degrees without bending the knee and return to the initial position. With improved condition and the ability to execute the movement without pain, begin weight training as follows:

Level 1: 3 sets of 10-30 repetitions without weight

Level 2: 3 sets of 30 repetitions with 0.5 kg

Level 3: 3 sets of 20 repetitions with 2 kg

Exercise 4: Leg Circle

This is a very important exercise for hip and knee control.

Lay down on your back, activate your core muscles, raise your right leg and rotate your hip, eight times clockwise and eight times counterclockwise. Keep your left hip and leg stable and aligned.

You can use a elastic band.

Exercise 5: Rear Thigh Muscles

Lying on your stomach, bend the knees 90 degrees and slowly return to the initial position. With clinical improvement and the ability to execute the movement without pain, begin weight training with:

Level 1: 3 sets of 10 repetitions without weights

Level 2: 3 sets of 10 repetitions with 20% of body weight

Level 3: 3 sets of 10 repetitions with 40% of body weight

Exercise 6:

Extension/flexing of knee: sitting on a table, completely raise the leg, then slowly lower it 45 degrees. Never go beyond this angle because it is possible to injure the patella. With clinical improvement and the ability to execute the movement without pain, begin weight training as follows:

Level 1: 3 series of 10 repetitions without weight

Level 2: 3 series of 10 repetitions with 1 kg

Level 3: 3 series of 10 repetitions of 2.5 kg

This is an example of an OPEN Kinetic Muscle Chain Exercise. It allows the athlete's foot to move freely during the flexing and extension of the knee. In this case, during the flexion of the knee, the action is controlled by the rear thigh muscle, while during extension it is controlled by the quadriceps.

Exercise 7:

Flex ring exercise for hip and knee muscle balance and core activation.

Lying on your back, with the knees bent, place the flex ring between your legs, just above your knees. Press the flex ring for 10 seconds and then relax. Repeat 10 times. If you have "knock-knees," put your flex ring around your ankles. Instead of a flex ring, you can use a ball. You can do it on a Feldenkrais Roll.

Exercise 8:

Bend the knees (as if you were sitting) until flexion reaches 30-40 degrees, then return to the initial position. Warning: Crouching more than 45 degrees can cause injury.

These exercises can also be conducted on a balance board, Bosu or mini-trampoline.

With clinical improvement and the ability to execute the entire movement without pain, begin weight training as follows:

Level 1: 3 sets of 10 repetitions without weight

Level 2: 3 sets of 10 repetitions with 20% of body weight

Level 3: 3 sets of 10 repetitions with 40% of body weight

Exercise 9:

Stretching exercises should include the quadriceps, the abductors and adductors, the rear of the thigh and the calf.

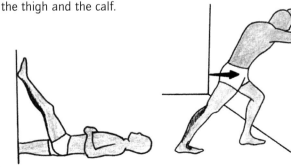

Exercise 10:

Proprioception and close kinetic chain exercises mainly include weight shifting exercises, exercises on balance platforms and exercises on a trampoline or mini-trampoline.

In Closed Kinetic Chain exercises, the foot maintains contact with the equipment surface, creating a closed multi-articular chain. This has the advantage of activating two muscle groups (rear thigh and quadriceps), both during the flexing and the extension of the knee (see page 150).

Back squats, front squats leg presses and lunges, concentrate on a combined contraction of the quadriceps, hamstrings, hip flexors, soleus, and gastrocnemius muscles. The joints of focus are the knees, hips, and ankles.

Everaldo "Pato" Teixeira – Training on the Bosu

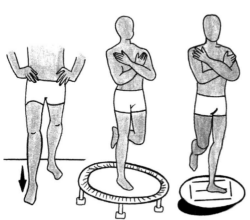

Fabio Gouveia – Core training on the ball

Exercise 11:

Closed Kinetic Chain exercises, with equipment: leg press

Exercise 12:

Standing hip flexion, quadriceps strengthening – standing up, raise the knee to the height of the hip and return to the initial position. Repeat the exercise 10 times. With improvement and the ability to execute the full range of movement without pain, begin to use weights as follows:

Level 1: 3 sets of 10 repetitions with 1 kg

Level 2: 3 sets of 10 repetitions with 1.5-2.5 kg

Level 3: 3 sets of 10 repetitions with 3-5 kg

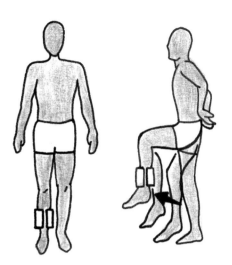

Exercise 13:

Standing hip extension, strengthening rear thigh muscles

Standing up with the hands supported on a table, raise the leg behind you (without bending the knee) and return to the initial position.

Repeat 3 series of 10.

With clinical improvement and the ability to execute the full range of movement without pain, begin to use weights as follows:

Level 1: 1 kg – 3 series of 10 repetitions

Level 2: 2.5 kg – 3 series of 10 repetitions

This exercise should be conducted with weights as soon as possible.

Exercise 14:

Standing hip abduction and adduction

Standing with the leg straight, raise the leg 30 degrees to the outside (abduction) and return to the initial position (adduction). Then raise it 30 degrees to the inside and return to the initial position. Repeat 3 series of 30. With clinical improvement and the ability to execute the full range of movement without pain, begin using weights as follows:

Level 1: 3 sets of 15 repetitions with 1 kg

Level 2: 3 sets of 10 repetitions with 2.5 kg

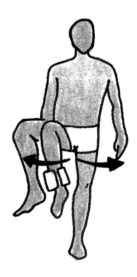

Exercise 15:

Standing internal and external rotation

While standing up; raise the knee to the height of the hips, rotate outwards and return to the initial position. Repeat the same sequence, this time rolling the hip inwards. With clinical improvement and the ability to execute the full range of movement without pain, begin working with weights as follows:

Level 1: 3 sets of 30 repetitions without weight

Level 2: 3 sets of 15 repetitions with 0.5 kg

Level 3: 3 sets of 10 repetitions with 2.5 kg

Advantages of closed kinetic chain exercises

These are also multi-joint movements, which are also labeled as sport-specific movements. The opposite of Closed Kinetic Chain are Open Kinetic Chain exercises.

Closed Kinetic Chain exercises include the following advantages:

1. They involve compressive forces, while Open Chain exercises involve shearing forces.
2. They are closer to common daily activities.
3. They involve multiple joints, while Open Chain exercises use a single joint.
4. They work with multiple muscle groups simultaneously rather than concentrating on just one, as do many Open Chain exercises.

Isokinetic

Rehabilitation through isokinetic training offers tremendous advantages for increases in muscular strength and endurance independent of the speed of movement, when compared to conventional muscular training programs. Such devices as a Cybex machine allow the athlete to work the entire range of the knee movement, reducing the effort at the point of pain. In addition, it allows quantifying the gain and decrease of muscular strength during the rehabilitation period. Due to the high cost, equipment such as this is usually only found in large rehabilitation centers and universities.

Returning to Surfing

As soon as possible, begin running on the ground in a straight line and then in a zig-zag. With increased muscular strength and stretching of the recuperated knee, you can safely return to surfing, progressively and carefully exploring maneuvers.

Remember, the principal cause of a sports injury is a poorly healed injury.

Prevention of Knee Injuries

A continuous and challenging core training program based on Pilates exercises and stretching is essential, especially for surfers with a predisposition to knee injuries.

Improved control and alignment of the pelvis and lumbar region allows improved alignment and control of the hips, knees, legs and feet.

Strong and stretched muscles help protect cartilage, tendons and ligaments. This does not mean that you need to become a weightlifter, but a few extra centimeters of muscles on the thighs and legs will help prevent injuries and improve performance. Regular exercise on a mini-trampoline or Bosu is an excellent option. Bicycling and swimming (avoid the breaststroke because of the frog kick) are excellent aerobic and knee-health strategies.

M. Giorgi

Photo: Aleko Stergiou

Kelly Slater
on a floater

Photo: Flavio Vidigal

Chapter 11

Ankle and Foot Injuries

Ankle sprains are the most common sports injury.

In sports such as soccer, skateboarding, snowboarding, martial arts, volleyball and basketball, ankle injuries are more frequent and serious than in surfing.

In surfing, ankle sprains account for about 27.2% of all sprains.

Sandboard

Skate

Surf

Snowboard

Wakeboard

Anatomy

An important instrument in surfing maneuvers, the ankle is a joint formed by leg bones (the tibia and the fibula) and foot bones (including the talus and the calcaneus), the cartilage between them, and the joint capsule that surrounds them and produces synovial liquid that functions as a lubricant.

The many ligaments in the joint provide stability to the ankle.

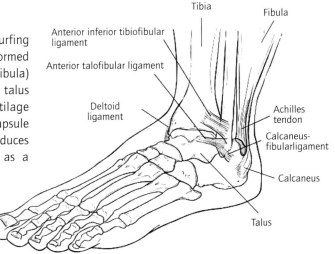

Illustration 1: Ankle anatomy

Ankle Fracture/Dislocation

Beach Assessment

The athlete has severe ankle pain, usually on the side of the ankle, caused by a twisting movement during a maneuver. Swelling is rapid, and a marked deformity may be obvious. The ability of the ankle to bear weight depends on the severity of the injury. The limb must be splinted and elevated (see Chapter 1). The athlete must be taken to a hospital for treatment.

Heitor Alves

Photo: Sebastian Rojas

Diagnosis

An X-ray is needed to make a correct diagnosis. At times, an MRI is also needed to evaluate ligament injuries.

Treatment

Ankle fractures and dislocations may require surgical procedures.

Rehabilitation

As soon as ankle stability allows, the athlete should begin to use a removable splint or brace and begin range of motion (Fig. 17.3) and strengthening exercises.

Return to surfing

The surfer may return to limited training with a protective brace. The progression of a return to training and sport is dependent upon the specific injury and treatment.

Sprained Ankles

Beach Assessment

The athlete has ankle pain, usually on the outside of the ankle, following a twisting movement during a maneuver. Mild to severe swelling appears over the next few hours.

The ability of the ankle to bear weight depends on the severity of the injury. The limb must be splinted and elevated (see Chapter 1). The athlete must be taken to a hospital for treatment.

Diagnosis

An X-ray is needed to make a correct diagnosis. At times, an MRI is also needed to evaluate ligament injuries.

The most common sprains take place with the ankle twisting inwards (called inversion). However, there are also eversion (or outward twisting) types of injuries.

The floater and the aerial are the maneuvers that most often cause ankle injuries. The ankle usually twists inwards on the already downwardly flexed foot during the landing phase of an aerial or floater.

The injuries can vary from simple, first-degree twists or eversions, where only a few ligament fibers are sprained, to a complete tear of one or a few ligaments, known as third-degree sprains.

First-degree sprains

In first-degree sprains, the ankle remains stable. The pain and swelling are not as serious, and an X-ray reveals no abnormalities in the anatomy.

Second-degree sprain
In second-degree sprains, the ligament injury is more severe and the ligament may be lightly to moderately torn.

First- and second-degree injuries usually require 4-8 weeks for complete recovery.

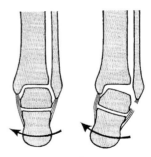

Illustration 2:
Second-degree sprain

Third-degree sprains
Third-degree sprains are more complex injuries. The swelling and pain are severe. There is a complete tear of the ligaments and the ankle loses stability. They are at times associated with a fracture.

Surgical correction is often necessary and the recovery period is longer. Questionable cases can be treated with immobilization in a plaster cast for a period of 3 weeks. If there is significant instability after this period, surgery should be considered.

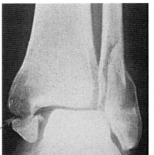
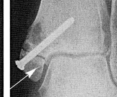

Ankle fracture **Surgical stabilization**

Treatment

Inadequate treatment can result in chronic ankle instability, with recurrent sprains and early degenerative arthrosis. The essentials of treatment are protected mobilization, followed by muscle strengthening and proprioception training.

The faster the initial treatment measures are conducted, the better the chances of fast recovery.

First phase:
• RICE therapy (Rest, Ice, Compression and Elevation)

• The initial steps include: Rest; Ice massages in the first 48 hours (about 20 minutes, four times a day); use of Compressive elastic bandages and Elevation of the ankle. This may be accompanied by anti-inflammatory medication; the use of crutches to prevent placing weight on the foot and consequently straining the ankle and acupuncture, to relieve pain and inflammation.

• Begin contrast baths 48 hours after the injury to further reduce swelling.

How to Take a Contrast Bath

First phase:

First step: place the ankle and foot in the coldest water that can be withstood. Add ice to keep it cold. Keep the ankle submerged for 30 seconds.

Second step: Immediately place the ankle in a vessel with the warmest water that can be withstood without burning (generally around 100° F, 38°C). Keep the ankle immersed for 30 seconds.

Third step: Place the affected area in the ice water again and keep it there for 30 seconds. Continue to alternate between ice water and warm water for a total of five minutes. The first and the last bath should be in cold water. Repeat the procedure three to four times a day.

In light and moderate sprains (first and second degree) an ankle brace with velcro should be used, in addition to rest. Remove the brace to apply ice.

For more severe sprains, a plaster cast should be used for one to two weeks.

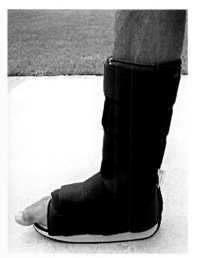

Ankle brace

Second phase:
- This includes a short period of immobilization and protection of the ankle (one to three weeks), with supportive bandaging, taping, or bracing in a neutral position and protected weight bearing to control pain and swelling.

- Continue the contrast baths and initiate physical therapy with ultrasound, laser and electrostimulation.

- Once the swelling and pain has subsided, the surfer may begin a functional rehabilitation program with mobilization and strengthening exercises using a low resistance elastic band.

- The exercises should not cause pain and should consist of light exercises conducted in a pool and on the ground (see the exercises below).

- Avoid exercises in which the foot is supported on the toes (exercises 12-14) because they place the ankle in an unstable position.

- The athlete can maintain aerobic conditioning by riding a stationary bike or swimming. Protection from "ankle twisting" is important during this phase to prevent overstretching of the healing ligaments.

- Hydrotherapy allows early walking without crutches and weight bearing, protecting the ankle from new injuries.

- With the progressive reduction of pain, crutches can be abandoned and exercises intensified, including exercises with resistance.

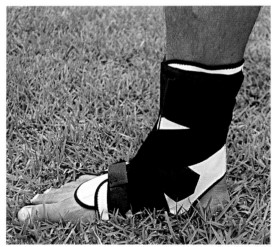

Functional brace

Third Phase:

- The third phase begins 3-6 weeks after the injury. Once weight-bearing and pain-free range of motion have been established, the surfer should begin muscle strengthening exercises.

- Proprioceptive training should also begin with a balance-board once muscle strength has improved sufficiently, typically three to four weeks after the injury. Proprioception training is continued for a minimum of 10 weeks for serious sprains.

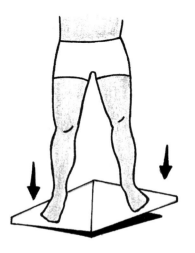

- The progression of exercise will depend on the symptoms.

- Continue ice massages if swelling persists, or only apply ice after exercising. Continue to use an ankle brace when walking. Remove it during movement and strengthening exercises.

- Continue the strengthening exercises using an elastic band or ankle weights.

- Use an ergometric bicycle and progress with aquatic exercises, such as steps, leg kicks, swimming and deep-water running.

Return to Surfing

The injured ankle must have pain-free, full range of motion. The surfer must be able to walk and run without limping.

Athletes with previous ankle injuries have a 2 to 3 times increased risk of re-injury, so continued use of a semi-rigid ankle brace should be considered.

- Continue exercising in the water.

- On the ground, increase the load of the exercises with resistance. Begin running on hard sand with proper sneakers. Walk in curves and run in a straight line clockwise and counterclockwise.

- An air-cast should be progressively substituted for a neoprene ankle brace.

- Progressively increase speed and continue the proprioception and stretching exercises.

- Run in a zig-zag pattern and in figure eights.

- Gradually return to surfing, at first avoiding vertical maneuvers, floaters and aerials.

Maintain your preventive core conditioning program (see Chapter 24).

Remember, surfers with previous ankle injuries have a 2 to 3 times increased risk of re-injury, so the use of a brace when first returning to the water may help.

Foot Injuries

Fractures/Dislocations

Beach Assessment

The athlete has severe foot pain following a twisting injury or a direct blow. Swelling is mild to severe. With the most severe of these injuries, the foot rapidly swells to twice its normal size and cannot bear weight. The athlete must be removed from the beach for further diagnosis. Apply ice, a splint or a compressive wrap.

Diagnosis

X-rays are usually needed for specific diagnosis.

Treatment

Depends on the type of injury. Surgery may be necessary.

Rehabilitation

After adequate healing of the fracture or dislocation, and sufficient stability is regained, weight-bearing activities can begin, progressing as tolerated. Exercises for stretching and strengthening of the foot muscles are particularly important.

Return to Surfing

When the fracture is completely healed – that is strength and flexibility have returned to approximately 95% of the uninjured foot – the athlete can return to unlimited surfing.

Chronic footpain

Due to surfing biomechanical needs during maneuvers, overweight and microtrauma are placed on the forefoot, specially on the transition at the base of the first metatarsal bone (the big toe) leading to soft tissue inflammation and pain. Treatment includes rest, ice and physical therapy. However, this chronic abnormal pressure on the side of the foot can develop a "bunion." You have to see a doctor to identify the cause of the bunion. Anatomical orthopedic problems, walking disturbances, and postural imbalance are among the usual causes. A baropodometry test can help to study abnormal foot pressures that may require a custom shoe insert to hold the foot in a better position. A flexible shield to keep pressure off the bone is also a good option. While surfing, use booties to reduce trauma and modify your feet position when surfing.

Rehabilitation Exercises

Core training exercises are essential for trunk stabilization and body and lower limb aligment. You should always have your core muscles activated when performing the exercises below. Always initiate with wave breathing exercises.

Exercise 1:

The initial exercises seek to increase the range of movement and include rotation of the ankle clockwise and counterclockwise, flexion and extension of the ankle and toes.

Exercise 2:

As soon as possible, begin to write the alphabet with your foot in a range of movement that does not cause pain.

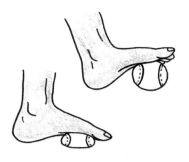

Exercise 3:

Foot Massage. Press and massage a tennis ball or a massage ball against the ground with the foot. Maintain the contraction for 10 seconds. Repeat 10 times.

Exercise 4:

Use the toes to pull a towel.

Hold it taut for 10 seconds. Repeat 10 times.

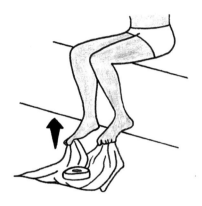

Exercise 5:

Using an elastic or similar band, lightly stretch the leg, with special attention to the calf muscles and the lower part of the leg.

Exercise 6:

Strengthening exercises should be conducted progressively. Using an elastic band, wrap it around the foot, and force the foot downwards. Begin with three sets of 10 repetitions.

Exercise 7:

Tie an elastic band around a fixed object. Place your foot inside the band.

Keep the heel down and move the foot inwards. Repeat three sets of 10 repetitions.

Exercise 8:

Tie the elastic band around a fixed object. Place your foot inside the band.

Move the foot up and inwards with the foot pointed up. Repeat 3 sets of 10 repetitions.

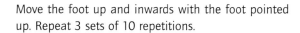

Exercise 9: Mobilization

Exercises with a skateboard can be done standing or sitting. Support the left foot on the skateboard and push it back and forth. Repeat the exercise on the opposite foot.

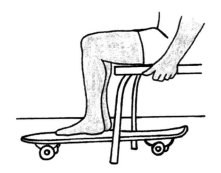

Exercise 10: Proprioception

Proprioception exercises are conducted on a balance board, Bosu, trampoline or on a Dyna disc. They allow three-dimensional balancing. Conduct one to two minute sets. Repeat a few times.

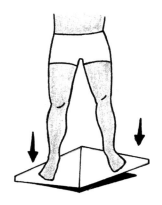

Exercise 11: Balance and weight shifting

Shift the base of support as in the illustration, training one's balance. Support for 10 seconds. Repeat 10 times.

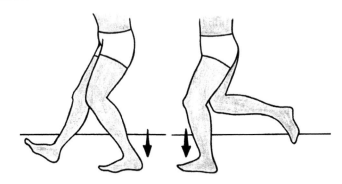

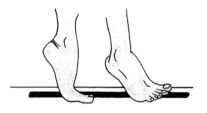

Exercise 12:

Walk on the toes in a straight line.

Exercise 13:

Walk in a straight line, crossing the feet to the front and to the sides.

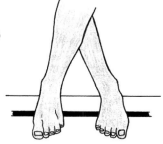

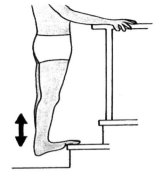

Exercise 14:

As soon as the pain subsides, exercise on the edge of a step. Begin stretching and then conduct three series of 10 elevations of the heel. Begin by exercising both ankles. Over time, conduct the movement with only the injured side.

Exercise 15:

Conduct isometric contractions. Press a basketball with the inside and outside of the foot. Hold the position for 10 seconds. Repeat 10 times.

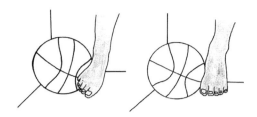

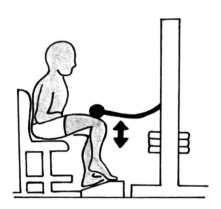

Exercise 16:

Develop muscular stamina on weightlifting equipment. Begin with three sets of 10. Progressively increase the number of repetitions.

Exercise 17:

Exercise on a mini-trampoline.

Exercises in Water

Include different types of steps, running in deep water, leg kicks and swimming.

SURFING & HEALTH

Photo: Flavio Vidigal

Teco Padaratz

Chapter 12

Teeth Injuries

Toothaches can place a surfer in the dentist's chair far from the swell of that long-planned surf trip.
Think prevention. Conduct regular visits to your dentist, especially in the weeks before your trip.

The most common dental problems that affect a surfer during trips are trauma, gum and teeth infections and problems with incisors.

Dental Fractures and Trauma

Dental fractures generally occur after a bang on the mouth from the board, which can frequently require stitches.

They can also be associated with other more serious facial or cranial trauma (such as a fall on coral or rocks) and should be very carefully evaluated (see Chapters 4 and 5).

The most commonly fractured teeth are those in front, known as the incisors.

Other causes of tooth fractures include:

*   The break of a tooth restoration

*   Trauma due to biting into a pebble in rice

*   Trying to open a beer bottle with the teeth

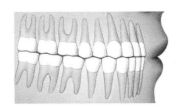

Complete dentition in adults includes four incisors, two canines, four premolars and six molars in each jaw.

Dental fractures are very painful, even in cases where the injury is minimal (Illustration 1)

Most fractured teeth can be restored, with the result depending on the treatment.

In the most simple fractures that affect the most superficial layer of the teeth, the dentin, try to save the broken piece. Immediate restoration is usually not necessary. Since teeth are very sensitive to air, cover them with wax or temporary dental cement, which is available in some pharmacies.

In the case of more complex fractures, X-rays are necessary to precisely locate the injury. Fractures that involve the root are the worst and frequently lead to a loss of the tooth. More comprehensive X-rays are needed to diagnose a broken jaw.

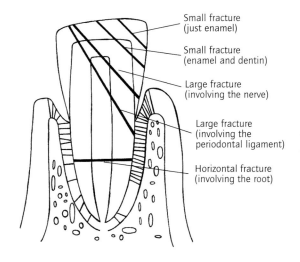

Small fracture
(just enamel)

Small fracture
(enamel and dentin)

Large fracture
(involving the nerve)

Large fracture
(involving the
periodontal ligament)

Horizontal fracture
(involving the root)

**Illustration 1:
Different types of fractures,
from the most simple to those
that reach the nerve root**

Treatment

Soft tissue injuries may require only cold compresses to reduce swelling.

Bleeding may be controlled with direct pressure applied with clean gauze.

Deep lacerations and punctures may require stitches. Pain may be managed with aspirin, acetaminophen (aspirin-free Excedrin) or ibuprofen (Motrin, Advil).

Treatment of a broken tooth will vary depending on the severity of the fracture. For immediate first aid, the injured tooth and surrounding area should be rinsed gently with warm water to remove dirt, then covered with a cold compress to reduce swelling and ease pain. A dentist should examine the injury as soon as possible. Any pieces from the broken tooth should be saved and brought along.

If a piece of the outer tooth has chipped off, but the inner core (pulp) is undisturbed, the dentist may simply smooth the rough edges or replace the missing section with a small filling. In some cases, a fragment of broken tooth may be bonded back into place. If enough tooth is missing to compromise the entire tooth structure, but the pulp is not permanently damaged, the tooth will require a protective coverage with a gold or porcelain crown. If the pulp has been seriously damaged, the tooth will require root canal treatment before it receives a crown. A tooth that is vertically fractured or fractured below the gum line will require root canal treatment and protective restoration. A tooth that no longer has enough remaining structure to retain a crown may have to be extracted (surgically removed).

Dental Dislocations

A loose or dislocated tooth should receive proper treatment. When a tooth is knocked out (evulsed), the socket is swollen, painful, and bloody.

When a permanent tooth has been knocked out, it may be saved with prompt action. The tooth must be found immediately after it has been lost. It should be picked up by the natural crown (the top part covered by hard enamel). It must not be handled by the root. If the tooth is dirty, it may be gently rinsed under running water. It should never be scrubbed, and it should never be washed with soap, toothpaste, mouthwash, or other chemicals. The tooth should not be dried or wrapped in a tissue or cloth. It must be kept moist at all times.

The tooth may be placed in a clean container of milk, cool water with or without a pinch of salt, or in saliva. If possible, the patient and the tooth should be brought to the dentist within 30 minutes of the tooth loss. Rapid action improves the chances of successful re-implantation; however, it is possible to save a tooth after 30 minutes if the tooth has been kept moist and handled properly.

Mouth protectors should be made to measure by your dentist and should be part of your first-aid kit. They can also be found in some pharmacies but these are unlikely to provide a perfect fit.

A young surfer's body usually rejects re-implantation of a primary (baby) tooth. In this case, the empty socket is treated as a soft tissue injury and monitored until the permanent tooth erupts.

A broken jaw must be set back into its proper position and stabilized with wires while it heals. Healing may take six weeks or longer, depending on the patient's age and the severity of the fracture.

Infections

Gum infections tend to bleed, swell and hurt. Infections of dental abscesses are usually caused by a deep cavity (Illustration 2).

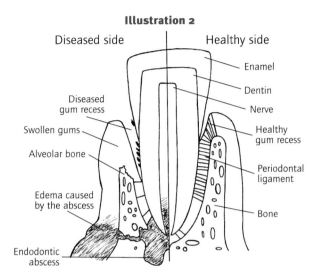

Illustration 2

Diseased side   Healthy side

Enamel
Dentin
Nerve
Diseased gum recess
Swollen gums
Healthy gum recess
Alveolar bone
Periodontal ligament
Edema caused by the abscess
Bone
Endodontic abscess

A tooth damaged from trauma, for example, can take years to become infected.

The pain appears when the nerve of the tooth is affected by the cavity. Generally, the nerve dies and the infection spreads to the jawbone, leading to a dental abscess. There is normally fever, pain to the touch and when biting, and swelling of the lymphatic ganglia below the mandible.

Treatment

The diagnosis should not delay the beginning of treatment, which includes the use of antibiotics and anti-inflammatories. The use of amoxacilina (500 mg, every 8 hours) is recommended. If the patient is allergic to this medication, use erythromycin at 250 mg, every 6 hours. To alleviate pain, use medication such as acetaminophen (Tylenol) or aspirin.

In most cases, if there is sufficient bone structure to save the tooth, root canal work will be necessary; if not, the option is extraction. Warning: the treatment of a dental abscess should be aggressive in order to avoid the risk of complications, such as meningitis. Thus, if improvement is not noticed within 24-36 hours after the beginning of treatment, see a doctor.

Alternative treatment

There is no substitute for treatment by a dentist or other medical professional. There are, however, homeopathic remedies and herbs that can be used simultaneously with dental care and throughout the healing process. Homeopathic arnica (Arnica montana) should be taken as soon as possible after the injury to help the body deal with the trauma. Repeating a dose several times daily for the duration of healing is also useful. Homeopathic hypericum

(Hypericum perforatum) can be taken if nerve pain is involved, especially with a tooth extraction or root canal. Calendula (Calendula officinalis) and plantain (Plantago major) can be used as a mouth rinse to enhance tissue healing. These herbs should not be used with deep lacerations that need to heal from the inside first.

Prevention

Dental trauma fortunately is not a common injury among surfers. However, some athletes could benefit from the use of a "mouth guard" to avoid dental trauma. Athletes who participate in contact sports like football, ice hockey, wrestling, and boxing commonly wear mouth guards.

Wisdom Teeth Problems

Regular visits to a dentist allow for the early detection of the lack of usable space within the jaw for the growth of wisdom teeth. If necessary, their removal should be set for an opportune time so that there can be complete control of the recovery. When the diagnosis is made early on, the roots of the teeth are not completely formed and their removal can be conducted more easily.

The deep position of the wisdom teeth makes good hygiene difficult, creating ideal conditions for dental and gum infection.

Do not let your wisdom teeth ruin your surfing. Visit your dentist.

Photo: Steve Ryan

SURFING & HEALTH

Marco Giorgi

Photo: Sebastian Rojas

Chapter 13

Ear Problems

The most common problems in surfing involve the outer and middle ear. If you are susceptible to ear infections, special care is essential for prevention.

External Inflammation

External otitis, or "swimmer's ear," is a very common problem among surfers. It is a skin infection that covers the external auditory canal. It occurs with greater frequency in warm and humid climates and is usually related to the improper use of cotton swabs, which remove the protective wax from the ear and to the accumulation of water, salt and sand inside the canal (See Illustration 1).

Symptoms

The skin becomes irritated, favoring the growth of bacteria or fungus. The most common symptoms are itching, pain, secretions from the ear and partial hearing loss. Movements of the head and ear exacerbate the pain.

Dampness in the auditory canal is one of the main factors that reduces the quantity of protective earwax, making the pH more alkaline and creating vulnerability to infection.

Treatment consists of ear drops that contain anti-inflammatory medication, antibiotics and anti-fungicides. The use of Otosporin is recommended in two or three drops four times a day, for a period of 7 days. This preparation should not be used in cases of a perforated tympanic membrane (eardrum), for which you must see a doctor. Avoid allowing water to enter the ear and stay out of the water for a few days. With improvement, you can surf with a silicon ear plug to prevent future infections.

Prevention is conducted with the regular use of a 2% boric acid solution or ear-drop solutions with acetic acid prepared in homeopathic pharmacies. Place two or three drops in the ears after surfing. While the alcohol helps evaporate water in the ear, the boric acid reduces the pH of the skin, thus reducing/preventing the growth of bacteria.

If there are recurring infections in the ears, repeat this procedure frequently. See a doctor.

Surfer's Ear

This is a bone growth beneath the skin of the outer ear canal that can cause partial or total obstruction (Illustrations 1 and 2).

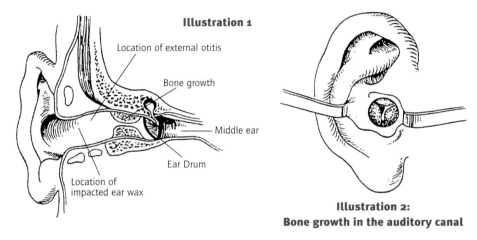

Illustration 1

Location of external otitis

Bone growth

Middle ear

Ear Drum

Location of impacted ear wax

Illustration 2:
Bone growth in the auditory canal

A first sensation of a clogged ear is followed by progressive hearing loss, buzzing and infection. Hearing loss is temporary and hearing returns with treatment, as long as there are no injuries to the delicate structures of the internal ear.

Surfer's ear is caused by repeated irritation from cold water and wind on the sensitive skin of the hearing canal. The hearing canal is the only place on the body where the bone is covered directly by a layer of skin with practically no fat or muscle. Hereditary factors also seem to be important because some surfers rapidly develop the problem while others do not.

Treatment is surgical, involving the scraping of the small bony protrusion that obstructs the canal. Prevention is exercised through the use of silicon ear plugs because, even after surgery, exposure to the wind and cold can result in new bone growth.

Impacted Earwax

Impacted earwax within the hearing canal is another condition that can interfere with surfing. While wax is a natural protection against infections, the improper use of cotton swabs can cause the impaction of wax, increasing pressure on the ear and causing pain.

A doctor's evaluation is recommended. If the wax is highly impacted, the use of a special device to suction the excess may be necessary. It is often necessary to use eardrops to dissolve the wax and facilitate the suction. Drops should be used for two or three days. On the fourth day the doctor washes the ear with jets of warm water and conducts the suction.

Otitis Media

This is a middle-ear infection. Pain and fever are the principal symptoms. It frequently occurs during a episode of the flu or infection of the upper respiratory tract. In some cases pus may be excreted from the eardrum. Treatment usually requires oral antibiotics. (Amoxicillin tablets 500 mg 3 times per day or ciprofloxacin 100 mg 2 times per day for 7-10 days).

Perforated Eardrum

A perforated eardrum (the fine membrane that separates the outer and middle ear) can be caused by a wipe out that bangs the surfer's ear against the water. Water penetrates the ear with pressure sufficient to perforate the membrane.

You must stop surfing and seek medical help.

Small perforations often close on their own in six to eight weeks, as long as they do not have contact with water.

Larger perforations may require tympanoplasty, a type of surgery that seeks to cover the perforation.

During Healing

Keep the ear canal clean, dry and free of any object while the eardrum heals. Insert earplugs gently into the ears when showering or shampooing to block any water from getting in. Don't use cotton balls since they absorb moisture.

Silicon earplugs are recommended to prevent other perforations or reperforations in the same location. The use of a helmet or neoprene caps is also recommended.

Heitor Alves
Goggles provide eye protection

Photo: James Thisted

Chapter 14

Common Eye Injuries

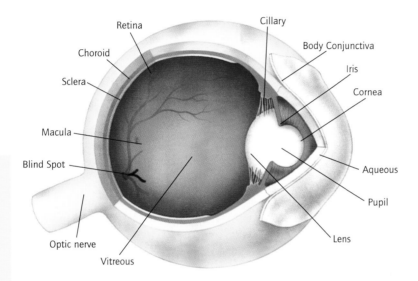

Retina   Cillary

Choroid   Body Conjunctiva

Sclera   Iris

Macula   Cornea

Blind Spot

Aqueous

Optic nerve   Pupil

Vitreous   Lens

Although they are not common in surfing (they account for fewer than 2% of surf injuries), eye trauma is potentially grave due to the risk of perforating the ocular globe. Sports that have a high-risk for eye injuries include basketball, baseball, tennis, water polo, fencing, boxing and contact martial arts.

In surfing, the most common mechanism of eye injury is impact with the sharp nose of the surfboard following a fall. This kind of eye trauma can rupture the eye like a grape and can be caused if the leash keeps the surfer too close to the board during or following a fall.

The symptoms that accompany a potentially serious eye injury include a sudden partial or total loss of vision, pain in eye movement, sensitivity to light (photophobia), double vision, vision of bright lights, alteration in the shape of the pupil, the sensation of a foreign body in the eye and red eye.

What to do in Case of Eye Injury

In case of eye injury, cover the eye with gauze covered with sterilized Vaseline and maintain light and delicate pressure. This will help keep the region clean and reduce any bleeding. Immediately seek emergency medical service for a careful optometric evaluation because there is risk of losing the eye.

In cases of significant swelling of the eyelid, place a bag with a small quantity of crushed ice on the region. Avoid ice cubes, the weight of which can aggravate the injury.

A simple modification in surfboard design, such as blunting the nose of the surfboard, or appropriate use of a nose guard, should lessen the severity of such injuries.

It is not uncommon for surfers to say that a nose guard saved an eye.

Surfing and Contact Lenses

Given this great technology, there is no reason not to be able to see the waves as they approach from over the horizon.

If you have problems seeing on land but use corrective devices, such as glasses or contact lenses, it is nearly always possible for the problem to be nearly totally corrected in the water as well. Contact lenses are perhaps the best option. However, while most eye-care practitioners advise against wearing contact lenses in the ocean, many surfers do anyway.

The number of surfers who now use contact lenses is increasing. A U.S. study with surfers using lenses in more than 5,000 hours of surf found no infection or eye wound related to the lenses and only one lens was lost for every 500 hours of surfing (an average of one lens per year). Nevertheless, there is significant variation in the number of lenses lost, that is, while some surfers lose one per month, others never lose them. The difference is probably in the way that the lenses adapt to the eyes and in the ability of the surfer to keep the eyes entirely closed during intense situations like a wipe out and duck diving.

Surfers who wear contact lenses while surfing must be aware of the various signs and symptoms that may precede an eye problem, for example, getting sand caught between your lens and eyeball. It's important to see an eye doctor immediately if there is any pain, redness, or decrease in vision.

Sports Lenses

Sports lenses are soft contact lenses that are much more comfortable than the old, hard ones. They are made to broadly cover the eyes, allowing an excellent adaptation during the practice of sports, including water sports and surfing.

The development of plastic lenses that are highly permeable to gases allows the cornea to receive more oxygen, which considerably increases comfort.

Daily cleaning and careful disinfection of the lenses can reduce the risk of infection during surfing in polluted water. Always rinse eyes with a saline solution to help remove any contaminants remaining on the surface of the eye.

If your eyes are very sensitive to the sun, contact lenses can contain ultraviolet protection, which is essential in avoiding the burning of the cornea and the development of pterygium (see below) caused by the sun. A one-day throw-away lens is a good option for surfers because the lenses are thrown out after getting out of of water.

Bruno Rodrigues
Eye protection

Photo: James Thisted

If contact lenses are not a good option, the optometrician can prescribe swimming glasses (goggles). These glasses for aquatic sports called "Spex" have a flexible, non-breakable structure that can be adapted for any type of lenses. In addition to protecting the eyes from traumatic injury, they also protect against ultraviolet rays. To resolve the problem of foggy goggles in the water, use one of the anti-fogging products on the market.

Pinguecula and Pterygium

Pinguecula and pterygia are different degrees of the same condition. Both are non-malignant, slow-growing proliferations of conjunctival connective tissue in the eye. They are caused by ultraviolet sunlight that directly or indirectly strikes the eyes (from the reflection of the sun on the water and sand) and are aggravated by wind and dust.

The reflection of the sun on water is one of the leading causes of the growth of blood vessels in the conjunctiva, a condition known as pinguecula.

Ultraviolet sunlight stimulates the proliferation of blood on the conjunctiva and on the periphery of the cornea. This phase of reaction in the eyes is known as pinguecula. This phenomenon appears as small, raised, thickenings of the conjunctiva. They may be yellow, gray, white, or colorless. They are usually on the side closest to the nose. A pinguecula may develop into a pterygium.

The disease progresses with the stimulus of sunlight, which leads to the formation and growth of a yellow fibrous tissue that slowly covers the cornea. Inflammation and reduced vision can occur, a condition known as pterygium.

Pinguecula and pterygium are mostly asymptomatic, however, they can produce the sensation of a foreign body in the eye.

Frequent washing of the eyes with isotonic saline solution or a 2% boric acid solution can help prevent the formation of salt crystals that cause eye irritation. The application of cold compresses using pieces of cucumber or gauze embedded in water with 2% boric acid helps clean irritated eyes. Artificial tears, as well, can be used to relieve the sensation of a foreign body in the eye and protect against dryness.

Surgical treatment for the removal of pterygium is the best option to eliminate the problem. In case preventive measures are not taken, a new pterygium can grow in nearly 10 % of cases, even after surgery. It is best to prevent these conditions with the regular and daily use of sunglasses with ultraviolet protection. Use boards with light colors and a dull glaze that reflects the least possible UV rays.

Photo: Daniel Ernst

Dislocated Retina

A dislocated retina can result from a severe blow to the head. Fortunately, this is not common in surfing. It occurs when the retina layers (in the rear of the eye) become dislocated. It can lead to blindness.

The first symptoms can appear days after an injury and include partial or complete darkening of vision. The treatment is surgical. Six months are generally needed for complete recovery.

Vitreous Floaters

Vitreous floaters appear in nearly 60% of people over 60 years of age and can also affect young people. Once they appear, this condition remains throughout one's life although it rarely requires treatment.

The vitreous humor is a clear gelatinous substance that fills the eyes and functions as a shock absorber, protecting the vital structures of the eyes and giving it the shape of a ball.

Indonesia

With age, proteins and cellular deposits or pigments can remain suspended in the vitreous humor. When light penetrates the eyes, these floating deposits produce a shadow on the retina (the rear portion of the eye) and the brain perceives them as little gray flecks just out of focus that appear to float before your eyes. Depending on the shape, they may look like spiders or worms. With the smallest movement of your eyes, they may disappear.

Although they disturb the vision, they are not a risk to sight or health. There is no operation or medication to remove them. In most cases, the brain learns to not see them. Nevertheless, a detailed ophthalmological examination should be conducted, since these vitreous floaters can appear as a consequence of a dislocated retina, surgery, eye infections, diabetes or high blood pressure.

Eyedrops

Eyedrops used to remove redness from the eyes are composed of substances that act in a manner similar to adrenaline, such as naphazoline or tetrahydrozoline, that is, they cause the veins on the surface of the eyes to contract and reduce the redness.

It is not recommended to use them more than 3 days per week. Constant daily use can cause tolerance to medication, meaning they will cease to function and the eyes will become even more red.

Develop the habit of washing the eyes with a 3% boric acid solution after surfing.

SURFING & HEALTH

Calunga, Hawaii

Chapter 15

Surfing in the Tropics and Common Infectious Diseases

To stay healthy during surf trips, it is important to be aware of the most common diseases found at the beach you are surfing. Prevention is the best way to combat illness that can keep you out of the water.

Common Infectious Diseases

Tetanus

This is a disease that is prevalent in tropical and underdeveloped countries. It is transmitted by the bacterium *Clostridiumtetani*, which is found dirt, dust and animal and human feces.

Tetanus can contaminate a wound, cut or a deep puncture injury caused by a nail or can that is infected by the bacteria. A skin puncture from contaminated needles used by uninformed drug users, or tattooing or body piercing considerably increase the risk. Wounds contaminated with soil, saliva or feces, if not properly cleaned, also increase risk.

It is a grave disease that can be difficult to treat and is often fatal because the toxin secreted by the bacteria provokes serious muscle contractions.

Prevention

Prevention is simple. A booster vaccine against tetanus should be received every 5 years. All wounds should be carefully cleaned and brushed with soap and water (see Chapter 4).

In case of contaminated wounds, it is advisable to administer a dose of intramsucular, anti-tetanus antibodies (immunoglobulin). When it is not known when a victim last had a tetanus booster, it is advisable to give another along with an injection of immunoglobulin.

Contaminated Sewage and Surfing

Millions of gallons of untreated and contaminated sewage are dumped daily into rivers, streams and oceans in many countries, transforming waves and surf into reservoirs of diseases such as hepatitis A diarrheas caused by bacteria and viruses, typhoid fever, conjunctivitis, mycosis and others.

The lack of infrastructure and planning for the proper collection and treatment of sewage is a public health problem that is the responsibility of municipal and state governments.

It is essential that the entire surf community participate in the struggle for the preservation of oceans and beaches and the quality of the water.

Contaminated sewage

Hepatitis A

Hepatitis transmitted by the A-virus is a benign disease found mostly among children, usually in poor regions that lack basic sanitation. It strikes regularly on surf trips in the Third and Fourth World countries.

Contamination can occur from:

1. Ingestion of food and water contaminated by human feces infected by the virus. This is the principal form of contamination.

2. Ingestion of small quantities of sea water while surfing in regions contaminated by sewage. Ingestion often occurs during surfing when small quantities of water penetrate the facial cavities and reach the back of the nostrils during duck diving or wipe outs and are spontaneously ingested.

Previous contact with hepatitis A during childhood offers permanent protection, and preventive vaccination is not necessary. If there has been no previous contact, three doses of a vaccine are recommended against hepatitis A before a surf trip.

Symptoms

After an incubation period of two to six weeks, non-specific symptoms arise, such as nausea, high fever, lack of appetite and vomiting. A few days later jaundice (the yellowing of the eyes and skin) sets in. A victim's stool usually becomes white and the urine brown. The diagnosis is confirmed by a laboratory test for the presence of antibodies in the blood and increased levels of liver enzymes called transaminases.

Complete recovery involves considerable care and can take three months.

Complementary medical treatment includes a low-fat diet based on brown rice. Lots of rest and continued medical supervision are required. This means no surfing until normal liver function returns.

There is no specific treatment. The body's defense system neutralizes and eliminates the virus.

Surfing in Peru

Prevention

On surf trips in poor regions, where hygiene conditions are questionable, basic prevention requires that you only drink water from safe sources or water that is boiled. Avoid raw food or vegetables and, whenever possible, carefully choose the source of your meals. It's worth inspecting the hotel kitchen.

There is a vaccine that offers partial protection for nearly two months but does not provide 100% protection, meaning there is still risk of disease in case of contamination.

Fortunately, the disease is benign and does not leave permanent damage.

Nevertheless, during surf trips to beaches in countries with poor infrastructure, seek information about the water quality.

It is common for local authorities to issue weekly water quality reports, analyzed from a test that counts the number of fecal coliforms present in the water. These are bacteria found in human and animal feces and the higher the number of bacteria found in the water, the greater the risk of contamination.

Hepatitis B

This is a potentially dangerous disease because it can cause chronic hepatitis and liver cancer. Hepatitis B is transmitted by the B-virus through sexual contact or contaminated blood, whether by the use of drugs or through blood transfusions. Tattoos and body piercings also increase the risk of contamination.

Symptoms

After a prolonged incubation period of three to six months, non-specific symptoms, such as tiredness, aches throughout the body, fever and nausea, appear. Then jaundice (yellow eyes and skin) appears. The liver generally increases in size. Recovery is slow, but the body's defense system is often capable of eliminating the virus. Nevertheless, some cases can develop into a chronic and persistent hepatic deficiency.

Treatment

Prevention is the best treatment. The good news is that the vaccination, in addition to being safe, offers 100% protection. Three doses are necessary for total and effective protection.

Hepatitis C

Transmitted by the C-virus, hepatitis C is also potentially dangerous because of the risk of liver cancer and hepatic deficiency and cirrhosis. Infection through sexual contact and contact with contaminated blood have been confirmed. Tattoos and body piercings increase the risk of contamination.

Be careful, there is no vaccination.

Once detected, antiviral drugs can limit the potential damage and, in some cases, clear the virus completely from the body.

Yellow Fever

Yellow fever is an infectious and dangerous disease caused by a virus from the family of arboviruses.

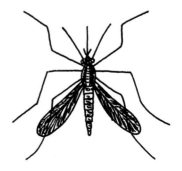

Symptons

The incubation period varies from three to six days.

**Yellow fever mosquito transmitter,
Aedes aegypti.**

The disease begins like a flu (with fever, headache, muscle aches, queasiness and weakness). In more serious cases, the victim may become yellow, for which reason the disease is called yellow fever. There is often vomiting, blood in the feces and the body may become covered with red splotches.

Yellow fever is most common in the tropical areas of Africa and the Americas.

In urban settings, the virus is transmitted by a sting from the same mosquito that transmits dengue, known as *Aedes aegypti*. Since this mosquito reproduces in clean and still water, the highest incidence of yellow fever is in the summer. Actions to eradicate the mosquito are essential. In the jungle, yellow fever is transmitted from monkeys to people by mosquitoes that breed in tree holes in the rainforests

Jungle surfing

Prevention

The only way to avoid the disease is by vaccine, which offers immunity for nearly 10 years. It is mandatory for someone who surfs in regions with tropical forests. Because it is a live vaccine, it should not be given to infants or people with immune system impairment

Typhoid Fever

This infectious disease is caused by the ingestion of contaminated food or water by the *Salmonella typhi* bacteria.

Symptons

After an incubation period of 3-25 days, there is a gradual appearance of fever, discomfort, lack of appetite, generalized pain in the body and diarrhea with mucus, pus or blood. The disease can become aggravated and fatal if it is not treated and can lead to hemorraging and intestinal perforation. Typhoid is generally associated with poor social economic conditions and found in poor countries such as Indonesia, the Philippines and Vietnam.

Treatment

Treatment consists of antibiotics, usually a combination of sulfa known commercially as "Bactrim." Hospitalization is often necessary.

Prevention

Only drink water from a safe source or that is boiled or treated with sodium hypochlorite. Drink only pasteurized milk. Avoid raw foods and vegetables. Always visit the kitchen when choosing a restaurant.

If these measures are impossible, a vaccine is recommended, but it does not offer 100% protection. There is an oral vaccination. See your doctor. The vaccine should not be taken by pregnant women.

Dengue

The dengue virus is transmitted by the same mosquito that spreads yellow fever. The mosquito is smaller than others, is dark and has white stripes. It bites during the day and lays eggs in clean and still water. Tahiti, Central America, Brazil, Indonesia and Vietnam are surfing locations with risk of dengue.

Symptoms

Symptoms include high fever, muscular and joint pain, pain behind the eyes and headache, accompanied by red splotches on the skin, weakness and lack of appetite.

One of the most dangerous forms is hemorrhaging dengue, which can lead to death. The first symptoms are the same as a flu, but when the fever passes, there is bleeding, a drop in blood pressure, the lips become purple, strong abdominal pain and the victim becomes either sleepy or agitated.

Treatment

There is no specific treatment or vaccine. Rest, plenty of liquids and the use of analgesics are recomended to alleviate pain and fever. Do not use aspirin.

Prevention involves avoiding proliferation of the mosquito through campaigns to eliminate areas where still, clean water gathers, such as plant pots, old tires, open water tanks and water in animal feeders.

Treatment of hemorrhaging dengue involves the administration of gamma-globulin.

Neco Padaratz
Tahiti

Cholera

Cholera is caused by a bacterium known as *vibrio cholerae*. It is transmitted through ingestion of food or water contaminated by feces or vomit from contaminated people.

Symptoms

With an incubation period of one to three days, the main symptom is watery diarrhea and vomiting that leads to rapid and grave dehydration, which if not treated, can be fatal.

Treatment

The treatment in milder cases includes oral rehydration. In the most severe cases hospitalization is needed for intravenous rehydration. Antibiotics are essential for eliminating the bacteria. Use tetracyclines, cloranfenicol or bactrim. The existing vaccine is not effective and is rarely recommended.

Prevention

Prevention is the same as that for hepatitis A and typhoid fever. Avoid contact with water and food contaminated by the virus. Water should be boiled or chlorinated. Always wash your hands after going to the bathroom and handling food. Always cook food before eating it.

Fortunately the risk of contracting cholera during an epidemic while surfing is small, but it does exist. The cholera bacteria is capable of remaining alive in seawater for 10-13 days at a temperature of 30-32°C and up to 60 days at a temperature of 5-10°C.

Although the virus remains alive for a long period of time in the sea, a surfer must swallow a considerable quantity of water contaminated with a high quantity of bacteria (i.e., 100,000 viruses per ml.) to become stricken. For this quantity of bacteria to be found in seawater, the entire community must be infected and passing the bacteria in their feces that run to the sea. But at a beach where sewerage flows into the sea and where part of the population is contaminated and passing the cholera bacteria into the water without treatment, there is a very high risk of contracting cholera if a small quantity of water is swallowed. The beach should be closed.

Malaria

Whether you are chasing barrels in Indonesia, West Java, Gajagang or Nias or exploring Vietnam or the Philippines, or surfing the pororocas in the Amazon, it's a good idea to seek protection from malaria.

Known for more than 2,000 years since the time of Hippocrates, it was first believed that malaria was transmitted by "bad airs." In reality, the disease is transmitted by the Anopheles mosquito. A bite can inject the *Plasmodium* protozoa that causes malaria into the victim's blood.

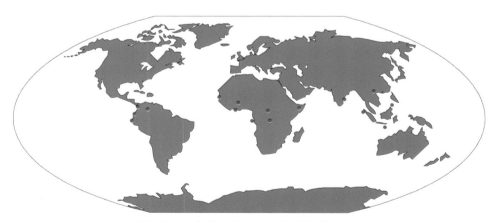

World map indicating malaria distribution

Symptoms

Symptoms vary with the type of *Plasmodium*. In general, they include, chills, fever, pain, lack of appetite and others.

A blood exam known as thick drop determines the type of *Plasmodium* that caused the infection.

If you are traveling to an endemic area, that is, a region where malaria is common, there is a large risk of contamination from exposure to mosquitoes. The most probable diagnosis fever at these beaches is malaria. Pay attention because during rainy seasons fever may mean malaria and not a simple flu.

The most common types of malaria are:

Indonesia has great waves, but be careful with malaria.

Vivax malaria

This is a benign disease, but it can be recurring if it is not adequately treated.

Malaria falciparum

This disease can be fatal if not promptly treated because there are risks of brain and kidney damage.

Treatment

In most cases, hospitalization is required for proper treatment. With vivax malaria, the medication used is chloroquine, associated with primaquine. Falciparum malaria, has been displaying increased resistance to various medications. Therefore, before travelling, consult your doctor to determine the predominant type of malaria at your destination. The World Health Organization (WHO) offers detailed reports on the locations where there may be contamination, with the most frequent type of malaria and the best type of medication. Among the medications most used are fansidar, doxiciclina, mefloquine, quino, malarone, and more recently, artemisinin derivatives (which are not licensed for use in the United States, but are often found in other countries.)

Even though there is no vaccine, prevention is the most important measure.

Preventive measures:

1. Stay under mosquito netting – especially at dawn and dusk, which are the feeding times of the Anopheles mosquito.

2. Use light colored, long sleeve shirts and long pants to reduce the areas of exposure to insects. Using dark clothing, perfume and aftershave can attract mosquitoes.

3. Use insect repellant on exposed areas. Protection can be strengthened with the use of repellant over clothes and inside mosquito netting.

4. The use of oral medications as prevention is advisable in cases in which your stay in the malaria region is relatively short (two to eight weeks). Medication, however, does not prevent contraction of the disease, but supresses the chance of symptoms, such as fever, chills and others, arising during the trip. No medication offers 100% protection.

    Thus, any fever that occurs months or even years after a surf trip should be suspected to be malaria.

    The use of preventive medication should be begun two weeks before leaving and continued for four weeks after return. The choice of preventive medicine should be made by your doctor and based on the itinerary, length of stay in the malaria region and degree of resistance that the malaria has to medications. Among the most common drugs for prophylaxis are: chloroquine, fansidar, mefloquine, doxiciclina, malarone and more recently artemisinin derivatives (which are not licensed for use in the United States, but are often found in other countries).

The Common Cold

Who hasn't missed a great day of surf because of a virus?

There are more than 200 types of viruses that cause colds and flu. While a flu can have symptoms that feel like a pounding from Mike Tyson, cold symptoms are milder and usually do not have complications, unless the immune system is weak.

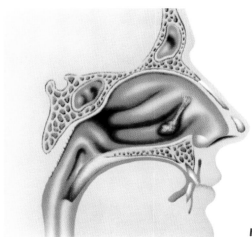

Mouth and nose – entrances for flu viruses

Transmission of a flu virus takes place by contact with a contaminated person, principally in the cold months of the year.

The virus is often initially transmitted by the hands and enters the body through the mouth, nostrils and eyes. Thus, hand washing helps to considerably reduce the transmission of this infection, which fortunately is self-limiting and benign.

Distributed through the four corners of the planet, the common cold affects men and women of all ages and is most common among small children, people who care for children and the elderly.

The symptoms appear two or three days after contact and nearly always include chilliness, stuffy nose, sneezing, sore throat, cough, achiness and headache. The associated fever is generally low and does not last more than two days.

More than two or three colds per year may be a sign of low immunity. If colds come with frequency, the culprit may be allergies.

The most effective method to prevent colds is to strengthen the immune system.

Flu

Flu symptoms are more intense and include high fever and body pains, as well as weakness. It is not a good idea to surf under these conditions in part because it will be difficult to do so.

Since surfing is also an aerobic exercise of medium to high intensity, the increased heart rate during training increases the risk of spreading the virus through the body.

In the final phase of the flu (the fifth or sixth day) when the symptoms are subsiding, light surfing helps to eliminate phlegm and clear the respiratory passages.

Considered a serious illness, the flu kills thousands of people each year, most of them elderly and those with immune system problems. Vaccination is the most suitable means of prevention.

The most common complications include viral or bacterial pneumonias and ear infections, sinus infections and bronchitis. They generally arise when treatment is delayed.

Treatment

There is no effective medication against the flu. Medicine only serves to alleviate some of the symptoms.

Among the principal measures that can shorten recovery time are:

1. Bed rest and lots of fluids.

2. Increased consumption of juices and citric fruits, especially those rich in vitamin C.

3. Use a syrup with honey and lemon, gargling with salt and lots of hot soup are part of the arsenal, in addition to onion and garlic, ginger and parsley, which are rich in zinc. Eucalyptus sprays also help decongestion.

4. The regular use of propolis, garlic and royal jelly, and echinacea also help prevention and reinforce the immune system.

The use of acetaminophen-based (Tylenol) analgesics are recommended to reduce pain and achiness. Nasal decongestants are helpful in case of severe nasal obstruction, when the symptoms are difficult to control.

Prevention

Flu Vaccination

For surfers – especially competitors – the flu vaccine is a good option for reducing the risk of contracting a flu. Since it is 89% effective, some people who are vaccinated may contract a flu, generally with weaker symptoms, like those of a cold. In addition, other viruses can provoke symptoms similar to those of the flu, wherein the vaccine will not function.

Since the vaccine is produced with pieces of dead viruses, there is no risk of being infected by the vaccination. Its use is very safe, however, in some people it may cause pain and mild reddening of the location of application. In a very small number of cases, the vaccine may trigger a low fever and achiness, which pass within 24-48 hours. As with any vaccine, after its administration, nearly two weeks are needed for the effects to be established.

Those who should avoid the flu vaccine because of possible side effects include:

1. People with allergies to egg protein.
2. Women in their first three months of pregnancy.
3. Children younger than 6 months.

It should be applied in the fall of each year, to exercise protection in the most critical time of year – winter – since the highest level of protection occurs 4-6 weeks after application.

Since the flu virus is mutant, the composition of the vaccine is altered annually by the World Health Organization, including the principal strains of flu virus circulating on the planet.

Sore Throat and Tonsilitis

The most common causes of sore throat are infections of the throat and tonsils.

The infections can be caused by a virus that leaves the throat red, causes pain upon swallowing, achiness and a low fever. There is usually improvement with the ingestion of lots of liquid, gargling with salt water and the use of propolis spray.

Treatment

The choice of homeopathic medicine depends on the symptoms. The most useful homeopathic medications include: Belladona 30C, Sulfureto de Cálcio 6C, Mercúrio 6C, Lucopodium 5C, Lachesis 6C and Phytolacca 6C.

At times, sore throats and infected tonsils can be complicated by a secondary infection generally caused by a bacteria known as streptococcus. In these cases, there is greater pain and higher fever with difficulty and pain in swallowing, in addition to swelling of the lymphatic ganglia in the neck.

The treatment is based on antibiotics. Amoxycycline bd 875mg. Take 1 tablet twice a day.

With the leaves, flowers and root of dried mallow, prepare a tea and use it for gargling in the case of mouth and throat inflammation.

Sinusitis

The facial sinus cavities are located above and below the eyes. They are connected to the nose and are full of air. Their principal function is to act as resonators for the voice.

Acute sinusitis is a frequent problem among surfers. It is generally caused by seawater that penetrates the nose and the facial cavities from a wipe out and duck diving, irritating the membrane that covers the cavities. Barotrauma, which is increased pressure on the facial cavities due to dives under the waves and individual conditions such as allergies, rhinitis and frequent flu, can lead to sinusitis.

Among the principal symptoms are headache, pain on one or both sides of the face, yellow mucus and fever.

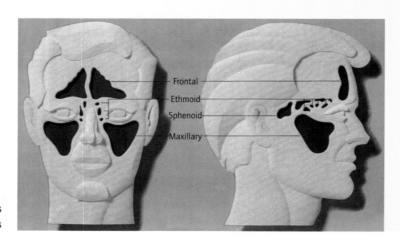

Frontal
Ethmoid
Sphenoid
Maxillary

Facial sinus cavities

Treatment

For less severe cases, the use of nasal decongestants, pain relievers and acupuncture is recommended.

For use of homeopathic medications, it is recommended that you see a homeopathic doctor. The most common medications are:

Hepar Sulfur 6C, for stuffy nose and irritability.

Pulsatilla 6C, for yellowish, green secretions and a lack of thirst and when symptoms get worse in closed environments.

Belladona homeopathic drops (30C) are used in the first phase of sinusitis, when there is pain and fever. Bryonia medication may be used for the cases of strong headache.

In case of severe headache and fever, you may need to see a doctor and take some antibiotics. Among the most commonly used are Clavulin (amoxicillin plus clavulanic acid, bd 875mg- take 1 tablet twice a day). Another option is ciprofloxacin hydrochloride 100 mg. Take one tablet twice a day. You may need to take this medication for 14 days in order to clear the infection.

Chronic Sinusitis

Surfers often develop an exaggerated and recurring sensibility in the sinus cavities, characterized by repeated pain, facial congestion and a runny nose, most often without a fever. This condition is known as chronic sinusitis and is often associated with the repetition of allergies that should be corrected.

The repeated inflammations can cause alterations of the membranes or even result in the growth of polyps (small benign tumors) that wind up obstructing the facial cavities. Whenever necessary, conduct a tomography of this region for a careful diagnosis.

Treatment

1. If allergic rhinitis is associated, it should be treated immediately because nasal congestion impedes recovery.

   Allergy tests of the blood and skin can confirm what elements are responsible for the allergic reactions, whether they be food (milk, wheat, chocolate, etc.) or dust, animal hair, medications, etc., and which should be avoided. Certain food additives, such as aspartame, monosodium glutamate and sulfites, can also cause allergic reactions.

2. The supplements lactobacillus acidophilus and lactobacillus bifidus are recommended in cases of food allergies because they are often deficient in the digestive flora.

3. The mites found in domestic dust are one of the leading causes of allergies in residential environments. They are microscopic arachnids that can cause dermatitis, rhinitis and asthma (see Chapter 19).

4. N-acetylcysteine is an amino acid used to break up the mucus. Take 50 mg, three times daily.

5. Juices that are rich in vitamins C and E, as well as B complex vitamins and minerals, such as molybdenum and zinc, help reduce allergic responses. They are found in spinach, asparagus, carrots, cauliflower, parsley and garlic.

6. Grape seed extract can help reduce sinus inflammation. Take up to 300 mg per day.

7. Garlic in tablets (odorless) also helps fight infections and to drain the sinuses. Take 250 to 500 mg twice a day.

8. Turmeric is an anti-inflammatory herb. Take 400 to 600mg of turmeric (active substance) three times per day.

Electric acupuncture is recommended in combination with nasal douching with warm saline solution.

Serious cases that are difficult to treat often require surgery.

Impetigo

Impetigo is a common superficial skin infection caused by bacteria. It appears as one or a number of infected wounds covered by a yellow-brownish crust (in the case of streptococcus bacteria) or as a large blister (in the case of staphylococcus bacteria).

It is highly contagious among athletes through direct contact with towels or other infected materials. The wounds should be carefully cleaned with washes of potassium permanganate solution and antibiotic ointment (neomycin). Permanganate is an oxidant that acts as a disinfectant in diluted solutions. The solution is made by adding tablet of permanganate to two liters of boiled water. Apply with gauze.

Treatment may require the use of oral antibiotics (amoxicillin bd 800 mg – take one tablet twice a day or eritromicine in case of allergies to amoxicillin). If they are not treated properly, the wounds can keep an athlete out of the water. See a doctor!

Boils

Furunculosis is a localized infection generally caused by folliculitis (inflammation of the pilose follicle, the origin of the hair on the skin) and principally affects the legs. Treatment involves warm compresses, application of calendula and neomycin ointment. It can lead to a skin abscess, which may require surgical drainage. Antibiotics are often necessary.

Simplex Herpes

The first time that an athlete suffers an infection from the simple herpes virus (HSV) small blisters may appear in the region of contact, generally around the mouth or the genitals.

There are frequently wounds within the oral cavity and lymphatic reaction in the region of the wound. Two to three weeks are usually needed for a cure. During this period, the virus hides in a nerve cell and remains alive. Any situation that lowers one's immunity, such as a flu, fever or excessive exposure to sun, can reactivate the wound and cause the virus' reappearance.

Treatment includes the use of a medication to eliminate the virus called Aciclovir that can be used in the form of pills or ointment.

The amino-acid L-lisina may be used to prevent recurrence. For prevention take 500 mg twice a day.

The topic ointment application of Melissa officinalis (lemon balm) can help on acute eruption and may help avoid recurrence.

Keep immunity strong by using garlic, royal jelly, propolis, vitamin C and zinc.

Acne

Acne is common among adolescent surfers and is characterized by skin pimples. Hormonal changes during this period of sexual maturation can cause the super-production of fatty acids by the skin that, in sensitive athletes, can accumulate and form acne. It initially arises as black heads that can trigger secondary infections and result in pustules, particularly on the face and limbs

Surfing can aggravate the condition due to the presence of sweat and the increase of oil production caused by exercise, especially in warm environments.

Treatment

Treatment consists in keeping the skin clean and removing excess oil. The skin affected should be carefully washed every morning, after surfing and before going to bed with a liquid and antiseptic soap with 1 % triclosan.

The daily use of benzyl peroxide at 5-10 % is recommended to dry the skin. In more severe cases, oral antibiotics (tetracycline) are used for weeks or months. Avoid chocolates, sweets, dairy fats but increase the consumption of fruits and vegetables. Reduce imbalances and impurities within the body by using potent antioxidants that can help eliminate the free radicals that are dangerous to skin and promote infections.

Specific homeopathic remedies for acne include lycopodium especially for those who are ashamed of the condition, pulsatilla to help clean the skin and graphite to help clear the pimples.

Athlete's Foot

An extremely common problem among surfers, this infection is caused by different types of fungi that grow in the damp, warm spaces between toes. It can also be found in the genital region.

Some athletes appear to be immune, while others have repeated infections. Itching and flaking skin between the toes are the first signs.

Treatment

Treatment involves washing and drying well between the toes and applying antifungal medication in creams or ointments that contain Ketoconazde, miconazol or clotrimazole. They should be applied for 10-15 days for complete elimination of the fungus.

Prevention is conducted through proper washing and drying of the toes, the use of clean cotton socks and daily antimicotic foot powder.

Digestive System Infections

Traveler's Diarrhea

Athletes traveling to other countries are particularly susceptible to a disease known as traveler's diarrhea. The symptoms include watery diarrhea five or eight times a day, generally

Digestive organs

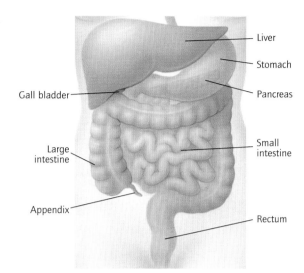

Liver

Stomach

Gall bladder

Pancreas

Large intestine

Small intestine

Appendix

Rectum

accompanied by cramps, upset stomach, vomiting, fever, body chills, and achiness. The symptoms begin 3-7 days after arrival. The disease is self-limiting, that is, it naturally subsides in 3-5 days, even without treatment.

Prevention is the best remedy:

1. Avoid tap water, ice cubes, raw salads, milk products and raw vegetables from unknown or questionable origins.

2. Do not eat old food or food left out of the refrigerator.

3. Avoid shellfish and partially cooked meals.

4. Only drink bottled and sterilized water.

5. Remove the skins from fruits before consumption.

Rehydration

The main treatment for diarrhea includes the restoration of fluids, solids and glucose. Dry mouth, thirstiness and reduced urine suggest dehydration. Begin rehydrating solutions that can be prepared at home. To do so, add a tablespoon of sugar and a teaspoon of salt to a liter of boiled water. Drink with frequency, especially after bowel movements. Commercial rehydration solutions can also be found.

Tahiti Photo: Ricardo Werneck

Check the labels. Coconut juice is an excellent rehydration fluid.

In case none of the above options are available, use Gatorade or even Coca-Cola. Herbal teas, such as chamomile, and guava leaves can help.

Stay away from coffee, alcohol and sweet and sugary foods. Avoid milk and dairy products, oranges, papaya and fatty or heavy food.

Eat crackers, light soup with carrots and rice. As the symptoms subside, have roasted and shredded chicken. Bananas and apples are fine.

There is no need for antibiotics, and the use of anti-diarrheal medication should be avoided. If there is mucus, pus or blood in the stool, see a doctor.

Viral Diarrhea

Many viruses can cause a disturbance in normal intestinal functions. The most frequent symptoms include loss of appetite, nausea, vomiting, diarrhea and abdominal cramps. These symptoms last a few days and improve spontaneously with rest, ingestion of a hydrating solution and a suitable diet as mentioned above.

Surf boat

Indo trip

Photos: Sebastian Rojas

Car loaded with surfboards

Indo trip

Photos: Sebastian Rojas

Worms

Worms are extremely common in tropical surfing destinations throughout the Third World.

Worms are contracted through contaminated water and foods. They become more frequent with contact with domestic animals, such as cats and dogs. Symptoms can include stomach ache, nausea, vomiting, headache and diarrhea. At times, they can lead to anemia.

Annual de-worming is recommended through the use of medication in the following manner: albendzole, in a single dose of 400mg. Repeat after two weeks. It kills the majority of the most common worms, including (roundworms, hookworms and pinworms).

Personal hygiene and sanitary measures are essential for prevention and include:

1. Always drinking only boiled water.

2. Washing hands after going to the bathroom and before eating.

3. Keeping nails cut and clean.

4. Avoiding salads and poorly cooked vegetables from questionable sources. Vegetables can be washed with a solution containing sodium hypochlorite (bleach).

5. Only eating fruits and vegetables after removing the skin.

6. Boiling non-pasteurized milk.

Southern Australia
**Enormous and icy waves
at Two Miles Bay**

Photo: Steve Ryan

Chapter 16

Surfing Cold Waters – Hypothermia and Cramps

The history of surf and the history of Mormaii are intimately linked to the creation of wetsuits that allow surfers to explore the thousands of icy waves on the planet.

Human physiology teaches that the normal body temperature is about 98-99° Fahrenheit (36° and 37° Centigrade) and that the ideal ambient temperature for humans, in dry air, is about 79-83°; (26 to 28° Centigrade).

Prolonged exposure to temperatures below 73° in shorts (23° Centigrade) can lead to a drop in body temperature.

Thus, surfing in the evening, with a water temperature between warm and cold (generally 68-70° F; 20-21° C) can cause a drop of 2° Fahrenheit (1° Centigrade) in the normal body temperature, which will result in the reduction of performance on the waves. Changes in one's state of consciousness, such as sleepiness, apathy or torpor, occur at body temperatures of 95° Fahrenheit (35° Centigrade) and is called hypothermia.

Body Adaptation Mechanisms to the Cold

One of the body's basic adaptation mechanisms against cold is peripheral vascular constriction, or reduced blood flow to the skin and muscles, to compensate for increased blood flow to the most important organs, such as the kidneys, brain and heart.

In addition to changes in the direction of blood flow, muscle tremors and shivering occur in an attempt by the body to produce heat and maintain its temperature. The tremors are involuntary muscular contractions of one or a variety of groups of muscles that raise the consumption of oxygen and make athletic performance even more difficult, impeding surfing, reducing control of the board and increasing the risk of accidents and injuries.

A decrease in body temperature, known as hypothermia, is even more aggravated in the following situations:

1. In the water, where heat loss is nearly 20-times greater than on land.

2. With wind, which stimulates the evaporation of water and aggravates the loss of heat.

3. The greater the body area exposed to cold, the greater the loss of body heat.

4. The lower the percentage of body fat (since body fat serves as thermal insulation). In general recreational surfers of school age have nearly 15% body fat, while professional athletes have an average of 8%.

5. When eating poorly, that is, when there is not adequate nutrition, especially in the two hours that precede surfing, since the burning of calories increases three times in the cold and can increase up to five times when tremors begin.

In addition, stamina – which is needed to recover from a wipe out – decreases in low temperature waters, considerably raising the risk of cramps (involuntary muscle spasms, principally in the legs) and drowning.

Avoid surfing icy waves in shorts and a shirt; not only will you quickly become cold and have difficulty surfing, but there is greater risk of accident and injury.

Cold kills in two steps: exposure and exhaustion. The colder the water, the less time you can survive (see Chart A).

Chart A: How Cold Water Affects You

Water Temp	Exhaustion	Survival Time
32.5° F	Under 15 min	Under 15-45 min
32.5-40° F	15-30 min	30-90 min
40-50° F	30-60 min	1-3 hrs
50-60° F	1-2 hrs	1-6 hrs
60-70° F	2-7hrs	2-40 hrs
70-80° F	3-12 hrs	3hrs to indefinite
Over 80° F	Indefinite	Indefinite

Morongo, a doctor and creator of one of the world's best wetsuits (Mormaii) helping his pupil Marco Polo find the safest route

Photo: Flavio Vidigal

The Solution

There are two ways to insulate your body from the cold and continue to surf:

1. Increase the percentage of body fat.

2. Use an excellent warm and dry wetsuit.

Thin surfers, those with a low amount of body fat, need thicker wetsuits. Surfers should put on a few extra pounds during the winter, within their normal weight range for their height (considering their biotype) since it is known that a thin surfer can lose up to 10-times more heat than a heavier one.

It is best to have a good wetsuit, have a good warm-up, stretch and have plenty of willpower to surf the planet's cold and giant waves!

A wetsuit, in addition to offering warmth, should allow total mobility. It is essential to use a good quality wetsuit. It is not worth skimping.

Guilly Brandão
Brazilian Kite Surfing Champion

Photo: James Thisted

Photo: James Thisted

Kauli Seadi
Brazilian Waves Wind Surf World Champion

Wetsuits work by insulating the skin from the water and in general the thickness is as important as the fit. The suit should adjust perfectly to the body and allow a complete range of movement. If possible, opt for the latest generation of clothes without seams (taped seams) and a dry zipper.

Since nearly 30% of the blood flow passes through the head and neck, a wetsuit should protect the neck in order to reduce heat loss.

For those who really get cold, consider the use of a cap or helmet, in order to reduce the heat loss from the head, as well as gloves and boots to avoid the sensation of icy toes.

Mark Renneker is a U.S. doctor famous for surfing large icy Maverick waves in Alaska, Canada, Iceland and Antarctica. With wetsuits thicker than 8mm, he was able to surf for 2 hours in water with a temperature of 0.5° C (see Chart B).

Chart B: Wetsuit Protection	
Water Temp	**Wetsuit Thickness**
Over 80° F	None (rash guard for sun)
60-79° F	2mm body 1mm arms/legs "Spring" or vest
50-59° F	3mm body 2mm arms/legs Full or "Steamer"
40-49° F	5mm body 4mm arms/legs Full
Below 40° F	Dry suit

Nutrition and Hydration

Surfing in the cold considerably increases the amount of calories needed because they will be burned to produce heat. A diet rich in carbohydrates (such as pasta or granola) is important 2-3 hours before surfing. Since the body's defense against the cold is to alter the flow of blood (which carries heat) from the skin to the kidney, heart and brain, a surfer urinates nearly three times more in the cold and can easily become dehydrated, which limits performance even more.

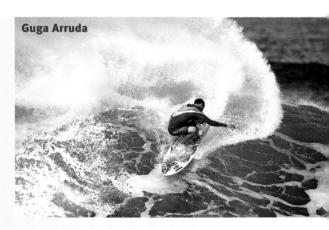

Guga Arruda

Therefore, drinking large quantities of water for more than an hour before and after surfing is a basic strategy to avoid dehydration, replace sodium and prevent sports injuries.

Other tactics for remaining heated and without cramps include:

1. A muscular warm-up before entering the water.

2. Short surf sessions, of moderate to high intensity, keeping active most of the time in the water.

Cramps while Surfing

Cramping is not a disease, but an involuntary muscular contraction. It can affect any person and is most frequent among athletes. Cramps are accompanied by sharp pain and make movement nearly impossible. Cramps are most frequent in the leg and arm muscles, which are more active when surfing. They can also come during rest or sleep.

We have no statistics about the incidence of cramps among surfers.

However, cramps afflict 39% of marathon runners, 79% of triathletes, and 60% of cyclists at one time or another.

Cause

Cramps are caused by the increased body temperature during exercise that causes muscular alterations and leads to a loss of sodium. This is generally associated with poor hydration and an imbalance in the proportions of water, sodium, potassium, calcium and magnesium in the muscle environment. The nerves then become hypersensitive.

The pain is due to the intense muscular contraction, leading to lack of oxygen and production of lactic acid.

Some medical conditions can lead to cramps, including narrowed blood vessels, usually from atherosclerosis, or some back problems that include compression of a nerve, as happens in spinal stenosis. Cramps also can arise from hypothyroidism or be the side effect of medication like diuretics (used to lower blood pressure), which can lead to a potassium deficiency.

Treatment

In most cases, a doctor is not necessary. Cramps, although painful, are generally easy to resolve. Treatment includes stretching the muscular group affected for a few minutes, which can immediately alleviate the pain. In case the calf muscle is affected, stretch the foot toward the face (Illustration 1).

Illustration 1: Stretching for cramps

Nevertheless, depending on the circumstances in which they occur, cramps can place a surfer's life at risk, especially those that take place in the zone of impact in large swells, for they can cause an athlete to panic. Fortunately, this does not occur frequently.

Stay calm, ask for help, stretch in the water, resist the pain, and take the first wave to the beach and stretch.

Guilherme Tripa
Aerial

Photo: James Thisted

**Special Mormaii wetsuit
for surf rescue!**

Photo: James Thisted

Preventing cramps:

1. Get suitable hydration before, during and after surfing. Drink plenty of water with electrolytes (sodium, potassium).

2. A balanced diet, rich in greens, vegetables, fruits, complex carbohydrates (rice, oatmeal, whole wheat bread) and small quantities of meat – preferably white meat (chicken and fish) – will supply the suitable fuel for muscles in addition to calcium (non-fat milk, low-fat cheese, spinach, broccoli and oysters), magnesium (leafy vegetables), potassium (bananas, tomatoes, etc.) and sodium (salt).

3. Improve cardiovascular conditioning. This will increase the amount of oxygen in the muscles. Ride a bike, swim and run at least three times a week, for an hour, in moderate to high intensity.

4. Stretch before surfing. It is important to stretch the quadriceps, rear thigh muscles and calves.

5. Keep warm in the water by paddling and surfing.

6. Avoid fatigue, and leave the water when you begin to shiver.

Everaldo Pato Texeira
Tahiti

Photo: Agobar Junior

Chapter 17

Sun, Surf and Skin Cancer

Surfers are a risk group for skin cancer: Be careful!

The sun is essential for maintaining equilibrium in the human body. One of the sun's functions is to stimulate the skin's production of vitamin D, which is important for bone health.

Nevertheless, the cumulative affect of considerable exposure over time is dangerous. Many years of surfing and sun exposure can cause serious damage to your skin and health. If you have light skin, the risk is even greater.

Australia has the world's highest incidence of skin cancer, a disease that is closely related to excessive exposure to the sun that has been affecting an increasingly younger population. In America, there are over one million new cases of skin cancer diagnosed each year, outnumbering all other cancers combined.

Before paddling out, these are some things you must know:

Sunlight

Sunlight is composed of electromagnetic waves of different lengths known as ultraviolet rays. They include:

1. UVA rays, long and short, are dangerous rays from sun-up to sundown. They are responsible for loss of skin elasticity, wrinkles, blotches and dehydration. They do not produce reddening (erythema) but direct pigmentation to the skin.

2. UVB rays dominate from 9 a.m. to 3 p.m. and cause sunburn to the skin.

3. UVC rays become more intense as the hole in the ozone layer gets larger.

247

All three of these rays increase the risk of skin cancer. Sunlight is responsible for 90% of all skin cancers. It is in the same class as other cancer-causing elements such as arsenic, asbestos, radon and tobacco smoke.

UV rays also easily penetrate clouds, so observe ALL sun-safety practices on cloudy days as well.

Scientific studies have shown that the earlier children are exposed to dangerous ultraviolet sun rays, without protection, the greater the chances of developing skin cancer as an adult.

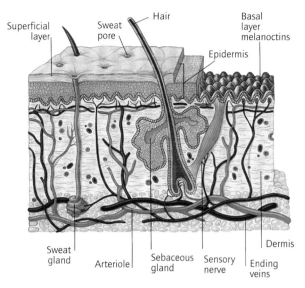

Skin Structure

Skin exposed to ultraviolet rays becomes red. This stimulates the production of the pigment melanin, which is responsible for tanning, functions as protection and leads to the appearance of freckles.

The degree of reddening or pigmentation depends on the type of skin and the number of hours of exposure to the sun.

Sun Protection

The principal problems related to prolonged and repeated sun exposure are:

1. Sunburn of first and second degrees

2. Premature aging of the skin (actinic keratosis)

3. Pre-cancerous lesions

4. Skin cancer and melanomas

5. Weakened immune system

6. Cataracts

Different Skin Types and Reactions to the Sun

Type 1: Ultra-Sensitive Skin

Skin that burns very easily and never tans. Very light skin with some freckles. Hair is often red and eyes blue.

Type 2: Very Light Skin

Skin that burns easily and rarely tans. Skin is lightly pigmented. People with this skin type usually have light colored eyes and blond hair.

Type 3: Light Skin

Skin that burns moderately and gradually tans. Surfers with this skin type usually have brown hair and eyes. They have some tolerance to the sun.

Type 4: Resistant – Light Brown Skin

Skin that burns minimally and regularly tans. Usually found among athletes with darker brown hair and skin.

Type 5: Dark Brown Skin

Skin that rarely burns but tans intensely. People with this skin type have dark hair and eyes.

Type 6: Black Skin

Skin that does not visibly burn. Surfers with this skin type have highly pigmented black skin.

Sunburns

Most sunburns are of the first degree, benign, affect the most superficial layer of the skin and improve with the application of hydrating creams with an aloe vera base.

Second degree burns are deeper and cause blisters. To treat them, plunge the affected portion of the body in cool or cold water and repeat the procedure a few times. If there are no blisters, apply an aloe vera-based cream. If there is intense pain, use aspirin or Tylenol. If there are blisters, avoid breaking them. Make a bandage with gauze and Vaseline or Furacine (nitrofurazone) and stay out of the sun.

Prevention of Skin Cancer

Fortunately, society in general – including parents, teachers, doctors, clubs, etc. – has assumed responsibility for teaching children about the effects of overexposure to the sun and how to avoid it. In the United States, for example, it is estimated that at 18 years of age a youth has received 75% of the sun exposure they will receive during their life. To avoid becoming another statistic in the incidence of pre-cancerous lesions, we recommend:

1. More surf and less sun. Avoid surfing from 10 a.m. to 3 p.m.. During these hours, the dangerous sun rays are at their strongest. Remember that the closer to the Equator, the greater the level of radiation.

2. Dress properly for surfing. Use total protection with lycra or long sleeves, hats, etc.

3. Use waterproof sun block, with a protection factor of 50 or more. Lotions are the most suitable because they offer more water resistance. Apply to all exposed areas of the body including the lips, nose and ears.

4. Keep hydrated. Drink lots of liquid, including fruit juices and carrot juice in particular because it has beta carotene.

5. Get regular check-ups. Carefully examine your skin. Currently, 1 in 7 people in the United States develop skin cancer. The good news is that most of the lesions can be completely cured, if diagnosed early.

What is Sun Protection Factor (SPF)?

The sun protection factor (SPF) indicates how much time a person can be exposed to the sun without burning the skin. A product with SPF 50, for example, allows a person to be exposed to the sun, without burning, for a period 50 times longer than if they are not using the product. Suppose that without protection the skin begins to burn in 5 minutes; with SPF 50, the skin will resist without burning for 250 minutes (50 x 5).

In addition to sun filters for UVA (used to prevent aging), UVB (used to avoid burns and allow tanning) and UVC, the best sun blocks include infrared filters and hydrating agents. They may also contain antioxidizing vitamins, such as E and C, that combat and prevent the formation of free radicals. Some sun blocks also contain opaque substances that reflect light, impeding radiation from reaching the skin. The most commonly used are zinc oxide and titanium oxide.

**Soraya Rocha –
Top world body boarder**

Waterproof sun block

Sun blocks must always be applied on dry skin 30 minutes before entering the water. For best results, use a sunscreen containing zinc oxide, commercially known as Z-Cote, 15 minutes before entering the water and reapply it every 30-60 minutes thereafter. Don't forget to apply sunscreen to often neglected, uncovered parts of the body including bald spots, the forehead, tips of the ears, backs of the hands, the neck, and the lower legs and feet.

If you intend to surf for many hours, you must apply a high level skin protector before going into the water.

An SPF 30 allows sun exposure for 2 hours, although repeating it after this time does not guarantee the same effect as using an SPF 60.

Sun filters can irritate and cause allergic reactions to eyes, including those products considered hypoallergenic. Thus, the greater the protection factor, the greater the risk of skin irritation.

In case of allergy, it is best to see a doctor to identify the responsible substance. One of the most allergenic substances is PABA (para-aminobenzoic acid). If an allergy is confirmed, test other sun blocks on the market until a less irritating and less allergenic chemical composition is found. Generally different lotions are indicated for different types of skin.

Blemishes – Beware

If you have skin blotches, also known as "nevi" or "moles," or a mark that begins to grow, change color or form, bleed or itch, see a doctor, because the lesion may be skin cancer in an early phase. A biopsy may be necessary, that is, a piece of the lesion is removed for medical microscopic analysis.

Older surfers should have their skin checked frequently by a doctor. The top of the ears, and the back and rear of the legs are high risk areas that are generally not checked.

When enjoying the waves and sunny days, always wear a hat and glasses and seek the shade.

Benign lesions

Common nevi (skin marks or blemishes) are round and symmetric, with regular edges, a single color and are smaller than 6 mm.

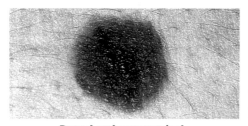

Round and symmetrical

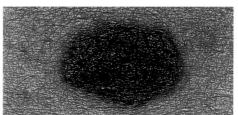

Regular border

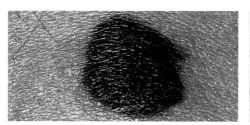

Uniform color

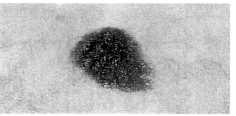

Smaller than 6 mm

Lesions that Require Medical Consultation

Skin blemishes with malign characteristics are usually asymmetrical, with irregular borders, two or more tones of color and a diameter greater than 6 mm.

Some forms of basal cell carcinoma and melanoma are asymmetrical, meaning if a line were drawn in the middle, it woud not create two comparable halves.

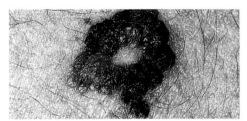 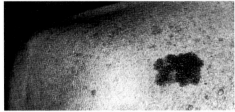

Malign skin tumors have irregularities, such as saliences and indents.

 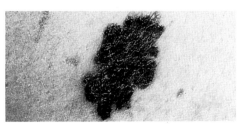

Melanomas usually have a variation in tone (first mark).

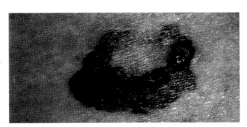 

In their first phases, melanomas are usually larger than 6 mm.

SURFING & HEALTH

Tom Carrol
Two Miles Bay - Australia

Chapter 18

Attacks by Sharks or Other Sea Animals

The risk of being hurt or killed in a shark attack is much lower than the risk of a car or motorcycle accident on the way to the beach. But it is important to stay alert and be careful.

Jellyfish

Although they are frequent in the summer waters, most jellyfish stings are fortunately not serious. There are over 900 known species. Usually they are solitary, but sometimes they gather in huge numbers, forming jellyfish blooms.

130 million tourists suffer jellyfish attacks worldwide.

They represent nearly 9% of surfing accidents.

These animals belong to the phylum known as Cnidaria that have tentacles (a type of skin) that surrounds the oral cavity. These tentacles are used to capture their prey and are characterized by the presence of a very special organ called a nematocyst.

Each nematocyst contains a venom capsule in which a harpoon is enclosed. At the surface of each nematocyst, a small cilium, once touched by a fish or a surfer, transmits a signal which triggers the mechanism of the nematocyst: the capsule breaks and the harpoon is launched, piercing the skin of the victim with high speed.

Hundreds or thousands of nematocysts are grouped in nodules or dense bundles along the tentacles or filaments, which can reach up to one meter in length, which facilitates the simultaneous discharge of a high number of nematocysts and the injection of a significant volume of toxin.

The Portuguese Man-of-War "jellyfish" are found in warm waters of the Pacific , Indian and Atlantic oceans.

Try to avoid any contact with this animal, especially its tentacles, even when it's dead at the beach.

Its painful toxin may be active for hours.

In Australia's Queensland region and West Coast some jellyfish species produce a very painful and high risk poison capable of killing a person.

No grave jellyfish attacks are known to have occurred in Brazil and few attacks in Hawaii cause medical emergency problems.

Jellyfish

Symptoms

Contact with jellyfish is most common on legs and arms.

The toxin is a mixture of proteins that, when in contact with the skin, causes stinging and intense pain at the location, which can last from a few minutes to a few days.

Red areas soon appear, with itching, stringy welts on the skin from contact with the blue tentacle – it is a painful eruption that can blister and cause necrosis of the skin in about 24 hours.

The most serious cases may be accompanied by headache, discomfort, nausea, vomiting, muscle spasms, fever, cardiac arrhythmia, sweating, fainting, rashes and even anaphylactic shock. The seriousness depends on the extent of the area affected, the type of animal and the characteristics of the victim.

A study by the Toxicological Information Center of Santa Catarina reported that the most frequent symptoms related to jellyfish stings were pain in 93%, redness in 23%, vomiting and nausea in 9% and blisters in 7%.

Treatment

When stung, carefully, pick or brush off any visible tentacles – try not to use your fingers – use your towel, fins, etc.

Rinse with fresh or salt water – do not use vinegar.

Bags of ice are often necessary to alleviate the local symptoms.

Immediate medical attention may be required as their stinging may bring about anaphylactic shock.

To remove the remaining nematocysts, apply a paste of sodium bicarbonate (baking soda), talcum power or flour and seawater, wait for it to dry and remove it with the edge of a knife. For persistent itching or skin rash, try 1 percent hydrocortisone ointment four times a day, and one or two 25 milligram diphenhydramine (Benadryl) tablets every 6 hours. These drugs are sold without prescription. Diphenhydramine may cause drowsiness. Don't drive, swim or surf after taking this medication. To relieve the pain, use an analgesic.

Sharks

While the strength of a lion or tiger bite is about 600 kg/cm^2 and that of a crocodile is approximately 800 kg/cm^2, that of a shark can be 3 tons per cm/^{2}. So keep your eyes open! Shark attacks on surfers are very rare in Brazil, except for the beach of Boa Viagem in Recife. When surfing, the risk of dying from a shark attack is basically nil (1 in 300 million), an insignificant number when compared to the risk of dying from other causes, such as drowning, heart attack or in an automobile or motorcycle accident on the way to the beach. In reality, you are more likely to be hit by lightning. Sharks are in sixth place among the wild animals that most frequently attack humans, far behind snakes, crocodiles, bees, hippopotamuses and elephants. In Brazil, nearly 20,000 people are attacked by poisonous snakes each year, with an average of 100 deaths.

As Wayne Lynch, the living legend of Australian surf advised those who surf large, icy, sharkinfested waves along the Great Ocean Road on the Australian Coast between Bells Beach and Two Miles Bay: Don't be paranoid, but keep your eyes open.

Sharks have been around for nearly 400 million years and have maintained their scary, pre-historic appearance. They cannot see colors, do not sleep and move 24 hours a day. With a reputation as fierce assassins, their size can vary from 15 centimeters to 18 meters. Some species have 8 rows of teeth, can reach speeds of up to 60 km per hour and live an average of 25 years.

Some can live for 100 years. Their eyes are covered by a layer that reflects light, which increases their vision in the weak luminosity of deep waters. Their sense of smell and accurate sense of vibration allow them to detect blood and movements dozens of kilometers away.

These characteristics probably make the shark the most efficient hunter in the oceans, which also makes them one of the most hunted. Nevertheless, sharks are part of the life cycle of oceans and should not be allowed to become an extinct species.

Fortunately, the large majority of sharks do not attack people.

Of the 380 known shark species, 30 have attacked humans, while only 12 are dangerous and truly attack swimmers, surfers, fishermen or divers when the shark senses an invasion of its space.

Sharks are found in coastal and ocean waters, from the surface to the depths, in practically all oceans and seas. Carnivorous, they are predators par excellence. They have a very primitive nervous system, with a small brain and nearly no sensibility to pain. Strong and resilient, they can take a long time to die even when seriously wounded. They operate exclusively by instinct, and their reactions to various situations are not predictable. Some species, due to their voracity, act like ocean garbage removers and eat wounded or dead animals (even those in decomposition). Nevertheless, each species has its alimentary preferences and sharks are habitually high on the food chain, which includes fish, crustaceans, squid, octopus, turtles, seals, sea lions, skates and other sharks.

The mechanism that leads a shark to attack a surfer is well known. The vibrations produced by the invaders, in this case surfers, trigger the instincts of the animal, which feels that its territory has been invaded. The leg and hand movements produce sound waves similar to those emitted by the fish that serve as their food. Thus, some of the attacks are made by mistake. It is common for a shark to bite to identify the animal in its territory.

Basically there are two types of shark attacks:

1. **Hit and run** – This is the most common and takes place in the wave-breaking zone where swimmers and surfers are found. In these cases, the aggressive sharks are not seen by the victim and usually do not come back after a single bite. It is believed that these attacks are provoked by errors of identification, which can occur under conditions of poor visibility or when the water is rough. Wounds caused by this type of attack are usually limited in most cases to small cuts, usually on the legs, below the knee, and rarely cause fatalities. The flat head shark is one of those often involved in this type of attack, especially in northeastern Brazil.

2. **Hit and bite** – Although less frequent, these attacks usually cause serious and extensive wounds, most of which lead to death. They involve bathers, swimmers, surfers and divers in shallow locations. The aggressor swims in circles, applying repeated blows before inflicting multiple and prolonged bites. The sneak attack is different because there is no warning. The species probably responsible for most of these accidents are the white shark, the "tintureira" and, at times, the flat-head.

Sharks on the Pernambuco Coast of Brazil

Shark attacks on the Pernambuco coast have become frequent in recent years and are attributed to the flat-head shark, a species that reaches 3 meters in length.

According to official statistics, 38 accidents were registered in this state since 1992, nearly half of the 91 attacks in Brazil in the entire century.

More than 40% of the attacks were against body-boarders. Most of these victims suffered mutilations. Not even in Florida, which has a terrible record of 109 attacks in five years, have the accidents been so serious. No deaths were registered in Florida. In addition, the attacks in Recife take place within a stretch of only 20 km of coastline, while the accidents in Florida take place in a range of 1,750 km of coastline.

To avoid new attacks, surfing was prohibited in Recife from the Pina Beach to Boa Viagem, near Paiva, on the Cape of St. Augustine. This measure includes 4 other municipalities in the region and violators are subject to arrest and fines.

There are various explanations for the shark attacks in Pernambuco. Some concern the temperature and concentration of nutrients in the water. A possible decrease in the food supply in the sea is related to the growing human occupation of coastal areas since the 1970s and the consequential environmental degradation and predatory fishing. In addition, the popularization of surfing facilitates encounters between humans and sharks. But specialists indicate that the attacks may be caused by other factors related to human activity in the region. One factor in the growth in the number of attacks is the construction of an Industrial Complex at the Port of Suape, 40 kilometers south of Recife. Installed in 1989, the port altered the sea currents near Recife. Currents that passed far from the coast are now closer to shore and the beaches in the southern part of the city. Since the sharks follow these currents, instead of remaining farther out to sea, they are feeding closer to the beaches. In addition, the movement of ships increased considerably and food is often thrown into the sea, whirch animals.

The surfers who risk these waves and reefs were naturally incorporated into the sharks' food chain. Surfing in these regions is like playing Russian roulette.

Fortunally, several preventative measures have eliminated the shark attacks in recent years.

How to Avoid Attacks

If you see a shark, take the next wave and get out! If it is not possible to escape attack, try to hurt the shark with a punch or kick, or with the tip of the board. There is a possibility it will give up the chase.

If immediately rescued, the majority of shark-bite victims survive.

If you are rescuing someone, do not be shocked by the gruesome quality of the bite and avoid panicking.

The main problem is the bleeding that should be rapidly staunched with a tourniquet, otherwise the victim will die from hemorrhaging. In case the victim cannot be taken immediately to the beach, try to staunch the bleeding using a hand, Lycra or a cord to compress the region above the bleeding.

At the beach, place the victim far from the waves, lying with the head lower than the legs and apply a tourniquet before taking him to the hospital.

A tourniquet should be applied above the wound, over a bone but not over a joint.

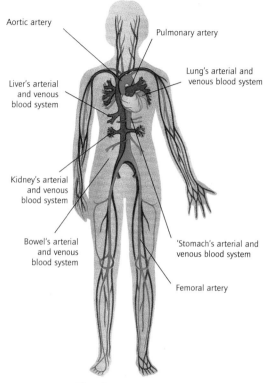

Aortic artery
Pulmonary artery
Lung's arterial and venous blood system
Liver's arterial and venous blood system
Kidney's arterial and venous blood system
Bowel's arterial and venous blood system
'Stomach's arterial and venous blood system
Femoral artery

Circulatory system

The blood enters from the left side of the heart and is then pumped to the lungs where it is oxygenated. It then returns to the left side of the heart from where it is expelled to irrigate the entire body.

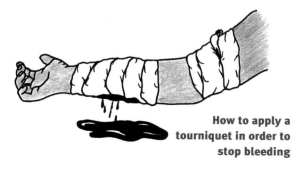

How to apply a tourniquet in order to stop bleeding

A belt piece of clothing, strap or cord can be used. If the bleeding continues, apply direct pressure with the hand. If the victim is using a wetsuit, do not remove it. Monitor the breathing and be ready to begin cardiopulmonary resuscitation, if necessary (see Chapter 31).

Blue Ring Octopus

This animal is found in the shallow waters of Australia. Although it is not painful, the bite of this octopus is fatal and mainly affects divers. The first symptoms include difficulty swallowing, blurred vision and numbness of the lips and tongue. There may be respiratory seizure.

The treatment includes cardiopulmonary resuscitation (see Chapter 31).

Blue ring octopus

Sea Snake

Found in the Fiji Islands, this marine snake with nocturnal habits has a deadly venom. The good news is that it feeds on fish and not humans, but stay away.

SURFING & HEALTH

Waimea – Hawaii

Chapter 19

Asthma and Surfing

Many surfers suffer from asthma.

In many cases, surfing is as good for the lungs as swimming.

The good news is most children improve significantly after adolescence.

Asthma makes breathing difficult for more than 22 million Americans, most of them children and teenagers. Fortunately, most of them improve significantly after adolescence and, with proper treatment, children and adults with asthma can surf quite well.

Bronchial asthma is defined as a hyper-reactivity of the air passages to different stimuli that cause:

1. Inflammation and constriction of the air passages; a condition known as bronchial constriction

2. Increased secretion of mucous in the bronchial passages

It is estimated that a high number of surfers suffer from asthma. An Australian study of more than 20 asthmatic surfers found that at least one stopped surfing because of asthma.

During an asthma crisis, there are bronchial spasms, hyper-secretion and inflammation.

265

Symptoms

Asthma symptoms include coughing, wheezing and chest tightness.

Asthma crises vary in intensity and frequency and should be given attention because untreated cases can be fatal. There are often no symptoms between crises.

Types of Asthma

Understanding the type of asthma you have can help you seek the most effective treatment when you have an asthma attack.

1. Allergies and Asthma: A Common Type of Asthma

Allergies and asthma often go hand-in-hand. Allergic rhinitis (also called hay fever) is the inflammation of the inside lining of the nose and is the single most common chronic allergic disease experienced by people. With allergic rhinitis, you may feel a constant runny nose and sneezing, swollen nasal passages, excess mucus, weepy eyes and a scratchy throat. A cough may result from the constant postnasal drip. Many times asthma symptoms are triggered by allergic rhinitis.

Allergic factors
The principal villains are dust, powders, pollen, animal hair; certain foods like chocolate or milk; certain artificial food dyes, etc.

| house dust mites | medications like AAS and propanolol | hair, feathers | emotions, stress |

2. Exercise-Induced Asthma

Physical exercise, including surfing, can trigger asthma (see section below).

intense exercise

3. Cough-Variant Asthma

In the type of asthma called cough-variant asthma, severe coughing with asthma is the predominant symptom. There can be other causes of cough such as gastroesophageal reflux disease (GERD or heartburn). Coughing because of sinusitis with asthma is common.

Asthma is a serious cause of cough that is common today. Cough-variant asthma is vastly underdiagnosed and undertreated. Triggers for cough-variant asthma are usually respiratory infections and exercise.

For any persistent cough, you should have pulmonary function tests to examine your lung functioning.

4. Climatic factors

Sharp temperature and humidity changes are among the main factors that aggravate surfers.

Temperature changes

5. Infectious agents

Flu and other infections of the air passages are capable of triggering a crisis.

Flu and colds

6. Occupational Asthma

Occupational asthma is a type of asthma that results from workplace triggers. With this type of asthma, you might have difficulty breathing and asthma symptoms on workdays but not on weekends.

Many people with this type of asthma suffer with runny nose and congestion or eye irritation, or have a cough instead of the typical asthma wheezing.

Some common jobs that are associated with occupational asthma include animal breeders, farmers, hairdressers, nurses, painters and woodworkers.

atmospheric pollution

cigarettes

cleaning products

Irritation factors include atmospheric pollution (carbon dioxide, sulfur dioxide, cigarette smoke and vehicle exhaust, chemical substances used in manufacturing surf boards and other industries), perfumes, soaps, cleaning products, etc.

7. Nocturnal (Nighttime) Asthma

Nocturnal asthma is common and dangerous. If you have asthma, the chances of having symptoms are much higher during sleep because asthma is influenced by the sleep-wake cycle (circadian rhythms). Your asthma symptoms of nighttime wheezing, cough and breathing trouble are common. You must see your doctor.

Exercise-Induced Asthma

Any physical exercise, including surfing can be a factor that triggers asthma. Sports such as running trigger crises more frequently. There are many people without asthma, including top surfers, who develop symptoms only during exercise.

In this form of asthma, the narrowing of the airways peaks 5 to 20 minutes after exercise begins but can also arise 6 to 8 hours later, making it difficult to catch your breath. You may have symptoms of an asthma attack with wheezing and coughing.

During surfing, or any other sport, the tendency is to breathe through the mouth (oral breathing). This reduces the warming and humidification of the air, which are tasks performed by the nose. As a result, the airways get dehydrated.

In addition, the increased quantity of air that passes through the lungs while surfing increases considerably, from 5 to 10 liters of air per minute at rest, to nearly 50 to 100 liters of air per minute during surfing. This aggravates the dehydration of the air passages even more, which, in turn, can trigger a crisis in a sensitive surfer.

The severity of the crises will depend on the individual characteristics of the athlete, as well as the:

1. Temperature and humidity of the air of the surf location

2. Duration and intensity of the surf session

3. Time since the last asthma attack

Surfing in general is a good sport for athletes who suffer from asthma because it is practiced in environments with high levels of relative air humidity. Nevertheless, sensitive and untreated athletes may trigger their asthma during a surfing session.

Recommendations

1. Do not surf in the winter, so as to avoid exposure to cold winds.

2. Pay attention during the spring, when offshore winds carry a large quantity of allergic material.

3. Be careful when surfing heavy waves, which require a lot of paddling, and wipe outs that are rough.

4. Pay attention because the salty environment of seawater can trigger crises for some surfers.

Evaluation and Treatment

An initial medical evaluation includes a test of lung function. It consists of blowing into a device linked to a computer, which conducts an analysis and offers important and precise data about the lung's functions.

Asthma treatment can vary from anti-inflammatory and bronchodilator asthma inhalers, to oral medications, drugs delivered in an asthma nebulizer or breathing machine.

Early and aggressive asthma treatment is key to relieving symptoms and preventing asthma attacks.

It is essential to completely recuperate from an asthma attack before returning to surfing.

A surfer with asthma must develop the ability to observe the reaction of his or her body, particularly the lungs, to different stimuli including temperature changes, physical exercises, perfumes, food, aromas, etc. You should also be aware of your breathing, to realize when a crisis is about to begin and when it is necessary to employ techniques to control and overcome asthma attacks.

Allergies

When asthma is caused by allergies, the treatment should be directed at the allergy.

In addition to being manifest in the lungs and causing asthma, an allergic reaction can also be expressed in other locations, such as:

1. The skin, causing a rash and eczema

2. The nostrils, causing rhinitis

3. The facial cavities, causing sinus inflammation

4. The eyes, causing conjunctivitis

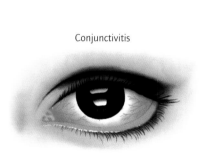

Conjunctivitis

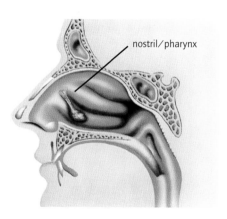

nostril/pharynx

Rhinitis and sinus problems can complicate the life of the athlete even more, resulting in difficulty breathing through the nose.

There are many dermatological and blood tests capable of identifying substances or foods responsible for allergies and which should be avoided. But the true test, however, is observing those agents in your daily routine that cause allergies.

Mites are also one of the main causes of asthma crises in domestic environments. They are microscopic arachnids found in dust, and are broadly distributed.

Hygiene: techniques for eliminating mites

The following solution is recommended to remove mites from homes and should be prepared in a homeopathic pharmacy:

1. benzyl benzoate, 25%

2. cetostearyl alcohol, 3%

3. triethanolamine lauryl sulfate, 100ml

Preparation for use: Dilute at the time of using, in the proportion of one tablespoon per liter of water. Apply the diluted solution once a week in the morning on a sunny day, with a clean cloth, sponge or spray, on furniture, mattresses, etc., then use a vacuum cleaner to remove the mites. Leave the space exposed to sun and air, and in the late afternoon, vacuum again. Repeat weekly for 3 months. After this period, apply monthly. Change linens on the day of application.

Athletes often have favorable responses to:

1. **Homeopathic treatment**

2. **Acupuncture**
    This technique uses needles on pressure points to relieve symptoms. While some people with asthma have found that acupuncture can significantly reduce asthma attacks and improve lung function, studies are not conclusive.

3. **Medicinal plants**

4. **Yoga**
    The breathing exercises used in yoga have been found to help some athletes and people with asthma control breathing and relieve stress.

5. **Asthma Diet**
    Restricting dairy products and sugar has reportedly helped some with childhood asthma.

6. **Biofeedback**
    Learning to increase the amount of air inhaled using biofeedback has reduced fear and anxiety during asthma attacks for some people.

Nevertheless, many athletes require some kind of medication to control and eliminate crises, whether in the form of a pump and/or inhalers. Pumps or inhalers are not considered doping as long as their use is accepted by the International Olympic Committee and used under medical supervision. The principal medications used in the inhalers are:

1. Bronchodilators: Airway openers that immediately alleviate the crisis and prevent asthma. An asthma inhaler sends medication directly into the lungs to help relieve

asthma symptoms faster and with fewer side effects, like a discrete acceleration in the heart rate for a short period of time and in most cases are well tolerated. They can also be used orally, or intravenously in emergencies.

2. Therapeutic and prophylactic medications that reduce inflammation of the aerial passages. These include sodium chromoglycate (Intal), the cortisone-based inhalers including Advair, Aerobid, Asmanex, Azmacort, Flovent, Pulmicort, Symbicort, Qvar, etc. and most recently the antileukotrienes. These medications are used regularly to control and minimize asthma symptoms.

All surfers who suffer from asthma should plan a treatment scheme with their doctor, in order to control their asthma and improve their quality of life and surfing performance.

Although it is not possible to guarantee that a medicated athlete will not suffer from an asthma attack while surfing, some measures can help to avoid this:

1. Always stretch, warm up and conduct exercises to open up the thorax before surfing (see following exercises). Never surf without warming up.

2. Maintain a regular program of aerobic exercises with special attention to swimming and bicycling. This will improve your cardio-respiratory capacity.

3. Respiratory exercises develop the habit of breathing through the nose; practice abdominal breathing.

4. Do abdominal exercises.

5. Surf frequently.

6. Avoid nasal obstructions.

7. Do not use drugs.

8. Begin a program of yoga, with special attention to the pranayamas, or breathing exercises.

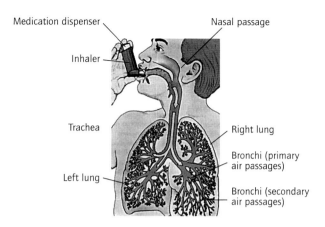

Medication dispenser · Nasal passage · Inhaler · Trachea · Right lung · Bronchi (primary air passages) · Left lung · Bronchi (secondary air passages)

An inhaler distributes the drug rapidly through aerial passages to immediately alleviate symptoms.

Exercises for Unblocking the Thorax for Surfing

Exercise 1

On your hands and knees in the "cat position," exhale and contract the abdomen, arching the back upward. Inhale and dilate the abdomen, inverting the backbone position. Conduct these exercises slowly keeping the hips and thighs at 90 degrees.

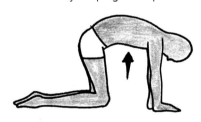

Exercise 2

On your hands and knees, stretch the arms to the front, keeping your trunk close to the ground. Inhale, exhale and contract the abdomen, returning to the initial "cat" position. Repeat 15 times.

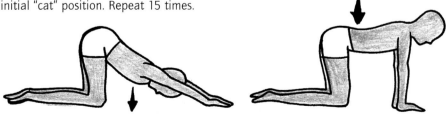

Exercise 3

On your hands and knees, with one of the arms supported, extend the other to the side and back, and turn the trunk and head to the same side as the arm. Repeat the exercise 12 times on each side.

Exercise 4

On your hands and knees, inhale while extending the left arm to the front, exhale and extend the arm to the right. Your head and trunk should accompany the movement. Repeat the exercise 12 times on both sides.

Exercise 5

Sitting down, raise the arms with fingers interlaced on the back of the neck, keep the elbows high. Bend the elbows back, as if you were trying to touch them behind the head. Keep the abdomen contracted for 30 seconds. Repeat the exercise 10 times.

Exercise 6

In the same initial position as Exercise 5, rotate the trunk to both sides. Then laterally bend the trunk to the side.

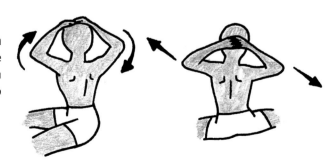

Breathing Exercises

Exercise 1

Practice nasal breathing. Shutting one of the nostrils, inhale from one and exhale through the other. Rest the tongue between the teeth.

Exercise 2

Lie on your back with legs bent and arms to the side of the body. Inhale from the nose, inflating the abdomen, exhale through the semi-closed mouth, contracting the abdomen. Repeat the previous exercise, this time controlling the length of exhalation by counting to 5, 10, 15 (increasing progressively).

Exercise 3

Lying on the back, inhale through the nose and exhale through the mouth, bring the legs and arms to the chest.

An asthmatic athlete knows from experience when the lungs are sensitive and are about to have a crisis. The use of an inhaler before surfing is recommended.

Always take the bronchial dilator inhaler when surfing, especially on trips. Place it in the sleeve of a wetsuit or sew it into a strong neoprene pocket for storage. If an asthma attack occurs while surfing, get out of the water. Use the pump twice (once to open the air passages, so that the second time the medication reaches the lungs). Wait a few minutes. If the attack is light and the surf allows, paddle slowly to the break zone. If the episode is more severe, repeat the use of medication. If there is no improvement in 20 minutes, repeat the dose. If the crisis persists, it is best to seek the closest emergency room.

Fortunately, most child surfers who suffer from asthma have significant improvement after adolescence.

Chapter 20

Testicular and Prostate Problems and How to Prevent Them

Early diagnosis is the key to a cure.

The Testicles

Cancer of the testicles is one of the most common types of cancer in men from 15-35 – the age group of most surfers. Fortunately, most cases are curable after chemotherapy and/or surgery. However, the earlier the diagnosis, the better the prognosis.

Testicular cancer is known to grow slowly. There is no relationship between its incidence and the consumption of alcohol or venereal diseases such as syphilis, gonorrhea or herpes. Trauma to the testicles has not been proved to be a determining factor. Among the principle risk factors are:

1. Testicles that delayed in descending from the scrotum. At the seventh month of fetal age (within the womb), the testicles migrate from a position in the abdomen (close to the kidneys) to inside the scrotum. If one or both do not complete the trajectory, it means they will be outside the scrotum, a condition known as cryptorchidism. Since they need the warmth of the scrotum to develop, this situation should be corrected in the first five years of life through medication or surgery in order to avoid infertility and the risk of testicular cancer.

2. Pregnant mothers who were submitted to radiation.

3. A genetic history of cancer.

It is recommended that every man from 15-35 years of age conduct a regular self-examination to detect any abnormality in the testicles.

Self-Examination Techniques

The self-examination is easy to conduct.

The best moment for the examination is after a warm bath and can be done lying down or standing up. It does not hurt and is not a form of masturbation.

Use your thumb and index finger as shown in the illustration and conduct a palpation of the entire surface of the testicles. There is no need to use force.

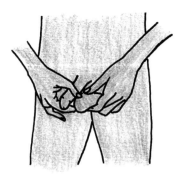

**Illustration 1:
Testicle self-examination**

Observe the size, shape, consistency and sensitivity to the touch. Compare both sides; the left is generally larger than the right.

Testicular cancer often begins as a painless lump in one of the balls. It may at times be painful, but the pain is a very late symptom. If you feel something different in your testicles, immediately see a doctor.

The Prostate

A large number surfers are in their 40s, the age when prostate problems begin to become more frequent and prevention is essential.

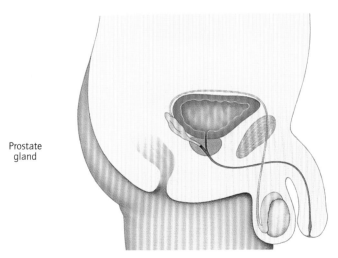

Prostate
gland

Illustration 2: Prostate anatomy

The prostate is a male sexual gland the size of a walnut that produces seminal fluid, which together with the sperm, constitutes semen. It is located strategically above the rectum and below the bladder, and within it is the urinary canal (urethra) that leads to the penis. Thus, any growth in the size of the prostate can cause obstruction in the passage of urine (Illustration 2).

After 40 years of age it is common to find a benign growth in the prostrate, a condition known as benign hyperplasia of the prostate. The cause is aging and relative increase of estrogen (female hormone) in relation to testosterone (male hormone).

Pay attention because many of the symptoms of benign hyperplasia of the prostate are similar to those of prostate cancer.

Prostate cancer is much less frequent than hyperplasia, grows slowly and usually affects older people. On the other hand, it is the second most common form of cancer in men after skin cancer.

The warning symptoms appear progressively and include:

1. Difficulty urinating

2. Weak urinary stream

3. A need to urinate frequently

4. A need to urinate at night

5. Urinating takes place in two steps; the urination is interrupted

6. Sensation that the bladder is not totally empty after urinating

7. Difficulty in beginning urination

8. Dripping after termination of urinating

9. Sensation of urgent need to urinate

10. Pain upon urinating or ejaculating

At times, there may be total urinary obstruction (in the most serious cases), infection or even bleeding.

In addition to a hormonal imbalance that stimulates its progressive growth, other factors that may cause a predisposition are advanced age (above 70), obesity, high blood pressure, diabetes and high levels of blood cholesterol.

Diagnosis

To confirm the diagnosis, an evaluation of the prostate through rectal touch is necessary for all men older than 40. There is no alternative. The doctor can then feel the size and consistency of the prostate, thus eliminating or confirming the possibility of a tumor.

A blood exam allows the identification of a substance produced by the prostate called the prostate specific antigen, which should have a certain level depending on age and size of the prostate. High levels can suggest hyperplasia or cancer. An ultrasound of the prostate allows evaluating its size and consistency. The diagnosis can be confirmed with a biopsy (the removal of a fragment of the prostate for analysis).

Treatment

Benign Prostatic Hypertrophy

Benign prostatic hypertrophy is treated with hormones, as well as medications that relax the bladder and prostate muscles. In serious cases, a doctor may decide to dilate the urinary canal that passes through the prostate, destroying the prostate tissue using radiofrequency or surgery.

Scientific research has demonstrated that the use of the dry extract of plants Pygeum africanum, Serenoa repens and Urtica dioica have satisfactory therapeutic effects on benign hyperplasia of the prostate.

Prostate cancer

Prostate cancer is rare in men younger than 55 and the earlier the diagnosis, the more effective the treatment, with a survival rate of 85%. Treatment depends on various factors and can include medication, hormones and surgery.

SURFING & HEALTH

Nat Young

SURFING & HEALTH

Otaviano "Taiu" Bueno

The great soul
of Brazilian surfing

Chapter 21

Surfing in Special Conditions

Surfing creates a healing energy that provides light and faith in self-realization.

When confronting a serious health problem, the medical team can work with the surfer to focus on the chance of getting back to the waves. Tremendous motivation and a healing force are generated.

Faced with the adventure of being able to surf again, it is not important what method is used, what is important is the ability to be able to ride a wave; this makes anyone a surfer.

Otaviano "Taiu" Bueno

In the early 1970s, I learned to surf by watching Taiu ride the waves of Manduka, at Guarujá. Today I still watch and study the lessons his life offers.

Our dear Taiu, Otaviano Bueno, with the soul of a warrior, continues to surf, despite the lack of movement in his arms and legs. He became quadriplegic when he broke his cervical column while surfing at Paúba Beach in São Paulo in 1992.

Enlightened, he continues to offer profound lessons of hope, humility, generosity, dedication to work and love for people, surf and God. He has created the group SMF, or Surfers Moving Forward — English-speaking surfers also know it stands for Smell My Fart.

Writing various columns in Surf magazines such as *Revista Fluir*, *Hardcore* and *Alma Surf*, Taiu is the author of the first surfing primer in Brazil, edited and published by Hardcore, in which he teaches the first steps of surfing. He also wrote the book *Alma Guerreira (Soul of a Warrior)*.

An announcer at various Brazilian and international championships, Taiu has created one of Brazil's best surf sites, www.Taiusurf.com.br. A great surf-reporter, from his perch above the waves at the Pitangueiras Beach in Guarujá, São Paulo, Taiu continues to surf his internal ocean and to send positive vibrations of courage and will-power to all of us.

In his book *Alma Guerreira*, Taiu emotionally describes his career as a surfer. Here is one portion of the book:

I wound up like this. My mission is in my simple presence. When someone looks at me and is touched in their heart, this is the time to thank God for the beauty of life, to appreciate the perfection of life, of health and of the functionality of our body.

I believe in the theory that life must be enjoyed, because it is a blessing, a gift from God. We should face each day as a present from God. Anyone with a healthy soul is a happy person. I am thankful simply for my breathing. Everyone is looking for happiness. Here is a formula to help find it:

Happiness is like a butterfly. If you run after it desperately you will never catch it, as with anything in life. But, if you sit down and relax and contemplate life and each moment with open eyes, letting everything flow, the butterfly will land on your shoulder... It's the good vibes... Otaviano Taiu Bueno

Pirata

Aleino Neto, better known as Pirata, is a great tube rider who has a passion for perfect, large, tubular waves. A living legend of Brazilian surf, he surfs majestic tubes and is not intimidated by the limits imposed by life.

Pirata is one of the few surfers in the world who, despite his physical disability, surfs a lot, with and without the use of mechanical prostheses. He had his left leg amputated after a motorcycle accident, but this is not a barrier in his life. He has a surf school in Guarujá, makes presentations in championships and loves to travel to find those perfect waves.

Pirata, Brazilian Surfer

Pauê

Surfer Paulo Eduardo Aagard, from São Vicente, São Paulo, is another Brazilian to rise above his difficulties. The victim of a serious accident that resulted in the amputation of his legs below the knee, Pauê, as he is known, trains intensively. He is the world's first known bilateral amputee to surf, using two mechanical prostheses. In addition to surfing, Pauê is preparing to compete in triathlons and the Paralympics.

Nem

Surfer Luciano Mercindo da Silveira is a native of Florianópolis where he has surfed for some 20 years. A victim of infant paralysis at six months of age, his left leg is stunted and atrophied.

Photo: Sebastião Pojas – Fluir

Paulo Eduardo Aagard

He explains:

I had to overcome discrimination from other people as well as my self, because I was ashamed to carry a surfboard on the beach, ashamed of people looking at me. I think that I am currently the only person with a disability surfing in Florianópolis, but I hope that this will change, that more people with disabilities can feel the thrill of riding a wave.

Given the excitement of surfing, its not important what method you use. You can surf with your mind, your feet, your knees, lying down, or without a board, what's important is riding the wave.

285

Gabriela Leite

Chapter 22

Female Surfers

Despite the differences between women and men, it is common to find that the best women surfers outperform many men.

Compared to men, women have:

1. A generally smaller and shorter skeletal structure

2. Wider hips

3. Narrower shoulders

4. Less muscle mass

5. A larger quantity of body fat

6. Lower blood volume

7. A lower maximum aerobic capacity

8. Lower quantity of testosterone

Considering all of these differences are in men's favor, women's athletic performance is surprising. Female records in track and field are only 8-10% below that of men.

The lower maximum aerobic capacity (VO_2 max) is probably mainly related to body composition and hemoglobin concentration. Typically, no difference in VO_2 max is found between trained men and women when VO_2 max is expressed relative to fat-free mass. In addition, iron deficiency is common among women because of iron loss during menses. This further decreases the oxygen-carrying capacity of the blood and decreases performance (see below – iron deficiency anemia).

Training Response – Strength and Endurance

By age 20, the difference in muscle area between young male and female surfers is 30% to 50%. The differences are greater in the upper than the lower extremities.

By adulthood, women have 50% of the upper body muscle size, but about 65% to 70% of the lower extremity muscle size of men. Similar differences are seen in the size of the bones as well.

Surfing men and women have little difference in training response to strength training if the parameters examined are relative increase in strength and muscle size.

Women can show muscle hypertrophy with strength training, although the maximum hypertrophy is typically less than for men. With regard to endurance training, the trainability of women has been found to be equal to men.

Musculoskeletal Differences and Injury Patterns

The women's wider pelvis and greater knee valgus (knock kness) make patellofemoral dysfunction more common among women surfers. The majority of cases of patellofemoral dysfunction in athletes can be controlled with Pilates and exercise programs that stretch any tight muscles that cross the knee joint and strengthen the quadriceps (particularly the vastus medialis), combined with the correction of other biomechanical problems, such as the excessive pronation of the feet.

In general, women have greater ligamentous laxity (loose ligaments) than men, which may lead to knee pain and shoulder instability. Most symptoms related to joint laxity can be controlled by increasing the strength and endurance of the muscles that control the painful, lax joint.

There is increased incidence of anterior cruciate ligament (ACL) injury among women when compared with men (see Chapter 10)

The causes for this are not yet fully known, but seem most likely related to conditioning and surfing technique differences.

Women have higher incidence of scoliosis, but scoliosis symptoms limit sports participation very rarely. Young athletes undergoing brace treatment for scoliosis may have limitations to surf competitions, but generally there are no limitations, and many athletes are allowed to train and compete a few hours per day without the brace.

Gabriela Leite

Photo: Sebastian Rojas

While men spend most of their life producing their principal weapon, the hormone testosterone, women have cyclic variations in the production of feminine hormones known as estrogen and progesterone.

This hormonal variation divides the menstrual cycle into well-defined phases, characterized by emotional and physical fluctuations, which can reflect directly on behavior, disposition and athletic performance.

Menstrual cycle

There are no changes in surfing performance, aerobic, anaerobic capacity or injury occurrence at any phase of the menstrual cycle.

The Most Common Menstrual Problems

All women have their own menstrual pattern, which begins at about 12 years of age, and in normal conditions, has a lunar rhythm varying from 23-35 days, with an average of 28 days.

Currently, women menstruate about 450 times during their life, while their great grandmothers menstruated only 1/3 that amount.

A lack of menstruation can indicate a health problem.

A normal menstrual cycle indicates that the nervous system and the hormones follicule-stimulating hormone (FSH), luteinizing hormone (LH), estradiol and progesterone are working in balance, which is totally compatible with a high level of surfing performance. Stress, travel, excessive training and changes in temperature can affect a normal menstrual cycle (see Graphic 1).

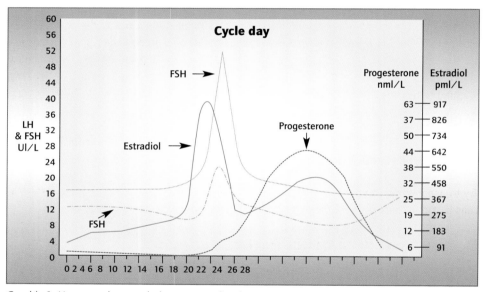

Graphic 1: Hormone changes during menstrual cycle

A normal menstrual cycle indicates that the nervous system and hormones follicule-stimulating hormone (FSH), luteinizing hormone (LH), estradiol and progesterone are working in balance, which is totally compatible with a high level of surfing performance. Stress, travel, excessive training and changes in temperature can affect a normal menstrual cycle (see Graphic 1).

1. The menstrual period

From the first to the fifth day of the cycle there is a menstrual flow with the shedding of the most inner wall of the uterus, the endometrium, causing typical vaginal bleeding. Among the principal symptoms are:

Physical:	Psychic/emotional:
• Swelling of the legs	• Greater sensitivity
• Breast tenderness	• Sleepiness
• Abdominal distention	• Attention
• Bloating	• Introspection
• Headache	• Discretion
• Cramps	• Lack of motivation to train

In this phase, it is advisable to eat food rich in vitamins K, A and C that help reduce menstrual flow. They are found in soy oil, wheat bran and green vegetables. Vitamin A, which is found in carrots, dried prunes, melons and peaches, helps in the restoration of the endometrium, while vitamin C improves absorption of iron and is available in pineapple, lemon, orange and kiwi.

Surfers who suffer from strong pelvic cramps can use an analgesic such as paracetamol (the generic name of Tylenol) or an antispasmodic (e.g., Midol). In the most serious cases anti-inflammatory medication is recommended.

Try to use internal tampons only when you are menstruating, since they can remove healthy cells that maintain vaginal lubrication, leaving them more exposed to infections.

2. The Post Menstrual Period

The space between the fifth and the tenth day corresponds to the post-menstrual period. Theoretically, it is the best phase of the month. Eat foods rich in soybeans, which can increase estrogen levels.

3. The Fertile Period

This is the best phase for competing.

With the normal variation of hormones during the cycle, the endometrium restores itself. Ovulation occurs between the 10th and 16th day of the cycle (when the egg leaves the ovary) preceded by a sharp rise in the rate of hormones (see Graphic 1).

In this phase, the skin becomes viscous and there is intense vaginal lubrication. A woman becomes more hyperactive, dominating, confident and competitive; she is more seductive and her sexual desire is at its peak. Foods rich in vitamin E, such as salmon, tuna, green leafy vegetables, wheat germ and canola and corn oil are recommended. Avoid animal fat. Increase the level of iron with the consumption of dark vegetables, such as broccoli, spinach or lean red meat (for non-vegetarians).

A woman knows if she is ovulating by observing some of the symptoms that occur in this period and include:

1. Lateral sensitivity of the breasts

2. Fluid retentions

3. Changes in appetite and mood

4. Basal body temperature

Jacqueline Silva
One of the world's
elite surfers

Photo: Flavio Vidigal

4. The Pre-menstrual Period

If conception does not take place – that is, if the egg does not find a sperm in the uterus – there is a reduction in the level of hormones, which will result in the shedding of the endometrium, with consequent menstruation.

In the normal pre-menstrual period a woman can become impatient, forgetful, or distracted, and may feel bloated, pain in her breasts, reduced sexual desire and greater appetite. To minimize these common symptoms, which can interrupt training and competing, the following measures are recommended:

- Reduce the intake of salt, which causes water retention.

- Eat lots of food with magnesium, which prevents water retention and decreases the compulsion for sweets, such as nuts, legumes and green vegetables.

- Consume foods with vitamin B6, which alleviates pain in the breasts and functions as an antioxidant. It is found in bran and the germ of grains, egg yolks, oatmeal, and legumes.

- Eat whole cereals and bananas, which are rich in amino acids and tryptophan and thus increase the quantity of serotonin, alleviating the symptoms of tension and anxiety.

At times, premenstrual symptoms are very intense and make surfing difficult. This condition is known as premenstrual syndrome (PMS).

Premenstrual Syndrome (PMS)

Premenstrual symptom is a condition without a defined cause that can cause a wide variety of physical and psychological symptoms with a particular characteristic: They improve or disappear noticeably as soon as menstruation begins.

PMS is more common among women from 30 to 40 but the symptoms generally begin at adolescence and can be associated with excessive bleeding, which increases the risk of anemia.

It is estimated that 20% to 30% of women have moderate to severe PMS and up to 10% suffer severely enough that it requires them to stay home. If the disease is not controlled, it can interfere with surfing. It is believed that many swells and waves are missed because of PMS.

The principal symptoms include:

- Anxiety, nervous tension, mood changes, irritability, fidgeting, impatience, excessive sleepiness, lack of concentration, lack of motivation
- Swelling, weight gain, painful breasts and bloated abdomen
- Depression, crying and insomnia
- Hypoglycemia (decreased blood sugar), headache, a desire for sweets and increased appetite
- Severe abdominal cramps, nausea, gas, muscular pain and fatigue.

Causes

The probable causes are a lack of serotonin (a chemical brain messenger), or vitamin B6, calcium or zinc. Hormonal disturbances and excess liquid in the brain due to retention are other possible causes.

Treatment

Competitors who suffer from PMS need to establish a suitable treatmeat with their doctor.

1. Diet

Treatment should include a change of eating habits, with a decrease of salt, refined sugar, alcohol and caffeine.

Caffeine, found in coffee, chocolate, many sodas and in some medications increases anxiety and emotional instability, and aggravates PMS.

Alcohol can cause headache, fatigue, and depression.

The decreased ingestion of salt reduces swelling caused by water retention.

Aerobic exercise (walking, bicycling, running and dance) and surfing help to reduce menstrual colic and improve one's mood.

Eat whole foods, adding complex carbohydrates to your diet (brown rice, whole grain bread and cereals).

Increased consumption of foods rich in calcium, such as milk products, broccoli, collards and fish, also helps to reduce bloating and mood swings.

Although vitamin deficiency has not been confirmed in PMS, some women report relief from symptoms by using vitamins A, B6, C and D. Use multivitamins regularly and consume lots of carrots, beets, papaya (rich in vitamin A), yeast (vitamin B6), citric fruits (vitamin C), and peanuts (vitamin D).

2. Acupuncture

Because it acts on the hormones and the brain's chemical messengers, acupuncture is recommended for the treatment and control of PMS. It reduces colic, anxiety and depression. In addition to its diuretic effect, it contributes to the regularization of menstrual flow and cycles. Treatment generally varies from 10-20 sessions, with 1-2 weekly applications for chronic disturbances and possible intervals between the series, according to the therapeutic responses. This treatment has been observed to cause a progressive decrease in the intensity and frequency of the symptoms.

The use of primula oil (Chinese primrose) and herbal remedies can offer good results. The use of dry extract of Hipericum perforatum (St. John's Wort) to control depression, and Piper menthisticum (Kava Kava) in anxiety are recommended.

Techniques that help alleviate stress and favor self-control and relaxation should also be sought. Tai Chi and Yoga are excellent options.

3. Medication

The contraceptive pill can be a good option for PMS since it helps reduce excessive menstrual flow, by facilitating the normalization of menstrual cycles and decreasing abdominal pain.

Nevertheless, because of its possible negative effects, such as reduced aerobic capacity and an increase of body fat, only 5-10% of female athletes use the pill.

In the most severe cases, a woman can decide to interrupt the menstrual cycle using injectable hormones or those implanted under the skin. It is common to use diuretics, analgesics and anti-inflammatories. Currently, there is no definitive cure for PMS.

Menstrual Disturbances

Excessive training may affect the menstrual cycle and can cause menstrual disturbances.

Among the most frequent are:

1. Total lack of menstruation (amenorrhea)
2. Decreased frequency of the cycle (oligomenorrhea)
3. Lack of ovulation

Menstrual disturbances can also be associated to anemia caused by an iron deficiency, due to excessive loss of blood, and to osteoporosis (loss of bone mass), caused by a lack of menstruation.

Athletic Amenhorrhea (Lack of Menstruation)

Women surfers submitted to intense and repeated training can have some alterations in their menstrual cycle. Among them are cycles without production of eggs, which can impede conception. The absence of a cycle (amenhorhea) increases from an incidence of 3-5% in the general population to 15-60% of women who exercise, which can significantly increase problems with fertility. A diagnosis requires detailed medical evaluation.

The main problems caused by the lack of a menstrual cycle are:

1. Infertility
2. Muscular-skeletal injuries
3. Osteoporosis
4. Aging of arteries
5. Greater incidence of cancer for reproductive organs

Treatment includes the use of hormones, reducing the intensity of training and slightly increasing body weight, in addition to a program of stress control that includes proper diet and sleep.

Photo: Sebastian Rojas

Gabriela Leite

Osteoporosis
(Lack of Normal Bone Mineralization)

Osteoporosis usually occurs in elderly women but can arise much earlier in life. It is known that 60-70% of bone mass is deposited during the rapid growth of adolescence and begins to decline between 35 years of age and menopause, when the reduction of female hormones accentuates decline of bone mass.

Among the main risk factors of osteoporosis in women are:

1. A positive family history

2. Reduced calcium intake

3. Lactose intolerance

4. An absence of menstruation for a significant period of time

5. Post-menopause period, whether natural or artificial

The absence of menstruation in athletes increases the risk of fractures and is similar to the post-menopause period, where there are also lower levels of hormones and an increased risk of stress fractures. Treatment includes reducing training, administering small doses of hormones to regulate menstruation and increased calcium ingestion, in doses of one to two grams per day. Formulations that offer greater absorption are preparations based on chelated calcium, calcium carbonate or calcium citrate associated with vitamin D.

Photo: Sebastian Rojas

The best treatment for premature osteoporosis is prevention through increased calcium intake with milk and dairy products, fish and dark green vegetables, such as spinach and broccoli.

Gabriela and her boards

298

Andreia Lopes Silvia
Brazilian surf champion

Photo: A. Junior

Iron Deficiency (Anemia)

Found in red blood cells and responsible for the transport of oxygen, iron is essential for good surfing. Its deficiency causes anemia (a nutritional deficiency) common among athletes of all ages.

The principal symptoms include fatigue and lack of energy. This is frequently associated with blood loss during menstruation and an improper diet, with reduced quantities of iron.

Blood exams can determine low levels of red blood cells, hemoglobin and/or iron deposits. The treatment consists in correcting the anemia and increasing iron deposits through ingestion of iron salts, such as iron sulfate or iron gluconate, and is usually combined with vitamin C, which helps its absorption.

Foods rich in iron, such as beans, lentils, egg yolks, fish, spinach and broccoli, should be part of the diet.

Women who restrict their caloric intake often have an inadequate intake of protein, vitamins, and minerals. They may require supplementation, particularly of B vitamins, folate, and iron.

Manipulation of Menstrual Cycle for Competition

Athletes can use two techniques if they want to manipulate the date of their menstruation for a certain competition. They are:

1. The use of the contraceptive pill
Normally, a dispenser has 21 pills that should be taken daily beginning at the first day of menstruation. After a rest of 7 days, begin once again with the new cycle. The beginning of menstruation can be postponed with the continuous use of the pill, with one dispenser used immediately after the other.

Interruption in the middle of the cycle leads to menstruation in approximately 3 days; while interruption at the end of the dispenser leads to regularization of the cycle, with menstruation occurring in about 7 days.

When a competition schedule is known, it is possible to begin manipulating the menstrual cycle 4-6 months in advance. In this way, one can progressively shorten the cycle, suspending the ingestion of the pill earlier in each cycle, programming menstruation for the desired day. It is not recommended to conduct this type of hormonal control for all 12 annual cycles.

2. Suspension of menstruation
Doctors are not unanimous about the issue of suspending menstruation for a prolonged period, either for competition or as a contraceptive method.

While some believe that menstruation is a thermometer of the proper functioning of the body and a sign that the egg is not fertilized, others argue that menstruation is a woman's option. For this reason, it is important to discuss the situation in depth with your doctor.

The suspension of menstruation is often a medical treatment used for surfers who have problems such as endometriosis (growth of the uterine lining outside of the uterus) and for those in who have symptoms of premenstrual symptoms, menstrual disturbances and menstrual cramps that are difficult to treat and/or interfere with performance in training and competition.

Menstruation and Shark Attack

Surfing during the menstrual period can attract sharks. Despite the use of tampons, small quantities of blood can flow into the water. Thus, in addition to a tampon, the simultaneous use of a contraceptive diaphragm and a wetsuit while surfing is recommended.

> Good sense recommends that if you are surfing waters that have sharks, stay out of the waves during menstruation.

Thermoregulation

There are differences in thermoregulation between men and women. First, women have cyclical changes in core body temperature during the menstrual cycle, increasing by 0.3°C to 0.6°C at rest.

The increased body fat of women surfers adversely affects their response to heat, but it is advantageous in cold environments. In equal heat, women's core body temperatures increase more than men's, both at rest and with exercise. Women sweat less, and they have a higher sweating threshold.

Women are at a disadvantage when exercising in dry heat, compared with men. However, they are at less of a disadvantage when exercising in humid heat, since continued sweating in humid exposure has a greater likelihood of leading to dehydration.

Photo: Flavio Vidigal

**Ana Cristina Steinman
pregnant with Gabriel**

Pregnancy and Surfing

Physiological changes until the second and third month of pregnancy appear not to have negative effects on performance. In the more advanced stages, competition is not compatible with pregnancy. An athlete can no longer focus on training and must turn her attention to preparing the ideal conditions for the development of the fetus. In addition, after the third and fourth month, the size of the stomach begins to be a problem for paddling on the board, as compression is not recommended. However, regular exercise during pregnancy enhances maternal fitness and physiological reserve, without apparent risk to the mother and/or the fetus.

Gestation increases the curve of the lower spine (lordosis or swayback) and shifts a woman's center of gravity. Back pain and changes in balance are common. Due to the weakening of ligaments, the risk of joint injuries are greater.

Women who were sedentary should begin a program of low-intensity activity, such as walking and aquatic exercises.

Regular exercise is better than intermittent exercise, but competitions and vigorous exercise, such as running and high impact aerobics, are not recommended. Surfing in cold water or in very hot temperatures should be avoided. Be very careful with abrupt movements, jumps and quick changes in direction. Consider avoiding exercise with risk of blunt abdominal trauma. Eliminate the risks of falls and be careful when bicycling. If you are in a weight-training program, it is recommended that you use light loads with frequent repetitions.

It is recommended to initiate exercise at least 3 hours after eating. It should be followed by a snack.

During pregnancy, a training program should be immediately modified if any musculoskeletal discomfort or other uncomfortable symptoms appear.

Additional modifications are indicated in the situation of multiple fetuses, bleeding, poor fetal growth or any other medical condition.

Finally, the exercising pregnant woman should monitor her training intensity carefully and avoid fatigue.

Postpartum

In general, it is safe to return to exercise a week after a vaginal birth and 10 weeks after a Cesarean section. Due to the weakness of the abdominal and back muscles, the return to surfing should be delayed until the third or fourth week after a vaginal birth.

As soon as possible, begin a training program that includes muscular strengthening, with special attention to your core muscles, including the abdomen and back. The return to competition should be treated with care, because weaker ligaments, muscles and joints significantly increase the risk of sports injuries, including herniated discs.

Female surfers should visit their gynecologist to conduct routine exams, such as a pap smear (to prevent uterine cancer) and after 30 years of age, prevention strategies for breast cancer.

Photo: Sebastian Rojas

Neco Padaratz
Teahupoo

Chapter 23

Principles of Exercise Physiology for Surfing Training and Competition

Twenty-five thousand sit-ups. Thirty hours of jumping rope. Lifting twenty tons of weights. Three hundred kilometers of pool laps. Ten kilometers of underwater swimming. Fifty kilometers of running in the mountains. Six hundred kilometers of biking, lots of steps. Two hundred pounds of sweat and lots and lots of surfing are some of the elements needed to become a champion.

There are various types of training that improve performance. A professional competitor must dedicate his or her heart and soul. For free surfers, a good training program, in addition to improving performance, will help prevent accidents.

Imagine a training program capable of making you faster and stronger with greater stamina – of turning you into a champion. Of course, you will have to give up training on that old, rusty bicycle and do a lot of functional core training exercise. It is increasingly clear to the great majority of surfers that natural talent and ability are not enough to win surfing championships. A specific training program is necessary.

Medical Evaluation Before Training Begins

A training program should begin with a medical evaluation six to eight weeks before the beginning of the season for any surfer, whether or not he or she is a competitor.

The principal purpose is to detect unnoticed problems that may limit performance or place the athlete at risk of injury.

The medical evaluation includes a general health check-up and one for physical aptitude. In addition to an examination of the cardio-respiratory system, a minute evaluation should

Dr. Steinman attending during Brazilian WCT

Photo: André Larrèa

Taylor Knox

Photo: André Larrèa

Mick Fanning

be conducted of the muscular-skeletal system, including a postural evaluation. The exam analyzes the entire range of movement and symmetrical strength of all muscles.

Anthropometric measurements have shown that elite surfers have become taller in recent years (average of 5'8'' and 6'1'') with a larger trunk area.

An evaluation of body mass allows determining the percentage of fat and muscle in the body. Elite surfers generally have 8-10% body fat, while recreational surfers have about 15%.

Laboratory exams should evaluate the blood, urine, feces and iron deposits.

Tests to determine the physical aptitude of the surfer study the energy transfer systems utilized in surfing.

Evaluations for physical aptitude include:

1. Anthropometry and body composition
2. Explosion (alactic anaerobic strength)
3. Stamina (anaerobic lactic strength)
4. Maximum aerobic capacity (VO_2 max)
5. Core stability and muscular strength
6. Velocity of movement;
7. Velocity of reflexes (reaction time)
8. Flexibility
9. Equilibrium

Based on the results of a complete evaluation, a training program can be developed to maximize performance in surfing, and give advice about health problems and rehabilitation measures for previous injuries.

Thus, all surfers, whether or not they are competitors, should use the knowledge of sports medicine and the physiology of exercise to develop the specific variables of their physical and mental aptitude.

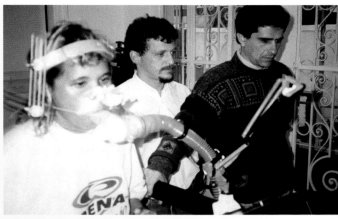

Sports medicine laboratory test

Energy Suppy Systems for Surfing

Surfing consists of many types of movements that require the use of the entire body and extract energy from three systems. They are: the alactic anaerobic systems (for explosion); the anaerobic lactic systems (strength) and the aerobic systems (stamina, see Graph 1). Energy for movement is released by the breakdown of the ATP molecule (adenosine triphosphate) within the muscle.

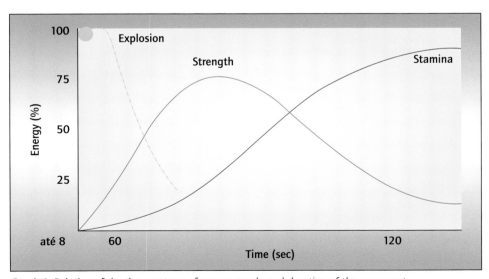

Graph 1. Relation of the three systems of energy supply and duration of the movement.

1. Source of Energy for the First Eight Seconds of Movement – Explosion

The alactic anaerobic system

This energy production system does not depend on oxygen but on the energy accumulated in the muscles in the form of phosphate and creatine. It supplies energy for explosive

movements that last up to 8 seconds, such as paddling to catch a wave, maneuvers such as bottom turns, cut backs, snaps, re-entries and fast movements to stand up on the board after entering a wave. Explosion training, that is, power surfing, is essential for competitive surfing, and is evaluated through the measure of alactic anaerobic strength. Thus, during fast, anaerobic, high-intensity maneuvers, the quantity of intramuscular high-energy phosphagens are very important.

Heitor Alves – Powerful maneuver

High-energy phosphates provide immediate energy for the initial acceleration to maximum speed. During the second phase of surfing, when maintaining the desired speed is the goal, other energy sources (i.e., the lactic anaerobic system – see glycolysis below) may have a more important role in the energy supply.

The types of training most often used to develop explosion include:

1. Plyometric exercises and weight training in explosive movements, conducted in order to gain speed but not for hypertrophy or building muscle mass.

2. Sprints (100-meter dashes), 25-meter swimming sprints and paddling spurts of 40 seconds are used in various sets with intervals of 30-40 seconds for recovery.

2. Source of Energy for the First Two Minutes of Movement – Glycolysis

The Lactic Anaerobic System

This system is responsible for muscular strength. It supplies energy through the burning of glycogen (sugars) in muscles and in the liver, without a need for oxygen, and results in the production of lactic acid. The system releases energy for movements of 60-90 seconds, which in surfing are used when paddling to catch a wave and in fast surfing, with repeated, powerful maneuvers.

Interval training is a good option to develop this system, using repetitions of various sets of exercises of short duration and high intensity. These include a 200-m freestyle swim, 400-m sprints, and strength-training activities with short rest periods (30 seconds) between sets. They rely primarily on glycolysis for energy liberation. This anaerobic energy system also contributes to energy production at the beginning of less intense exercise, when oxygen lags behind the total energy demand placed on the system.

Repeated and explosive exercises, in addition to increasing the capacity of this system, help eliminate lactic acid from the muscles being exercised. It is important to remember that improved aerobic capacity also helps remove lactic acid.

Plyometric exercises are also a good option. These help the surfer gain strength in the legs and thighs, and include squats, push-ups, jumps, jumping jacks, leg lifts etc.

To evaluate explosiveness and muscular anaerobic resistance (alactic and lactic anaerobic strength), use the maximum strength test, known as the Wingate test, conducted in an exercise physiology laboratory, preferably with ergometers for arms and legs.

Photo: Flavio Vidigal

Waves at Campeche in southern Brazil, surfing a long ride

Joaquina Beach

Photo: Flavio Vidigal

3. Source of Energy for Stamina

The Aerobic System

This system provides energy by burning glycogen and fat.

It is vital for surfers, and it represents the body's maximum capacity to assimilate and distribute oxygen to the muscles during long-duration activities of medium intensity, or to supply energy for basic surfing in repeated sessions on the same day (on large waves and against the current). While the anaerobic energy system provides a high amount of energy in a limited supply, the aerobic system provides a continuous and steady supply of energy to the muscles at rest and during lower-intensity, long-duration activities due to intensive energy-yielding capacity.

The table below indicates the high values of maximum aerobic strength of elite surfers compared to those of other athletes.

This maximum test is specific for each sport. Thus, the ergometric evaluation of the surfer conducted on a treadmill (or riding a stationary bicycle) does not indicate his or her real aerobic condition, given that a surfer is not a runner or a bicyclist.

Table 1: VO_2 maximum values measured in ml/kg/min or amount of oxygen consumed per kilo of weight

Elite athletes	Men	Women
Skiers	76	65
Marathon runners	72	59
Surfers	70	52
Triathletes	69	66
Rowers	60	49
Soccer players	58	
Amateur surfers	50	45

The best aerobic evaluation in surfing is conducted through the maximum test realized on a cyclometer modified and adapted for the arms or in a pool with the evaluation conducted while paddling on a board, (simulating the paddling in surf) with a collection of respiratory gases, which measures the quantity of carbon dioxide produced and the quantity of oxygen consumed in each breath.

The evaluation of the lactic curve (blood lactate) during swimming sprints can also be used for aerobic evaluation.

Blood Lactate

From resting values of about 1 mmol/kg, muscle lactic acid may increase during maximal surfing activity to more than 25 mmol/kg.

In an exercise test with an increasing workload, the blood lactate concentration (as an indirect measure of the lactic acid produced in the working muscles) remains stable during the first few minutes of the test because the energy demand is adequately supplied by the consumed oxygen.

Then, at a certain point in the exercise, the blood lactate concentration will quickly increase. At this moment, called the onset of blood lactate accumulation (OBLA), or anaerobic threshold, the levels of blood lactate concentrations reach about 4 mmol/L.

Untrained surfers reach this concentration level at around 50% to 60% their maximum aerobic capacity (VO_2 max). Trained surfers reach it at around 80% to 90% VO_2 max.

M. Giorgi

Photo: Sebastian Rojas

To improve aerobic capacity, you must train at the maximum point of this system, or that is, at the anaerobic limit, which corresponds to maximum intensity of exercise, where the blood lactate levels remain stable.

The intensity of this training can be controlled and monitored by the athlete's cardiac frequency, which permits personalizing the training.

Thus, the closer the training is to the anaerobic limit, the greater the development of cardiorespiratory endurance and the ability to surf large swells.

Another indirect parameter used to monitor aerobic capacity includes the recovery of normal cardiac frequency after the end of each training session or wave. Athletes with greater aerobic capacity will recover from anaerobic exercises (explosion and strength) more quickly.

Determined principally by genetics, aerobic capacity can improve by 20-25% with aerobic training. The best sports for this purpose are bicycling, swimming, running, rowing and surfing.

If one is far from a laboratory equipped to perform these tests, one can prescribe an aerobic training zone based on maximum cardiac frequency with the following formula:

Maximum cardiac frequency = 220-age (beats/minute)

The zone of aerobic training is between 60-85% of the maximum cardiac frequency, with the anaerobic threshold closer to the upper level. For example: A 28-year-old surfer has a maximum cardiac frequency of 192 beats per minute and his zone of training would be between 115 and 163 beats per minute.

You have
to be fit

Specific Training for Surfing

Training for surfing, whether recreational or competitive, reflects the combination of many factors that combine to improve the act of surfing and increase resistance to surfing-related injuries and enhance motivation for training.

Physical preparation includes basic and specific components that comprise the base of the training pyramid (see below).

Inadequate physical preparation will lead to technical mistakes and incomplete and poorly executed maneuvers due to the effects of muscle fatigue that will be evident. In turn, the technical mistakes will lead to tactical errors that may cause psychological distractions.

A coach can help to establish a training program for the season based on individual characteristics, physical aptitude and objectives.

PSYCHOLOGICAL

TACTICAL

TECHNICAL

PHYSICAL

Training pyramid

313

Keep a Daily Training and Competition Diary

Daily notations about all aspects of training and competition will facilitate the diagnosis of your difficulties, mistakes and strong points. The information that can be extracted after a period of record-keeping will be very valuable in the preparation, review and improvement of the training program.

Fundamental Training Principles

The principles of training include specificity, overload, progression, supercompensation, reversibility, tapering, and periodization.

Specificity

Specificity Principle

Training for surfing requires core strength, flexibility, cardiovascular conditioning, and balance (neuromuscular).

Core muscle strength is needed to improve your stability; arm and leg strength and power to paddle and surf with power and speed; reflex speed, endurance and cardiovascular conditioning to paddle out through the waves, flexibility to surf longer and balance to surf fluidly.

Therefore, you need to improve the 3 energy supply systems:

1. Aerobic
2. Explosion (anaerobic alactic)
3. Strength (anaerobic lactic)

Photo: André Larrèa

Taylor Knox

Muscle strength is a basic requirement for surfing. Together with core training, the strengthening of leg and arm muscles used in paddling and maneuvers, in addition to improving the quality of surf, is essential for preventing sports injuries. Weight training should follow the principle of overload. The usual strength training is done with free weights or on gym machines. Start with low resistance and plenty of repetitions. Progressively increase resistance and reduce the number of repetitions.

The maintenance of muscular strength and power after a period of training should include at least three sessions per week.

Speed of movement is essential and related to muscle strength, also known as power surfing. It is the result of muscular strength training and acceleration.

Elite surfers have greater reaction speed and move more quickly than amateur athletes.

Flexibility

Good flexibility allows increasing the range of movement in the joints, improving performance and decreasing the risk of injuries. Flexibility is essential for surfing. Although genetically determined, it can be improved through stretching exercises. They should be conducted immediately after a brief muscular warm-up, before and after each training session. Each stretching exercise should be conducted in a static position and held for 40-60 seconds.

Heitor Alves stretching

Proprioceptive neuromuscular facilitation (PNF) training is usually performed with a partner and involves both passive movements and active (concentric and isometric) muscle actions. There are different types of PNF stretches, but they typically involve a passive (done by a trainer) prestretch of the involved muscle (done by a trainer), a contraction against opposition, and finally relaxation and further stretching. Common PNF stretches with a partner are used to enhance hamstring, quadriceps, and chest flexibility. Because they facilitate muscular inhibition, PNF stretching is a very effective method of gaining flexibility.

Reflex Speed – Reaction Time

Reflex speed or reaction time is also genetically inherited and refers to the time of a surfer's reaction in different maneuvers and his or her adaptation to the wave. It should be improved through surfing itself, in training with skateboards, balance boards and in simulations of maneuvers on a trampoline.

In summation, in addition to surfing, you'll need: swimming, bicycling, and running to improve cardiovascular function and provide stamina for long and repeated surf sessions; core strength training to provide greater muscle stability, power and flexibility (pilates) and yoga.

Meditation will help center your mind and improve concentration and awareness.

Capoeira, skate and carve boarding, trekking or hiking, among other activities, can also be used to exercise biomechanics similar to those used in surfing.

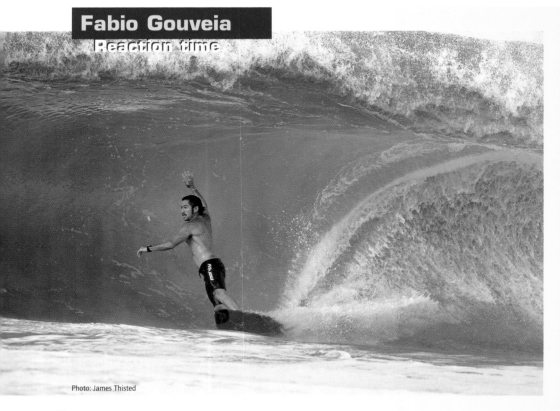

Fabio Gouveia
Reaction time

Photo: James Thisted

Supercompensation is related to properly balancing the overload and the regeneration period. The amount of recovery required after a training session is directly related to the magnitude and duration of the stress created by the action. During the recovery period, the restoration balance processes will progress to a higher level, which is often called supercompensation.

Tapering is related to peak performance and requires maximum physical and psychological stress tolerance. After periods of intensive training, the athlete's exercise tolerance and performance capacity may start to decrease. Coaches may therefore reduce the training volume and intensity after a "hard training period" before the next training cycle or a major competition. Tapering may increase muscle power, enhance surfing performance and decrease the risk of overtraining.

Training Components

A training program should adjust the volume and intensity of activity to the athlete's goals.

Volume

The volume of training refers to the total quantity of training activities, or that is, the duration of the sessions, the number of waves surfed and the number of repetitions of a certain maneuver. A high volume of training increases the capacity of the energy systems and muscles. When free surfing, special attention should be given to intensifying the training load, paddling, surfing and performing as if it were a competition.

Table 2 shows the number of training hours per week for athletes of different levels.

Table 2. Level of total hours trained per year and the athlete's performance level

Athlete's level	Number of training hours per year	Number of training hours per week
Top 20	1000	20
International level	800	16
National level	600	12
Regional/local level	400	8

It is important to note that the number of hours of training presented in the table above refers to supervised training with defined goals and not to the number of hours of free surf or irregular and ineffective training.

Intensity

The intensity of training is related to the stress placed on the surfer, the speed of movement and the variations in the intervals of rest between them.

Table 3 defines the different levels of intensity in training in maximum percentage of effort made.

Table 3. Different levels of intensity

Intensity	Maximum % of strength
Easy	30-50%
Balanced	50-70%
Sub-maximum	70-90%
Maximum	90-100%

Kelly Slater
Imbituba – Brazilian WCT – 2007

Photo: James Thisted

Relation Between Volume and Intensity in Preparation for a Competition

The relationship between volume and intensity is essential to the success of the program and should be carefully planned as a function of the competitive calendar (Graph 2).

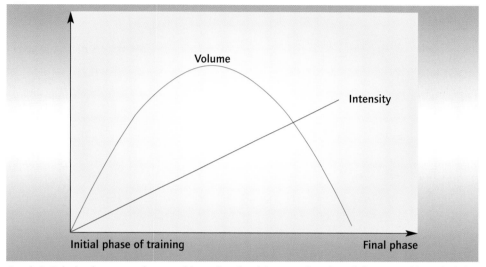

Graph 2: Relation between volume and intensity of training as a function of the competitive schedule

In the initial phases of training, generally in the preseason, greater emphasis is given to volume, that is to cardiovascular endurance training and body muscle strength (especially the core), which includes surfing, swimming, running and bicycling for a few hours at low or moderate intensity.

Improved aerobic conditioning allows increasing the intensity of training. This corresponds to the moment at which the curve of volume begins to fall and the intensity begins to increase. In the week before an event, the intensity and volume should be drastically reduced in order to allow the surfer adequate recovery and an ideal competitive situation.

Supercompensation and tapering strategies must be used.

The Principle of Overload and Cycles

The overload principle is based on the need to train the body at a level beyond that to which it is normally accustomed. Overload can be achieved by increasing the frequency, intensity or duration of exercise (see below). High performance training is divided into cycles. Each of them should begin at an intensity level lower than the conclusion of the previous, which should then be progressively increased. Recovery is essential to allowing the body to assimilate the training load. Insufficient recovery can lead to chronic fatigue, over-training syndrome and injury.

Maintenance

Upon reaching peak performance, the load and intensity of training should be maintained or even decreased to prevent a deterioration of capacity.

Frequency

Training should be conducted six days a week. Ideal preparation includes 1-2 daily sessions of surfing, with weight-training sessions on alternate days.

Duration

It is relatively difficult to recommend the duration of a surf session, which will vary with the size of the swell, the quality of the waves, etc.

Nevertheless, the introduction of intense sessions of 20 minutes, simulating heats, should be started as soon as possible.

For the other training forms, 1-2 hour sessions, including warm-up and relaxation, are adequate.

Break with routine

Breaking the training routine with fun can lead to a successful training program. In addition to free surf, include fun activities, such as sailing, dancing, skateboarding, rollerblading, skiing, and other sport activities.

Rest, relaxation and sleep

Rest is of vital importance in the life of an athlete and refers to the interval and time used to recuperate between the repetitions of a set of exercises, as well as relaxation and rest within the training program. It is during rest that many of the physiological adaptations from training occur.

When training at a gym, prolonged recovery periods (two – three minutes) between intense series of exercises are recommended for the development of strength and power (stamina).

Neco Padaratz on a day off

One day of rest per week is advised so that the physiological systems, in particular the muscles, can completely recover and be prepared for the coming week's training. Acupuncture and sports massage, including do-in, Chinese massage or shiatsu, allow recovery and relaxation.

Meditation is one of the forms of rest most used by elite surfers; it is a form of so-called "active rest."

A minimum quantity of sleep is essential for restoration, which varies from seven to 10 hours a day, depending on the intensity and length of the day's training. Naps after lunch and relaxation sessions after training are very efficient.

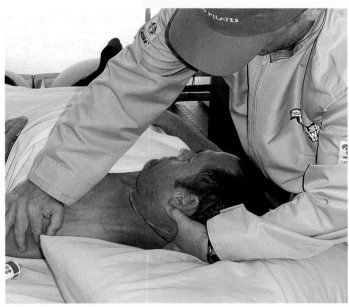

Neck mobilization during WCT

Periodization Strategies

Periodization is a planned variation in a training program. Without a planned variation in the training schedule, which includes periods of adequate rest, surfers may lose motivation or suffer from excess training. The classic periodization divides the training program into specific time periods. In general, a macrocycle is about one year, a mesocycle about or four months and a microcycle about one to four weeks.

A yearlong periodization model generally comprises several mesocycles, which begin with high-volume, low-intensity exercise and gradually progress to lower-volume, higher-intensity training close to competition.

The Macrocycle of a Competitive Athlete

Training for peak performance is quite different from training for optimal health. Macrocycle planning is essential for a competitive surfer and will help a commited free surfer prepare for an important free surf trip to Indonesia, Hawaii, Fiji, Tahiti, Peru, Chile, etc.

In summary: Periodization involves variations in the training stimulus to optimize gains in performance and reduce the risk of fatigue and overtraining. While this does not mean that new exercises should be performed every training session, noticeable changes in the volume and intensity of training should be made every few weeks.

The schedule of competitions strongly influences excessive demand.

An athlete who participates in the World Championship Tour (WCT) and the principal phases of the World Qualifying Series (WQS) has an average of 27 competitions per year in different countries. This is equivalent to 2-3 competitions per month, including travel and adaptation to different time zones (from which the surfer can suffer from insufficient rest) and to the cultural and eating customs of the location.

The surfing preseason (period before competitions begin), which usually starts in late December and January, should be used to start specific training, with the objective of improving physical capacity, particularly cardiovascular endurance (high volume – low intensity). Training should continue before competitions begin (low volume – high intensity) and between competitions, seeking maintenance of the preparation acquired: A cross training program is a good example.

Table 4 provides a possible macrocycle for a competitive surfer. The period marked with an "X" corresponds to the specific training and the remainder is maintenance training.

If the period between competitions is three weeks or more, the athlete should return to the specific training program, remembering the importance of reducing it progressively on the eve of the event.

Table 4.

Pre season:	Maintenance:
Late December – January, increase cardiovascular capacity strength/resistance.	From February to December, circuit training
The competitor's macrocycle power	Alternating: high volume-low intensity between competition with low volume-high intensity

Joel Parkinson
WCT 2007

Photo: James Thisted

The Competitor's Microcycle

The microcycle represents the weekly training program (see Table 5). Given the difficulty of precisely planning great surf days, training should give priority, of course, to the waves. Arriving tired for a surfing session because of physical training, in addition to limiting performance on the waves, will increase the chance of injury.

Training for core stability and strength, progressing to explosive or muscle strength, in addition to flexibility and cardiovascular exercise are essential for performance on the waves.

Table 5 offers a suggested weekly training program known as a microcycle, used in the pre-season or between competitions by a competitive surfer. The program should be flexible and of course should be adapted to individual goals.

You should concentrate on weight training when the waves are weakest.

Table 5. Weekly training program, pre-season and between competitions for competitors

Day	Morning	Afternoon
Monday	Pilates/yoga/surfing	Pilates with weight training/surfing
Tuesday	Bicycling/run/swim/surfing	Surfing
Wednesday	Pilates/yoga/surfing	Pilates with weight training/surfing
Thursday	Swim/bicycle/surfing	Surfing
Friday	Pilates/yoga/surfing	Pilates with weight training/surfing
Saturday	Surfing/pilates/yoga	Tennis/relax
Sunday	Surfing/relax	Relax

See Chapter 24 on Pilates.

Exercises are done on the swiss ball, Feldenkrais roll, Bosu, dyna disc or magic circle.

If you are a free surfer and able to surf almost every day, you may need cardio workouts three to four times a week combined with core strength training. Go easy on the strength training when you are surfing a lot.

Never do strength training two days in a row unless you train different muscle groups. Don't forget to rest and repair after a workout, because by training too soon after a workout you can injure yourself and hinder the strength building program.

**Dean Morris –
Pilates training on the Cadillac**

Fabio Gouveia – Roll up – Warm up

Table 6. Weekly training program for a free surfer

Day	Morning
Monday	Bicycling/run/swim/surfing
Tuesday	Pilates/yoga/surfing
Wednesday	Bicycling/run/swim/surfing
Thursday	Pilates/yoga/surfing
Friday	Bicycling/run/swim/surfing
Saturday	Pilates/yoga/surfing
Sunday	Surfing/Relax

**Pigmeu, a top surfer, adjusting the
position of his lumbar pelvic complex**

Dean Morris work-out

Everaldo Pato Teixeira
On Bosu balls

Technical-Tactical Training

It's essential and very helpful to film training and heats to provide a deeper and more detailed analysis of your technique and tactics, to visualize errors committed and enhance and consolidate the well-executed work.

For technical training, working to improve various maneuvers is suggested, including bottom-turns, cut backs, re-entrances, snaps, floaters, aerials, tubes, tail slashes, 360s, and others. They should be executed with verticality, speed and power, on a wide variety of waves. Much emphasis is given to the bottom-turn, considered one of the principal maneuvers given that the explosion of the turn creates the energy for the subsequent maneuvers (top turn, etc.).

The goal of tactical training is to develop and improve competitive strategies and performance. The principal tactical variables include: the variety and repertoire of maneuvers, the speed of surfing, the verticality of the maneuvers, the positioning, the quality of waves selected and the first maneuver, observation of the sea, simulation of heats, the length of the wave surfed, the completion, knowledge and analysis of the opponent, surfing for the judges and others.

Psychological Training

The psychological factor is decisive and occupies the top of the training pyramid. It provides the fine tuning of a competitive surfer. A negative idea at the wrong time can cause loss of concentration and of a heat.

Mental training involves motivation, positive thinking, self-confidence, self-control, a high degree of concentration, aggressiveness and other quantities. Additional behavioral strategies include familiarizing oneself with contact with the other competitor in the heat, the possibility of switching boards during a competition, knowing how to win and lose, knowing how to relax, meditate, visualize etc. Pilates and yoga has been used by many elite athletes.

Mike Fanning
ASP 2007 World Champion
Meditation is a terrific strategy
for competition and life

Photo: James Thisted

327

Everaldo Pato Teixeira
Back door Hawaii

Chapter 24

Pilates for Surfers – Control, Core and Functional Training

The core of your body is the support system for your entire body. The core usually refers to the abdominal and lower back muscles. However, the core also includes the pelvic floor, upper back, hip and shoulder girdle muscles.

The core muscles stabilize the trunk and connect it with the upper extremities (shoulder, arms and hands) and the lower extremities (the hips, legs and feet) during movement.

They provide body alignment and stability allowing optimal functioning of your limbs during surfing.

Pilates is the most efficient method of core conditioning and is an excellent strategy for improving surfing performance.

The Pilates method is focused on core rehabilitation and conditioning.

It was developed in the 1920s by German boxer, circus performer and exercise creator Joseph Pilates, and has been incorporated to several sports training programs.

It requires patience, attention to detail and consistent training, but the results are great.

The original name of the method, named by Pilates, "Contrology" explains the deep and broad meaning of his ideas: "The science of control."

Pilates focuses on the integration of body and mind.

Surfing requires this same integration of mind and body.

Taylor Knox warming up –
Bosu Pilates with Dr. Joel Steinman

Your core is the center of your body. It is where your center of gravity is located and is also the center of your strength. It plays a fundamental role in your balance and equilibrium. Pilates' balance approach ensures that no muscle group is overworked; the body flows as an efficient, holistic system while surfing.

In other words, the central stability of your body promotes functional strength, flexibility and mobility for your surfing maneuvers.

The greater a surfer's initial level of stability, the easier it is for his or her body to master the specific requirements of surfing.

Muscle and joint stability is the key prerequisite for efficient development of muscle flexibility and durability.

You need a well-developed core to protect your body during surfing.

The results and benefits from a well-defined Pilates program include:

1. Improved strength, flexibility and balance

2. Challenging the core muscles

3. Engaged mind and enhanced body awareness

4. Reduced stress, relieving tension and boosting energy through deep stretching

5. Restored postural alignment

6. A stronger and flexible spine

7. Increased range of motion

8. Improved circulation

9. Enhanced mobility, agility and stamina

10. Improving the way your body looks and feels

You must challenge your core by conducting training exercises that can be performed in a variety of ways: on the beach, using a mat, a Swiss ball, a Bosu ball, balance board, magic circles, Feldenktrais roll, or other props. You can also train on Pilates equipment, such as the reformer, Cadillac, chair, ladder barrel, and wall unit, or on the high-tech "vibration platform" or gyrotonic equipment.

In all cases, the emphasis is on the quality of movement.

The principles of the Pilates Core Training Program are:

1. Control

2. Concentration

3. Centering

4. Conscious costal lateral breathing

5. Flow

6. Precision

7. Training routine

Core training through Pilates focuses on coordination in order to create flowing movements and results by helping the brain and body work in perfect synergy. The aim is smooth, continuous motion, rather than jarring repetitions. Repetition is used to train your brain. Concentric, eccentric and isometric muscle contraction are balanced to create and maintain a flowing motion.

Core training at the vibrational platform, Brazilian WCT

**Pilates during Brazilian WCT.
Dean Morris**

You'll gain tridimensional stability (like your surfboard). Your entire body will be connected during each exercise. That means that your core control will allow for the efficient transfer of strength and efficient movement.

Core training works simultaneously with strength and flexibility, developing great motor control. This facilitates controlling the surfboard.

The development of core strength and control will create what is called the "powerhouse" of the body. This allows one to absorb the impact of motion in the appropriate region, at the right time. It synchronizes the body with the motion.

Pilates offers a large range of core stability exercises, the suitability of which varies according to the rehabilitation and training perspective of each surfer.

Core training is by no means confined to the rehab clinic, however. It is essential for preventing injuries.

The rational for this "prophylactic" training is that increased recruitment of the stabilizer muscles and increased strength in the "prime movers" (main movement muscles) will create better posture and motor control during surfing movements.

It is important to develop your core training as soon as possible – before you are injured. Progression, functional and specific surfing, and dynamic variety are the keys to optimizing the benefits of a strengthening program.

The core training menus presented here are designed to range from prophylactic core stability to a highly functional surfing performance program, using a wide variety of movement and accessories to maximize adaptations for improvement.

Stability and Breathing

Core training involves a breathing pattern known as lateral thoracic breathing.

You must master this technique in order to develop your stability.
You'll begin to paddle and surf using this breathing stabilizing strategy.

You'll use this breathing during all core exercises.

Wave breathing pattern: This is the master key to core training.

You have to master it during all exercises:

1. Facing up
2. Facing down
3. On your side
4. Sitting
5. Kneeling
6. Standing

To master this breathing pattern, conduct the following basic breathing wave exercise:

- Lie on your back
- Bend your knees with your feet on floor and hips, legs and feet aligned
- Keep your head and cervical, lumbar and pelvic regions in a neutral position

Maintain this neutral spine position while inhaling and exhaling.

- As you exhale, lower your chest (chest down) with the lungs
- Contract your ribs (using your intercostal and oblique muscles)
- Engage your abdominals, pulling your navel to your spine, without flattening the natural curve in your back
- Engage your pelvic floor muscles
- Activate your adductor muscles
- Keep your head and cervical, lumbar and pelvic regions in a neutral position

You are activating your core muscles. Concentrate on your core. This will connect your entire body at once. This will strengthen your muscles, stabilize your spine, protect your neck and back, and improve your balance and posture.

Maintain this muscle activation while inhaling and exhaling.

333

The Flex Ring Strategy for Core Control

You may train the breathing wave by using the magic circles or flex ring.

Place and hold the flex ring between your thighs just above the knees or between your ankles. It will help tone your core muscles and align the hips, knees and feet.

The flex ring is an important accessory for improving core control! You can use this device for all exercises.

WCT Surfer Phil McDonald

Core Training Program on the Ball – Pilates on the Ball

Always initiate your training with a self-massage in order to wake up your body, including your core's muscles.

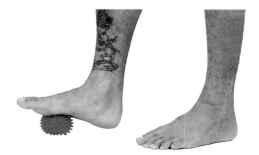

You can use a "point ball" or a kind of a brush to massage.

Begin with your feet. Progress to the abdomen, hips, lower back, upper back, neck, head, face, chest, back. Then massage the front and side thigh and leg muscles.

Introduction – Warm Up

1. Sit on the ball

2. Maintain a neutral spine from the base of your head to your tailbone.

3. Initiate "wave breathing." This is the key to your workout. It is also called lateral chest breathing.

> Remember you are always working on your stability. Try to maintain your balance longer, do a few more reps and attempt to progress to the next level. This practice will make a difference out on the surf!

During each exercise always maintain your control, concentration and centralization. Try to perform each exercise with precision. Maintain fluidity by using lateral chest breathing.

All exercises incorporate multiple muscle groups, challenging core stability.

These warm-ups connect you with your core.

1.   Pelvic tilts

Sitting on the ball, warm up by tilting your pelvis in all directions.
Conduct 12 to 20 reps in each direction

Front to back

Side to side

Moving from the right to the left ischium bone

Circles (right/left)

Drawing a circle with the pelvic bone, moving from right to left ischium bone

Figure eights

2.   Rollbacks, sit–ups

Sitting on the ball, maintain complete body alignment. Begin the breathing wave. Roll back, vertebra by vertebra, as if you were conducting a "lay back." Do not apply pressure to your neck. Return slowly, vertebra by vertebra.

You can intensify this exercise by placing your hands behind your head.

3.   Rollbacks, Twist-Activating the Oblique Muscle

Method 1

Sitting on the ball, maintain complete body alignment. Place your hands behind your head. Conduct the breathing wave. Roll back, vertebra by vertebra, as if you were doing a "lay back." Stop at your shoulder blades.

Sit up, twist and rotate your back, crossing your right shoulder to your left knee. Return to center and repeat the motion on the opposite side. Return to neutral spine. Do not apply pressure to your neck. Return slowly, vertebra by vertebra to the side position. Do 30 reps.

4.   Rollbacks Twist-activating Your Oblique Muscle – The Cross Muscle System

Sit on the ball with complete body alignment. Begin the breathing wave. Keep your arms stretched out in front of you with the shoulders aligned.

Roll back, vertebra by vertebra as if you were doing a "lay back," then twist to the right side, placing your right arm to the back and left arm to the front. Return slowly, vertebra by vertebra to neutral spine. Repeat the exercise to the opposite side. Do not apply pressure to your neck.

6. Shoulder Bridge

Sit on the ball with complete body alignment. Begin the breathing wave. Roll back, vertebra per vertebra, as if you were doing a "lay back." Keep going until you rest your neck on the ball. Keep your pelvic bone up and aligned with your trunk. It will give you strength at the back hip and thigh muscle. Return to neutral spine. Do not apply pressure to your neck. Return slowly, vertebra by vertebra.

This is a very important exercise to roll the pelvic and lumbar bones and counterbalance overused lower back muscles.

Always keep your pelvic floor muscles flexed.

You can disrupt your core stability by extending one leg.

Repeat 8 to 20 times.

7. Shoulder Bridge – Side-to-side Roll

Sit on the ball with complete body alignment. Begin the breathing wave. Roll back, vertebra by vertebra, as if you were doing a "lay back." Keep going until you rest your neck on the ball. Keep your pelvic bone raised and aligned with your trunk. Roll from one shoulder to the other, pressing the shoulder on the ball. Return to neutral spine. Repeat the exercise on the opposite side. Do not apply pressure to your neck. Return slowly, vertebra by vertebra.

8. Leg Circle

Lie on your back with your feet on the ball. Keep your spine neutral with your arms parallel to the body.

While exhaling, lift your right leg, point your toes and make circles clockwise and then counterclockwise.

This is a very simple but very important exercise that must be mastered.

You must isolate the movement on the right hip. That means your left hip should remain stable. Do both legs.

9. Roll Up – Sit Up From Floor

Lie on your back with your feet on the ball. Keep your spine neutral with your arms parallel to the body.

While exhaling, roll up your head, neck and upper chest, and stretch your knees.

Breathe in and out and return slowly to the floor vertebra by vertebra, bending your knees.

Be careful to not place stress on your neck and always return your head and neck to a neutral position.

10. Roll Up from Floor – Teaser

Lie on your back with your feet on the ball. Keep your spine neutral with your arms parallel to the body.

Exhaling, roll up your head, neck and upper, middle and lower back and stretch your knees.

Breathe in and out and return to the floor vertebra by vertebra, bending your knees.

Be careful not to place pressure on your neck and always return your head and neck to a neutral position.

11. Rolling Like a Ball

From a sitting position, bend your hips and knees with feet off the ground. Place the ball over your knees. Keep your back in a C position. Be careful to not lift your shoulders or flex your neck too much.

While inhaling, roll back; while exhaling roll up. Maintain the distance between your chest and knees. Do not touch the floor with your head or feet.

12. Open-leg Rock

Conduct the same exercise as above, while extending your knees.

13. Roll Over

Lie down on your back with legs up and knees extended. Place the ball between your ankles with your hands parallel to the body.

Roll over vertebra by vertebra to the point you are comfortable on your neck.

"Deep on the powerhouse" (put strength on the central part of the body). Breath out and return vertebra by vertebra.

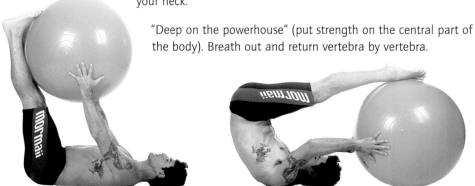

14. Corkscrew

Lie on your back with your legs up and knees extended. Maintain perfect body alignment and your spine in a neutral position with the ball between your ankles and hands parallel to the body.

Roll to one side, vertebra by vertebra, until you are comfortable on your neck.

Deep on the powerhouse. Breathe out and return vertebra by vertebra. Repeat on the other side.

This is a very important exercise for surfing maneuvers.

15. Control Balance

Lie on your back with your legs up and knees extended. Maintain perfect body alignment and your spine in a neutral position with the ball between your ankles and hands parallel to the body.

Roll over, vertebra by vertebra, to the point you feel comfortable on your neck. Place and hold the ball over your head. Control your balance while alternating hip flexion and extension.

Deep on the powerhouse. Breathe out and return vertebra per vertebra.

This is a very important exercise for surfing maneuvers.

16. Cross Strength

Lie on your back. Place the ball between your left foot and your right arm. Keep spine neutral. Press the ball for 30 seconds. Repeat on other side.

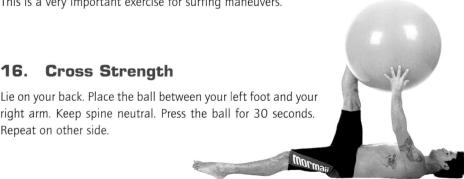

17. Shoulder Bridge from Floor

Lie on your back, in a neutral position. Keep your hips and knees aligned and bent. Place your feet on the ball. Begin the breathing wave. While exhaling, roll your pelvic bone and your back, vertebra by vertebra, up to the T7 (the lower point of your shoulder blade). Return to the neutral spine.

You can strengthen your core further by extending your knees.

18. Shoulder Bridge, Single Leg Stretch

Conduct the exercise above, but with only one leg support, keep the pelvic bone aligned and execute 3 hip flexions and extensions.

Perform with each leg.

19. Spine Stretch from Floor

Sit upright on the floor. Initially you can try keep your knees bent. Breathe out and roll your head forward. Keep rolling vertebra by vertebra. This will stretch the spinal muscles. Return the movement vertebra by vertebra.

Intensify the exercise by extending your knees and lifting your toes.

20. Spine Stretch from Floor

Sit upright on the floor with your knees initially bent. Breathe out and bend your trunk forward. Always maintain your alignment.

Challenge the exercise by extending your knees and moving your arms.

21. Neck Stretch – Flexion/Rotation

Sit on the ball with body completely aligned. Begin the breathing wave.

Stretch your neck through slow flexion and rotation on both sides.

22. Obliques Muscles Stretch – Mermaid

Sit on top of the ball with your feet wide apart. Keep your spine neutral. Begin "wave breathing" to connect all the core muscles.

Lift and outstretch your right arm (with shoulder blade down). With left arm on the ball, lean one side to another. Keep your waist aligned on the ball. Hold each stretch for 30 seconds.

23. Lower Back Stretch

With the side of your waist on the ball, split your legs for balance. Put your lower hand on the ground and stretch the opposite side. Keep your trunk aligned. This will stretch your spine's lateral and back muscles, hips and waist, as well as the most important paddling muscle – the latissimus dorsi.

24. Abdominals and Chest Stretch

Sit on the ball and roll gently down to the lower back. Ease yourself back slowly. Increase your range gradually. Avoid painful range of motion. Outstretch your arms to stretch abdominal and chest muscles.

25. Hamstring stretch

Sit up right on the ball with your knees bent. Straighten both your legs. Lift your toes. Breathe out and reach forward, while keeping your back flat. You will feel the stretch from your buttocks to your calves.

26. Spinal Stretch

Sit upright on the ball with your knees bent. Breathe out and roll your head, backward and forward, vertebra by vertebra. Remember to keep your chin off your chest (you can use a tennis ball). This will stretch the para-vertebral muscles. Return the movement vertebra by vertebra. Intensify the exercise by extending your knees and lifting your toes.

27. Spinal Stretch 2

Sit upright on the ball with your knees bent. Breathe out and bend your trunk forward. Always keep your alignment from your head to your pelvis.

Intensify the exercise by extending your knees and moving your arms.

28. Twist

Sit on the ball with complete body alignment. Begin the breathing wave. Twist your trunk to each side. Keep your pelvic bone aligned.

29. Saw

Sit upright on the ball with your knees bent. Conduct the exercise above, twisting your body to the right side and complete the motion by rolling your head, neck and back forward (bringing the left hand in the direction of the left foot). The right arm should be stretched backward. Do the other side. Intensify the exercise by extending your knees and lifting your toes.

30. Quadriceps and Ileopsoas Stretch – Hamstring Stretch

Straddle the ball with one leg forward and one leg back. Roll slowly and press your hip forward and backward. This will stretch the ileopsoas and quadriceps of your rear leg. Roll back and stretch the back of your front leg.

31. Sit on the Ball and Stretch your Levator Scapulae Muscle

Sit on the ball with the spine neutral. Reach one arm as far down between your shoulder blades as possible. Look as far as you can to the opposite side. Take a deep breath in and hold for 5 seconds.

As you exhale, look downward as far you can toward your shoulder.

Always remain in a comfortable position.

32. Chest and Shoulder Stretch

Kneel on the floor and place your forearm over the apex with your shoulder resting on the ball as seen in photo.

This is an excellent way to stretch your medial shoulder rotators and pectoralis major muscles (the largest chest muscle).

This is an excellent exercise for stretching the pectoralis minor muscle.

Keep your shoulders parallel to the ground. Allow your body to drop forward. Remaining in a comfortable position, inhale and press the forearms into the ball for 5 seconds. Exhale and move into a stretch.

This is an excellent exercise for stretching the pectoralis minor muscle that gets tight from paddling.

Place your shoulder on the ball. As you drop your upper body downward, allow your shoulder blade to move toward your spine.

Once you feel the stretch, inhale and press your hands and shoulders into the ball for five seconds. Remaining within a comfortable position, inhale and press your forearms into the ball for 5 seconds. Exhale and move into a stretch.

If this stretch bothers your shoulder, you should start a shoulder strengthening program (see Chapter 8). Many surfers may have some instability in the front region of their shoulder joints from past injury and lifting weights with poor technique. This stretch may serve to stretch areas that are already too loose. If symptoms persist despite training, you should see an orthopedic surgeon.

33. Upper Back and Shoulder Stretch – Rhomboid Muscles

The rhomboids and related muscles are used to stabilize the shoulder blade.

Kneel in front of the ball, placing your elbow on the ball and press forward. Move your arm at different angles to explore the thigh muscles.

When you complete the stretch, activate the rhomboid muscles as if pulling the shoulder blade toward the spine.

Hold the pressure for 5 seconds. Repeat the circle three to five times on each side.

NOTE:
It is very important that you not perform these stretches if they cause any discomfort in the shoulder.

Prone Exercises – Facing Down

Always find your stable zone and progress from there!

A stable, comfortable core training zone should allow you to progress safely!

1. Push Up on Ball

Kneel on the floor with the ball in front of you. Fall forward with hands on the floor and place the ball under your feet. The further the ball is from your navel, the harder the push-up will be. Keep your pelvis and your trunk aligned during the exercise. Do not allow your back to lose stability.

You can challenge yourself by doing the push-ups with only one leg on the ball.

2. Hip Extension

Kneel on the floor with the ball in front of you. Fall forward with hands on the floor and place the ball under your feet. Do alternating hip extensions. Keep your core stable!

3. Push-Up on Ball

Kneel on the floor, place hands on the ball in a push-up position. Bend your elbow and shoulders until your chest touches the ball.

350

You can intensify the exercise by stretching your knees and supporting your core on your feet and hands.

This core functional exercise works on the stabilizing muscles.

4.   Roll Out

Kneel on the floor with the ball in front of you. Fall forward with hands on the ball, using your elbows. Roll the ball forward, keeping your trunk stable and aligned. You can intensify the exercise by stretching your knees and transferring the support to your feet!

Be careful! You shouldn't feel discomfort in your back.

Return to the straight kneeling position!

5.   Double Hip and Knee Flexion and Extension

Start from the push-up position with your feet on the ball. Bring your knees to your chest, rolling the ball under your legs. Keep your core activated all the time. Roll the ball in and out. Do 20 reps.

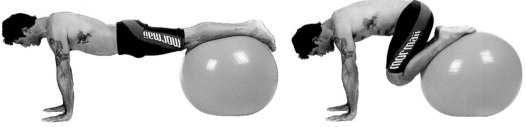

6. Duck Diving – Single Leg — Hip and Knee Flexion and Extension

Do the same exercise as above using one leg, as in the duck diving position.

7. Elephant or Pike Press – Hip Flexion and Extension with Knees Extended

Start from the push-up position with the feet on the ball.

Bend your hips, rolling the ball up to the tips of your toes. Position your hands beneath your shoulders. Try to keep your trunk aligned.

This is an excellent core exercise and will help during duck diving.

You can intensify this exercise by alternating push-ups and pike presses.

8. Single Leg Pike

Repeat the exercise above; from the final position, raise one leg off the ball.

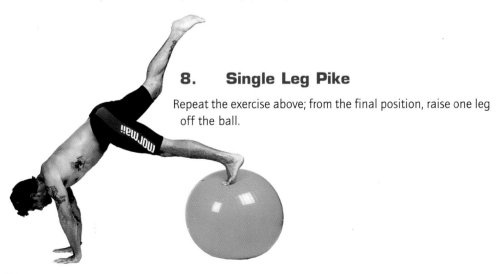

9. Side Strokes

From the push-up position, bend your hips and knees, rolling the ball forward and to the right side. Return to neutral. Then to the left side.

This is a powerful trunk core exercise.

10. Paddling Exercise – Superman 1

Most surfers' back problems come from imbalance in the muscles used for paddling. You must master core stability for paddling

Go slowly, always maintain control.

Lie prone with ball under chest/abdomen, legs hip-width apart, pelvis neutral. Place your center of gravity on the ball.

Master the breathing wave technique to have your core provide total trunk stability.

Exhale and extend your trunk with your arms outstretched in front of you. Maintain your alignment; avoid lower back and neck compression! Keep your shoulder blades down!

Inhale, exhale and return to the rest position.

Repeat 8 to 20 times

You can make this exercise more challenging by using an elastic band.

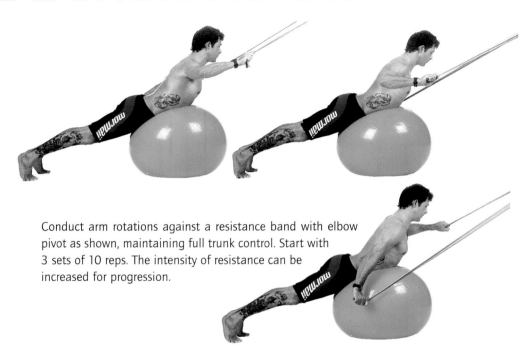

Conduct arm rotations against a resistance band with elbow pivot as shown, maintaining full trunk control. Start with 3 sets of 10 reps. The intensity of resistance can be increased for progression.

11. Paddling Exercise – Superman 2

Repeat the exercise above; from the "superman" position, extend your arms to your hips (as if paddling using both arms together), and at the same time increase trunk extension. Exhaling, return to the rest position.

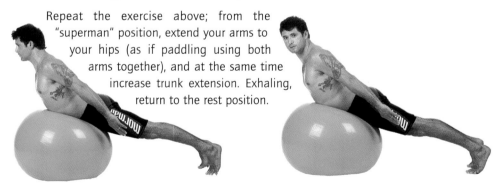

Maintain your alignment, avoid compressing the lower back and neck! Keep your shoulder blades down! Repeat 8 to 20 times

Intensify the exercise by paddling with an elastic band

12. Hip and Lower-Back Stretch

Lie on your stomach with your core stable. Place the ball between your ankles, and while exhaling, rotate the ball to one side. Inhale and exhale, then return to the rest position. Do the other side.

13. Spinal Rotation

Lie on your back, with the ball between your ankles and roll the ball to one side and the neck to the other. Keep shoulders on the ground.

Side Exercises

1. Side-Up

To find the proper position, roll down the ball from a sitting position into a supine position and then roll onto your side.

You can use a wall to anchor your feet.

Keep the right arm along your body and the left arm outstretched. Shoulder blades positioned.

Lift your trunk sideways. Keep trunk stable and aligned.

Do 30 reps on each side.

2.   Side Leg Bend (Abduction/Adduction)

To find the proper position, roll down the ball from a sitting position into a supine position and then roll onto your side.

You can use a wall to anchor your feet.

Keep the right arm on the ball and the left arm outstretched. Shoulder blades positioned.

Lift your leg sideways.

Keep trunk stable and aligned.

You can modify the exercise with hip circles and forward kicks.

3.   Snakes

Place the ball on your side as in the above position. Rotate the trunk, placing both hands on the floor, with legs apart. Find your balance and stretch. Keep full on your powerhouse. Perform on the other side.

Balance Exercises – Functional Training

1.   Sit on the Ball

Sit on the ball in neutral position with both feet on the ground. Lift one leg straight and hold for 10 seconds. Repeat on the opposite side.

2.   Sit on the Ball in Neutral Position with Both Feet on the Ground

Lift the left hip and the right arm. Alternate each side. Hold for 10 seconds. Repeat on the opposite side.

3.   Kneeling on the Ball with Hands on the Ball

Find your balance with your knees and hands on the ball. Maintain for at least for 30 seconds.

357

4.   Kneeling on the Ball – Hands off the Ball

Find your balance with your knees on the ball for at least 30 seconds.

5.   Stand Up on the Ball – Progress to Squats

Stand up on the ball - Squats with trunk rotation.

Simão Romão

Stimulating the Nervous System

Exercises on a Bosu, dyna disc or a rocker board can add a some fun and challenge. The core muscles tone instantly!

1.   Face Up Pilates Exercises on the Bosu

2. **Face Down Pilates Exercises on the Bosu**

3. **On-the-Side Pilates Exercises on the Bosu**

Standing Pilates on the Bosu

1. Bosu Balance and Double Leg Squat

Standing on the bosu, keep your pelvis and back flat. If your chest is drooping, reduce the range of motion until you get control. Do 20 squats.

You can add some weights (3 to 5 kg).

2. Bosu Balance and Rock

Standing on the bosu, keep your knees slightly bent. Press the bosu, alternating sides. Try 5 sets of 30 seconds with 1-minute intervals.

3. Bosu Balance and Single Leg Squat

Stand on the bosu and raise one leg. Keep the other knee slightly bent.

Hold balance for up to 1 minute.

Alternate a few squats with each leg.

4. Bosu Lunge

Lunge forward with your leg, placing your front foot on the bosu. Bring your back knee to the ground.

Lunges are excellent for the legs and buttocks. Return to rest position. Alternate feet. Do 10 lunges.

You can make the exercise more challenging by placing your rear foot on the bosu and bending your leg forward. For advanced training, place only the toe of your back foot on the bosu or ball.

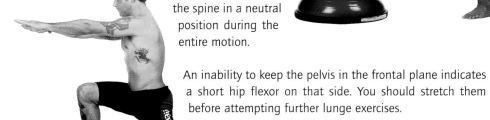

Always maintain good upright posture. Keep the spine in a neutral position during the entire motion.

An inability to keep the pelvis in the frontal plane indicates a short hip flexor on that side. You should stretch them before attempting further lunge exercises.

ATTENTION:
Female surfers should avoid pushing off the forefoot. This movement increases the risk of anterior cruciate ligament injury of the knee.

Benefits:

*   Improved strength and function in multiple planes of movement

*   Improved knee and pelvis stability

*   Strengthened buttocks and thighs

*   For progression use a swiss ball

5. Bosu Side Lunge

The same exercise as above, just on the side.

6. Lunge and Reach Forward

As you lunge forward over the bosu, extend your hands out in front of you.

7. Two Bosus

Do 10 lunges with one foot on each bosu! Bend as if you are going to grab the board.

You can do the exercise on the rock boarder or dyna disc.

8.   Bosu – Dyna Disc Lunge

Do 10 lunges to the side with one foot on each bosu! Bend as if you are going to grab the board.

You can do the exercise on the rock boarder or dyna disc.

9   Bosu Balance – Saw

Standing on the bosu, roll and twist/rotate your trunk forward. Place your right hand on your left foot. You can bend your knees to facilitate the exercise.

NOTE:
You can use free weights or an elastic band for arm and shoulder resistance training!

Carlos Burle, over 60 feet – Mavericks

Photo: Frank Quirante

Foam Roller Mobilizations

1.   Feldenkrais Roll

NOTE:
Prior to mobilizing your spine with a foam roller, it is very important that you are in good condition. Some people may have arthritis of the spine that precludes them from performing this mobilization.

Place your foam roller perpendicular to your spine, slightly below your shoulder blades; cradle your neck with your hands. Make sure that you do not hold your head or else the movement may cause neck discomfort.

With your neck supported, begin mobilizing your spine by exhaling as you slide backward over the roller toward the floor. There is often some discomfort when performing these mobilizations, so go slowly and only go as far back as you can comfortably go.

Hold the end point three to five seconds. Each vertebra should be mobilized into extension three to five times.

Mobilization should be done before and after surfing. Daily training is needed to improve spinal flexibility. If you feel discomfort in the spine after performing these mobilizations, it is likely that you are doing too many. Reduce the number of repetitions.

2.   Longitudinal Mobilizations

It is very helpful to lie on the roller lengthwise before and after surfing.

This allows gravity to stretch the ligaments in front of your spine, which helps restore optimal spine curvature. The better your alignment, the more efficiently you will rotate during surfing maneuvers.

Place the roller along your spine from the base of the skull to the tailbone. The knees should always be bent and the feet flat on the floor.

Hands can be placed on the floor or on the chest.

Start with a few minutes a day.

To improve the rotational mobility of your spine, allow your stabilized pelvis and shoulder to roll in opposite directions. Repeat this process until you feel loose.

3.   Sit-Ups on the Roll

Full on the powerhouse: use a flexi ring. It will help stabilize your lumbar, pelvic and hip areas.

Lie on the roller lengthwise; with your spine neutral, begin wave breathing.

Exhale and roll up vertebra by vertebra. Do not place excessive pressure on your neck.

Deep on the powerhouse! Sit up with your spine in a neutral position.

Exhale, rolling back vertebra by vertebra.

Note at which point (vertebrae) you lose control.

4. Double Straight Leg Stretch

On the roller lengthwise, with the spine neutral, begin wave breathing. Bend at the hip with knees aligned at 90 degrees. Exhale and roll up vertebra by vertebra. Extend both legs and execute a hip flexion and extention (knee extended). Do not overload your neck. Deep on the powerhouse! You can use a "magic circle" to challenge your training.

This is a great exercise to improve your core and lower leg strength. Return, exhale, roll back, vertebra by vertebra.

5. Roll Over

On the roller lengthwise, with the spine neutral, begin wave breathing.

Bend 90 degrees at the hip, knees extended.

Exhale and roll back vertebra by vertebra. Stop the motion before placing excess pressure on your neck. Return with full control vertebra by vertebra. Deep on the powerhouse!

This exercise improves spinal mobilization and control.

6. Knee Flexion/Extension

On the roller lengthwise, with the spine neutral, begin wave breathing. Bend at the hip with knees aligned at 90 degrees. Exhale and roll up vertebra by vertebra. Extend both legs and execute a knee flexion and extension. Do not overload your neck.

Deep on the powerhouse!

This is a great exercise to improve your core and lower leg strength. Return, exhale, roll back, vertebra by vertebra.

7.   Scissors

On the roller lengthwise, with the spine neutral, begin wave breathing. Bend at the hip with knees aligned at 90 degrees. Exhale and roll up vertebra by vertebra. Extend both legs and execute a scissortype motion (alternated flexion/extension of the hips, with extended knees). Do not overload your neck.

Deep on the powerhouse!

This is a great exercise to improve your core strength and stretch the hamstrings. Return, exhale, roll back, vertebra by vertebra.

8.   Swan Exercise

Lie on your stomach with trunk and shoulder blades aligned in neutral. Stretch out your arms and place hands over the roll.

Use your powerhouse for stability!

Exhale and pull the roll toward your chest, keeping your trunk extended. Maintain stabilization and control. Do not overload neck or lower back.

At the highest point, look back and rotate your neck to each side.

Do 12 reps and compensate with the fetal position.

This is a very important exercise for trunk stability during paddling.

9. Double Knee Flexion-Extension

In a cat position, place the roll under your knees. Keep your trunk in a neutral position.

Exhale and extend your hips and knees. Return to the cat position.

Intensify this exercise by alternating the legs.

10. Shoulder Mobilization

Keep your core stable all times.

11. Roll Back Massage and Mobilization

This is a very important exercise for surfers!

Place your foam roller perpendicular to your spine at the point slightly below your shoulder blades; cradle your neck with your hands. Keep your hips up and aligned with your trunk. Extend and bend hips and knees, moving the roll along your back from the neck to the tailbone.

Feel each vertebra.

Keep on the massage along the buttocks and legs.

12. Roll Hip, Leg and Side Massage

Place the roll under your thighs. Maintain side stabilization and alignment on your trunk at all times.

Move the roller along the side of each thigh and leg.

Always keep your core stabilizing muscles activated.

The stretch should be repeated three to five times on each side.

Suggestions for Strength Training with Weights at the Gym

Always use your deep powerhouse muscles for motion control.

Lower body

Begin weight training three times a week (on alternate days), followed by swimming and apnea. Weight training includes:

Lower body			
Weightlifting 1	Series	Repetitions	Interval (minutes)
1. Leg extension	3	20	1
2. Leg flexes	3	20	1
3. Squats	3	20	1
4. Spine on neutral (Land)	2	20	2
5. Balance training	3	20	2

Training load

The training load should be defined with your physical trainer. A good parameter is to use from 60-70% of the maximum tolerated load in each exercise.

1. **Leg extension**

2. **Leg flex**

3. **Squat**

Initial movement   Final movement

4. Strengthening back and legs

This is one of the most important exercises for the strengthening the rear thigh and lower back muscles, which, in the paddling position, are in a shortened and tense state. It should be conducted with the supervision of a physical trainer. Always keep your back straight and your belly muscle contracted.

Initial movement

Final movement

5. Work with the balance ball

See core training (p. 335-364)

Exercises with a balance ball help to improve stability on the board, develop balance and muscle control, and improve the capacity to adapt to the instability of the board in the wave.

Upper body

Upper body			
Weightlifting – arms and back	**Series**	**Repetition**	**Interval**
1. Back pull	2	30	1
2. Surf paddling (Two cables)	2	30	1
3. Inverted cross	2	30	1
4. Lateral lift	2	20	1

Swimming Program After Core Training

This training session is designed to prepare the musculature for situations common in surfing when legs and arms are exhausted, such as from paddling through the breaking waves while holding your breath and exploding to get a wave or to improve general physical ability in general.

Training suggestions:

- 1-5 pool lengths as warm-up; relaxed swimming in crawl style

- 2-10 pool lengths with 7 strokes to each breath (with just the upper body, place a float between the legs)

- 3-7 pools with 9 strokes for each breath (just the upper body, using a float between the legs)

- 4-5 pools with 11 strokes for each breath (just the upper body, using a float between the legs)

- 5 pool lengths with explosion training using 80% of maximum intensity

- 6-5 pools of backstroke

- Relax

Apnea training in the pool

Training suggestion: while holding the breath, take 1-3 strokes and do an Olympic free turn without touching the wall of the pool; do 4 series just below the limit; progressively increase your time underwater, developing hyperventilation techniques.

Always keep water nearby for rehydration.

Circuit Training Between Competitions

If you don't like health clubs, circuit training on the beach in conjunction with Pilates, yoga and surfing is a good option to maintain physically and mentally prepared for competition.

A sequence of 8-20 exercises is selected because they are related to surfing. It is common to use plyometric exercises (those that use one's own body weight). Plyometrics, also known as stretch-shortening cycle exercises, are activities that allow the muscles to reach maximum force in the shortest possible time. Because of the stress placed on the muscles, connective tissue and joints, plyometric exercises need to be carefully executed and progressed. Athletes must have a sufficient base of muscular strength, speed, and balance to avoid risk of injury.

Progressively increase the number of executions each 30-60 seconds. With the development of your physical capacity and speed, increase the length and load of the exercises using weights or a flexi band. These exercises are very effective for increasing the leg strength needed to perform bottom turns, snaps and other maneuvers.

A circuit-training program is suggested for the period between competitions and on flat days.

You can use the mat, the balance ball, Feldenkrais roll, flex band, magic circle. You can take these items everywhere!

- Always keep your core muscles activated!
- Always start training using self-massage!

Warm Up!

Warm up with a light 10-minute jog on the beach. Pick up your pace until you are working at 70% to 80% of your maximum heart rate. Run into the water and swim beyond the breakers and back to the shore again. Run for 6 minutes. Repeat these intervals a few times.

Or

Running in knee-high water increases the intensity of work. Vary the intensity by changing the depth of the water. Run in ankle-high water for low intensity and knee-high water for high intensity. Work at sub-maximum intensity. Conduct three sets of one minute with one and a half minutes of rest/slow beach running in-between.

**Mormaii Training Center –
Aragua, Praia Mole,
Florianópolis**

375

Exercises

1. Sit ups
- Conduct 3 series of 30 repetitions, with 1-minute intervals

2. Oblique sit ups
- Conduct two series of 20 repetitions, with 1-minute interval

3. Hip flexion/extension

4. Double straight leg stretch

5. Scissors

6. Teaser

7. Roll Over

8. Corkscrew

9. Swan

10. Push-ups
- Conduct four series of 10 repetitions, with 1-minute intervals; changing the position of your hands helps to challenge different muscles.
- Do one series with your arms wider than your shoulders. In the next series, place your arms directly beneath your shoulders.
- Do the next series with one arm out wide in front and the other arm down to the side. Then switch sides.

11. Duck diving

12. Elephant

13. Side bend

14. Jump split – squats on soft sand.
- Standing in a lunge position, jump and switch your foot position. Conduct two series of 20 repetitions, with 1-minute intervals.
- Attention: Do not go beyond a half squat because this creates a risk for knee injury.

15. Count body builders-10 reps
- From a standing position, squat down, placing your hands on the ground. Kick your legs back and take a stable, aligned push-up position.

- Exhale, spread your legs out wide.
- Inhale, then exhale and bring them back together.
- Do three push-ups as slowly as you can.
- Return to squat position.
- Return to standing position.

16. Star jumpers – 15 reps
- Stand in a squat position, with feet shoulder-width apart. Place your hands on the ground while keeping your back straight.
- Leap up, getting both feet off the ground and extend your hands toward the sky. Keep your shoulder blades down.

17. Rotator cuff rotation
- Fix the elastic band under your foot and rotate your arm to shoulder height.

18. Lateral raise/lift
- Raise an elastic band or 2lb to 5lb dumbbells out and up to the shoulder height. Do not go higher than shoulder height.

19. Forward lunges
- Lunge forward; bring your back knee to the ground.

20. Lunge and reach forward
- As you lunge forward, reach your hands out in front of you.

21. Side lunges

22. Lateral leg hops
- Stand on one leg and hop along an imaginary line. Do 15 with each leg.

23 Three 25-meter sprints with 1-minute intervals (on hard, flat sand)
- Recover with a light run in soft sand – 10 minutes – or bicycle sprints of 400 meters, with one-minute interval or jump rope for three series of 1 minute each.

24. Swim underwater – dynamic apnea
- Conduct 3-4 series at sub-limit capacity.

25. Recover by swimming freestyle for 5 minutes and relax

This circuit training guide is just a suggestion. You can choose the exercises. Be aware of your fitness level in order to progress. Always activate your core muscles to stabilize your spine.

What to do Before a Surfing Session

Conduct at least 10 minutes of warm-up. The benefits include:

1. Increased blood flow to the muscles and joints

2. Prevented injuries

3. Reduced muscle tension

4. Increased range of movement

5. Development of body awareness

6. Improved mental control of your body

7. Improved reaction and movement speed

Capoeira, natural gymnastics and some series of yoga positions can be used as a warm-up.

Suggestions of Warm-Up Exercises to do Before Surfing

1. Light running for a few minutes

2. Jumping jacks (jump in place, while alternating the position of the feet in synch with arm movements)

3. Jumps with half squat

4. Saw-trunk and arm twisting/rotating alternately from one leg to another

5. Oblique sit-ups

6. Lie on the ground and jump to your feet in the surfing position (regular and goofy) (30 each)

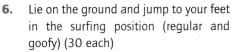

Stretching

If you do not stretch, you will progressively note:

1. Limitation in torso rotation, limiting vertical maneuvers

2. Limitation in back flexibility, which will limit the speed of getting to your feet from a prone position

3. Chest and arm muscles will be shortened, making paddling more difficult

4. Back muscles will be shortened, making it difficult to arch the back to see the waves and paddle

5. Groin and rear thigh muscles will be shortened, making the squatting position difficult

Stretch before and after each training session.

Suggestions for stretching

General stretching

These static stretches should be held for 30 seconds.

1. **Neck stretch**

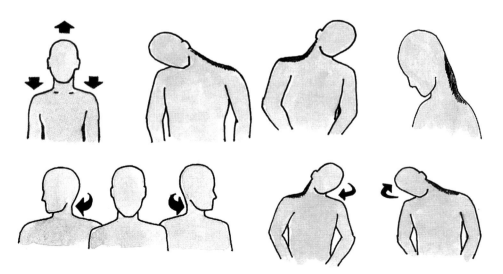

2. **Rotate the torso and head with knees bent**

3. **Stretch the arms and pectoral muscles**

 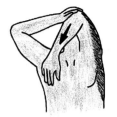 

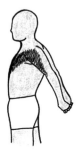  

4. **Spine stretch: While sitting, contract the abdomen and stretch hands in direction of feet**

5. **Swan. Support the hands and extend the elbows, raising the back and neck. The neck should follow the trunk extension.**

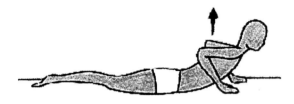

6. **Stretch the groin**

7. **Stretch the quadriceps and calf**

Some sequences of yoga postures (asanas) should be used!

Teco Padaratz and Julia Reis

APT presents

mormaii
TOW IN
WORLD CUP
PE'AHI · 2009 · JAWS

Log onto: APTWorldTour.com
North Shore Maui, Hawaii aka: JAWS

Chapter 25

Techniques for Surviving Wipe Outs

Since you love surfing, you are going to have to get used to wipe outs. Surfing giant waves is dangerous and requires willpower, attitude, courage and tremendous physical and mental preparation.

For beginning surfers, the first lessons involve lots of wipe outs and time underwater.

Lets face it, if a surfer doesn't wipe out, he or she is not exploring his or her limits or those of the waves.

Survival Techniques

Wipe outs take place with greater frequency during take-offs (drops) and bottom turns; usually when a surfer stands up too slowly or is positioned incorrectly on the board, often too far to the front. After countless wipe outs, the surfer learns how to keep calm and better withstand the soup.

The principal strategies for surviving wipe outs include:

• Protect your head and ears with your arms and hands during the fall.

• Hold your breath to avoid letting air escape from your nose and mouth.

• Flow with the wave for as long as possible to get away from the impact zone as quickly as possible.

There are four dangers during a wipe out:

1. The lip of the wave: When surfing shallow water and falling headfirst from the board, try to protect your head from a possible collision with the bottom, using your hands and arms to reduce the impact. When falling in a sitting position, or on your side, try to avoid

being pushed against the bottom, using your arms as a cushion, as if falling from a parachute. A blow from the heavy lips of giant waves can cause serious injury including fractures, dislocations and torn ligaments.

2. The board: A bang from a surfer's own surfboard is the cause of most surf injuries. Therefore, always try to fall as far as possible from the board. The use of a nose guard and a leash that is a foot or two longer than the board can help prevent it from coming back and hitting you (see Chapter 3).

3. The ocean bottom: Serious injuries can be caused when a surfer hits the bottom (see Chapter 3). Fortunately, fractures are not frequent, but they do occur, including those of the spinal column. Injuries from sharp coral or rock, in addition to fractures, can cause cuts that often require stitches. The use of a helmet can reduce the risk of head injury (see Chapter 5).

4. A collision with another surfer or board.

What to do to withstand the wipe out and do not run out of air?

A few minutes without oxygen can be fatal for the brain. Although in most cases the 'wipe-out' does not last more than 30 seconds, it can seem like forever because of the high level of anxiety and the low volume of air in the lungs.

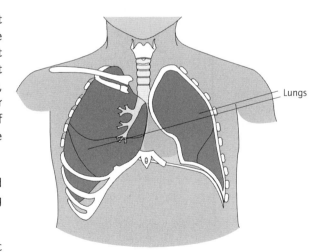

Lungs

It is important to understand how the lungs and breathing function.

The lungs are a pair of elastic sponges located within the chest (known as the thoracic cavity) that have thousands of alveolas, which are the structures responsible for the exchange of gases, absorb oxygen from the air, and eliminate the carbon dioxide (CO_2) produced by the body.

The principal muscle used in respiration is the diaphragm. Located at the base of the lungs, it separates the chest and the belly. The muscles between the ribs (intercostals) and the abdominal muscles, including the obliques, are called accessory respiratory muscles.

The act of breathing is an automatic process that can be controlled to a point by a special area of the nervous system called the respiratory bulb. This limit of control is determined by the level of carbon dioxide (CO_2) in the blood; it is the carbon dioxide and not the oxygen that commands the respiration. The higher the level of CO_2, the greater the stimulus to breathe. In the same way, the lower the level, the lower the stimulus to breathe. Divers and surfers use this function to increase the time and depth of their dives through the technique of hyperventilation.

Hyperventilation

Hyperventilation consists of breathing rapidly and superficially for 20-30 seconds before diving. This eliminates large quantities of CO_2 from the body, reducing its level in the blood and thus decreasing the stimulus to breathe, which allows you to stay underwater longer.

But this technique can create a serious risk of drowning and is not advisable for use by inexperienced surfers, because the reduced stimulus to breathe can cause unconsciousness from the lack of oxygen and, as a result, drowning.

Important points to remember when in the juice or diving:

- When surfing large waves, spontaneous hyperventilation is frequent (anxiety causes faster breathing). This reduces CO_2 levels, which in turn reduces the warning signals that trigger the respiratory centers to function.

- During a wipe out and when diving to pass under a wave, the series of impacts of water on the body – known as the washing machine effect – can remove a large quantity of air from the lungs, leaving less available oxygen.

- A deep, underwater dive is required to escape the turbulence of the waves.

- The deeper the dive, the greater the water pressure against the thoracic wall, which also reduces the volume of air in the lungs.

- Swimming underwater burns a large quantity of calories and oxygen, and in some cases, the levels can reach critical levels unsupportable by the brain.

- At the surface, the water may be covered by foam, which makes breathing difficult while more waves arrive.

- Fatigue causes a stagnation of blood in the muscles and arms, reducing the quantity of blood pumped by the heart; in addition, less blood gets to the brain. The situation becomes more critical, as O_2 levels drop and CO_2 levels rise. Tiredness increases, dizziness appears, and fainting and drowning can occur.

SURFING & HEALTH

Surfing giant waves involves conviction, courage and willpower. Excellent physical and mental conditioning is essential.

Romeu Bruno
Jaws, Hawaii

Suggestion for a training program to help withstand wipe outs and surf large waves

To surf big waves, you need endurance. You need to be able to hold your breath, and you need to be able to paddle and swim strongly. You need to be in control!

Rigorous training is needed to develop this control.

1. Conduct cardiorespiratory training, including swimming and lots of surfing! Cycling and running will also help to increase aerobic capacity.

2. Stay strong – Do Pilates and core training exercises (see Chapter 24).

Kauli Seadi
World Wave Wind Surfing
Champion, Jaws, Hawaii

3. At the ocean or at the pool: hyperventilation and apnea training.

a) Conduct exercises using different breathing control techniques. Start underwater swimming. Begin with 3 sets of 25 meters of underwater swimming. Increase the distance progressively. As you become fitter, your confidence with big waves will grow.

b) Practice diving to the bottom of a pool or the ocean and returning to the surface. Repeat the process in a series of 10 dives every day for at least two weeks. This will increase the time you can stay underwater.

c) Practice diving relatively deeply and quickly. Inhale deeply and dive approximately 6-9 meters per minute (using a mask, snorkel and fins) with supervised training. Move on to using weights. You must be prepared for the juice.

4. **Warning, the following exercise is very dangerous**, and it should only be practiced by highly experienced athletes and when accompanied by a coach. On surface dives, try to prolong your time underwater until you see stars or feel tingling in the arms and legs, or even a sensation of fainting, also known as shallow-water blackout. There are risks involved in this kind of respiratory training, because the technique, often used in free diving, is simply meant to prepare you to adapt to overcome the urgent need to breathe.

5. Continue with the dives, trying to achieve increasingly deeper depths.

6. Practice diving from a board, and then swim underwater to the farthest part of the pool.

7. If you are training in the ocean, practice looking for objects and bringing them to the surface.

8. When you reach the bottom, float on your back. At the surface, breathe naturally, allowing the sensation in your head and body to return to normal.

9. This training will provide a sense of happiness and relaxation. This is known as the hypoxic high. It raises the question: Why was I so scared down there? One thing is certain, as you push your limits and stay longer underwater, you will begin to feel like a superhero.

Be careful: Only conduct the following exercise with the presence of a team trained in cardiopulmonary resuscitation.

10. Practice walking under water while carrying a stone. Progressively increase your time in the water.

11. Always use a floatation jacket in surfing. It can make a difference during prolonged wipe outs.

12. Thanks to the knowledge and experience acquired from tow-in surfers, jet ski surfing rescue is the quickest way to get out of trouble.

Make sure you have an concentrated jet ski team around when you go paddling for big surfing.

Wipe out

Many elite surfers consider the leash to be a hazard when surfing large waves. The late Donnie Solomon, was dragged a long distance by his board at Waimea. Nevertheless, the more modern leashes, with safety pins that can be unlocked when pushed, or easy-to-remove velcro, free the surfer and are a safe alternative.

In addition to risking surfing very large waves, many athletes chase giant swells and generally need to cross various time zones, with long, slow trips, and often, in order to catch the swell, do not have time to properly adapt their biological clocks, which increases the risk of injury and accident.

There is an elite group of surfers that stays in constant tune with the low-pressure weather systems that generate giant waves. They have been setting new limits in traditional surf and in tow-in surfing. They include, Joe Sweeney, the late Eddie Aikau, Marcos Shaw, Brian Poynoton, Bob Pike, Dave Jackmana, John Monie, Lans Cairns, Simon Andersom, Peter Mel, Laird Hamilton, Flea, Jeff Clark, Eraldo Guerreiro, Silvio Mancusi, João Mauricio, Rodrigo Resende, Carlos Burle and Everaldo Teixeira (Pato).

If your trip is giant waves, train hard, go for it and good luck!

Homage to Mark Foo,
who died while surfing at Mavericks

SURFING & HEALTH

Everaldo (Pato) Teixeira
Big rider

Chapter 26

Nutrition for Competitive and Free Surfing

Dr. Joel Steinman and Dr. Tânia Rodrigues

We Are What We Eat

The purpose of this chapter is to help surfers of all levels to understand in what way nutrition influences their physical and mental performance.

Nearly 2,000 years ago, the father of Western medicine, Hippocrates, declared: *We are what we eat.* In other words: Tell me what you eat, and I'll tell you who you are.

This scientific truth, increasingly more evident in this century, has inspired man's continued search for nutritional balance.

On one hand, a lack of food causes hunger and with it come malnutrition, anemia and diseases otherwise related to poverty. On the other, excess food causes obesity, nutritional imbalance and its consequences include heart disease, cardiac arrest, high blood pressure, cerebral stroke, diabetes, cancer and even accelerated aging.

The most important element in this scenario is that these and other diseases can be avoided and some even cured through a balanced diet. Proper nutrition has a direct effect on mood, temperament, impulses and thoughts. A balanced diet is essential for general health, reduces the possibility of diseases that can interfere with training and competition, and allows for a longer duration of amateur, recreational or professional surfing.

Balanced Nutrition and Surfing

A sound diet that is especially planned for training and competition can improve performance on the waves, reduce fatigue, allow a greater number of surfing hours per training session, facilitate faster muscular recuperation, reduce chances of injury and help maintain ideal weight.

It should be clear to those who take surfing and health seriously that it is important to study and understand nutrition and stick to a balanced diet.

The proper choice of food will complement muscle deposits of energy needed for competition, which can be decisive for victory.

Indonesian fish

While nutrition cannot substitute genetic gifts, well-planned and executed training, psychological techniques used in competition and the will to win, a balanced diet will certainly improve performance on the waves.

How is it possible to have a balanced diet when one day you are in Australia and another in Indonesia, the next in Fiji, then Japan, and another on the pororoca waves of the Amazon River?

What is the best diet?

How should you deal with and escape fast food and junk food?

Food and diets vary as a function of location (geography), time of year, religion, culture, economic conditions, and other factors. But various food groups and sources of basic nutrients are available any place in the world.

In general, we recommend natural and whole (non-refined) food, preferably without genetically modified elements. They should be free of pesticides, herbicides and chemical additives. A sound diet should have plenty of whole grains, vegetables, legumes, salad greens and fruits, a reduced quantity of animal fat, sugar and salt, and a moderate quantity of white meat (fish and poultry).

Food Energy and Surfing

Food is the main source of energy for humans. The quantity of chemical energy stored in food is measured in calories.

The energy from food is accumulated in the form of the compound adenosine triphosphate (ATP). ATP supplies energy for the contraction of muscles, nerve transmission, the production of hormones, digestion, respiration, circulation and the production of proteins.

Where Does the Energy to Surf Come From?

When surfing, the muscles use energy in direct proportion to the duration and intensity of the movement.

Energy Consumed in Surfing

The more active the sport, the greater the need for energy. In one cycling race, such as the Tour de France, or in Ironman competitions, athletes can burn nearly 10,000 calories.

In general, 350-400 calories are burned per hour of surfing. Recreational adult surfers need an average of 30-40 calories per kilo of body weight per day. This should be distributed between 55-60% of carbohydrates, 10-15% proteins and 25-30% fats (Graph 1).

Meanwhile, surfers that train or compete regularly need 40-50 calories per kilo of weight per day, composed of an average of 65-70% carbohydrates, 10-15% proteins and 15-20% fats (Graph 2).

To restore the energy consumed, a minimum of 4-6 meals a day are advised. That is, between the three principal meals of breakfast, lunch and dinner, nutritional snacks are recommended at 10 a.m., 4 p.m. and at night.

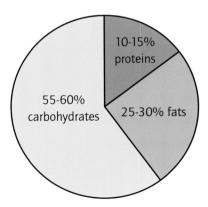

Graph 1.
Composition of the diet of recreational surfers

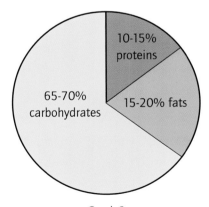

Graph 2.
Composition of the diet of competitive surfers

Needs are individual and depend on the length of training, as well as the level of conditioning, which affects the amount of energy consumed by the muscles.

If energy deposits are reduced and energy is not supplied at the same rate at which it is used, the movements become slow until they are interrupted.

The Choice of Fuel

In general, nutritional guidance is the same for free surfers as for competitors. It's not just a question of how much you eat but the food quality. Eat a broad and colorful variety of food because no single food alone offers all the needed nutrients.

Special attention should be given to eating before and after training and during and after competitions, when the quantities of specific nutrients for performance, yield and recovery are generally greater.

The nutrients are commonly broken into three classes: carbohydrates, fats and proteins.

Carbohydrates – the Core

Carbohydrates are the principal energy source for muscles when surfing. They form the base of energy reserves, which are accumulated in the liver and in the muscles in the form of glycogen. The amount stored in the body will directly affect the athlete's stamina and endurance.

Photo: Maria Vidigal

Whole grain bread

The base of the pyramid consists of foods that are sources of carbohydrates. This nutrient is found mainly in grains and cereals, roots and tubers.

Whole grains are the best sources of complex carbohydrates, because they contain other nutrients, such as fibers, B vitamins and minerals. Because of their ability to produce energy, they should constitute 60-70% of an athlete's diet. They play an important role in the recuperation of tissue.

Once eaten, carbohydrates are broken into smaller sugars, known as glucose, fructose and lactose, that circulate through the blood and are made available to the cells that need energy.

Any glucose not needed right away gets stored in the muscles and the liver in the form of glycogen; the excess is stored as fat.

Glycogen is the energy source most often used for exercise. It is immediately accessible for any sort of motion in surfing, from explosion to long distance paddling. A decrease in glycogen reserves will lead to tiredness and fatigue, compromising performance on the waves. Optimal carbohydrate intake also helps prevent protein from being used as a source of energy, thus avoiding muscle loss.

Carbohydrates also have specific functions for fueling the central nervous system (CNS) and brain.

Complex Versus Simple Carbohydrates

Simple carbohydrates are produced naturally in fruits and vegetables, but can be found in sweets and candies.

Complex carbohydrates are polysaccharides, which include the digestible cereals like rice, wheat, corn, oats, rye and barley, and are found in such foods as pasta, bread, granola, legumes and starchy vegetables and fibers.

The Glycemic Index

The glycemic effect of a food is very important in competition and training, and refers to how high and fast the blood glucose rises, and how quickly the bodily responses return the blood glucose to a normal level.

Highly glycemic food is absorbed quickly and can raise blood sugar levels rapidly; low glycemic food is absorbed slowly and has a moderate effect on raising blood sugar levels.

Junk food, like heavily processed food including "low or nonfat" cookies and cakes, tend to have a high glycemic index because of the addition of simple sugars.

Foods with whole, minimally processed grains that are high in fiber, such as multigrain bread and granola, tend to have a lower glycemic index. Low GI food is thus generally recommended before athletic activity.

Table 1. Carbohydrates, calories, and glycemic index of commonly consumed food.

Food Carbohydrates	(gm)	calories	Total Glycemic Index
Spaghetti/macaroni/noodles (1 cup)	40	200	Medium
Brown rice (1 cup)	90	106	Medium
Parboiled rice	90	100	Low
Baked potato (1 large)	55	240	High
Starchy vegetables			
Corn (1/2 cup)	18	80	High
Carrots (1 medium)	10	60	High
Peas (1/2 cup)	10	40	High
Tomato sauce (1/2 cup)	10	80	High
Legumes 35 220			
Baked beans (1 cup)	50	330	Low
Lentils (1 cup)	40	215	Low
Kidney beans (1 cup)	33	204	Low
Split-pea soup (11 oz)	35	220	Low
Bread products			
Bread, whole grain (2 slices)	25	150	Medium to High
Submarine roll 855 (1 large)	60	280	Medium to High
Bagel (1)	30	210	Medium to High
English muffin (1)	25	130	Medium to High
Bran muffin (1 large)	45	320	Medium to High
Corn bread (1 large slice)	29	198	Medium to High
Graham crackers (2)	11	60	Medium to High

Cold/hot cereals			
Grape nuts (1/2 cup)	46	200	Medium to High
Shredded wheat (1 cup)	37	180	Medium to High
Raisin bran (1 cup)	42	180	Medium to High
All bran (1 cup)	27	180	Medium to High
Oatmeal (1 oz)	30	140	Medium to High
Pancakes 455 (2)	30	140	Medium to High
Fruits			
Orange/Apple	20	80	Medium
Banana	26	105	Medium
Raisins (1/2 cup)	60	240	Medium
Grapes (1 cup)	16	58	Medium
Dried apricots (8 halves)	30	120	Medium
Fruit yogurt (1 cup)	50	250	Medium

In general, we advise the consumption of six to 11 daily portions of complex carbohydrates, while avoiding the consumption of refined carbohydrates, such as white bread, white rice and white sugar, candy, etc., from which important nutrients have been removed and which are associated with diabetes, heart disease and cancer.

In addition to carbohydrates, fruit and vegetables supply vitamins, minerals and fibers (see Table 2).

They are nutrients that do not contribute significantly to the calorie total but are important in regulating the entire body since proteins, carbohydrates and fats depend on vitamins and minerals for their metabolism.

Vitamins A, D, E and K are fat soluble, or that is, they reach the blood linked to fats, while B complex and C vitamins are hydrosoluble – they reach and leave the body through water (see the principal functions and food sources of vitamins at the end of this chapter).

Photo: Flavio Vidigal

Salad

Fiber, which is present in skins, stalks, leafy vegetables and fruits, increase the volume of food, which improves the functioning of the intestines and the regulation of glucose and cholesterol levels in the blood.

Many studies show that the daily consumption of fiber helps prevent intestinal cancer.

Vitamins A and C increase immunity, improve the action of antibodies, and function as potent antioxidants, helping to neutralize free radicals produced by stress, excess training, improper nutrition and some diseases.

Because they have reduced caloric value, they can be consumed freely, with recommendations for a minimum of five portions of fruit and five portions of vegetables per day.

Proteins

Proteins have a fundamental role in cell maintenance. They are used for the growth, repair, and maintenance of body tissue. Their deficiency leads to low immunity, loss of muscle mass and hormonal imbalance, in addition to other associated problems. Proteins consist of combinations of 20 amino acids necessary for human growth and metabolism, 8 of which cannot be synthesized in the body and must come from proper nutrition. Adequate, regular protein intake is essential because they aren't easily stored by the body.

The body's use of protein to produce energy during exercise becomes most apparent when carbohydrate reserves are low.

The best sources of proteins are food of animal origin, such as meat, eggs, milk and cheese.

400

In surf training, the consumption of 1.4–2 grams of protein per kilo of body weight per day is recommended, depending on the athlete's level of training.

Proteins should represent 10-15% of a surfers' total calorie intake. Although they are essential to muscle contraction, increasing their ingestion can cause gastric discomfort (because they take time to digest) and can overload the kidneys.

Photo: Sebastian Rojas

M. Giorgi

The dairy group, including milks, cheeses and yogurts, should preferably be consumed without fat, when it is necessary to control cholesterol. It is food that is rich in calcium, participates in bone development and in teething, and supplies vitamins A and D.

In a balanced carnivorous diet, two portions of animal protein are recommended per day (lean beef of any kind, eggs, milk and dairy products) and a portion of vegetable origin (beans, lentils, soybeans, tofu, chickpeas, and peas). Guidance for vegetarian surfers is provided below.

Below are examples of the amount of protein in food.

Food	Amount	Protein
Fish	3 oz.	21 grams
Chicken	3 oz.	21 grams
Turkey	3 oz	21 grams
Meat	3 oz.	21 grams
Milk	8 oz.	8 grams
Tofu	3 oz.	15 grams
Yogurt	8 oz.	8 grams
Cheese	3 oz.	21 grams
Eggs	2 large	13 grams

Lipids (Fat)

An Important Source of Energy

Lipids are a fundamental source of energy that provide up to 70% of the total energy used at rest and about 50% used during light exercise. This means that most of our energy is delivered from adipose tissue depots.

When exercise starts to increase in intensity, the balance of fuel utilization crosses over and energy is provided predominantly by carbohydrates.

Nevertheless, endurance training increases the metabolism of fat in the muscles, so that during intense surfing sessions, fat metabolism will account for a greater proportion of the energy demands of a surfer who conducts intensive training compared with a casual surfer.

When surfing continues for more than 3 hours, the role of stored fat becomes even more important and may provide more than 80% of the energy requirements.

The basic importance of fat:

1. Fat is the essential component of all of your cell membranes (over 50 trillion).

2. Nerve fibers depend on it to transmit information.

3. All steroid hormones in the body are produced from cholesterol.

4. Vitamins A, D , E , K are known as fat-soluble vitamins.

5. The insulating subcutaneous fat layer also helps preserve body heat.

Fat is stored mainly in adipose tissue with some in muscle cells.

Fat is Important for Health and Energy Supply

Some surfers excessively reduce their fat intake, fearing they will get fat! Female surfers in particular can be at risk of the "female athlete triad."

Surfers need an intake of 20% to 25% of calories from fat, with each gram of fat supplying 9 calories, more than double the energy supplied by proteins and carbohydrates.

Unsaturated, monounsaturated and polyunsaturated fats are good for your health and performance. They are the richest in essential fatty acids and found in common vegetable oils (linseed, corn, soy, sunflower, olive and others – but not palm oils). The fatty acids, Omega 3 and 6, are found in beans, string beans, snow peas, soybeans, linseed and oily fishes like salmon, herring and tuna. Their consumption helps protect the heart and blood vessels.

Saturated fats are not healthy. They are found in beef, pork, egg yolks, cream, butter and coconut milk. They are rich in cholesterol and should be limited to 1/3 of the daily total fat intake. Excess consumption can lead to cardiovascular diseases.

The consumption of food high in fats and sugars, such as desserts like ice cream, chocolates and other sweets, is related to obesity, heart disease and diabetes.

Suggestion of a Diet of Nearly 4,000 Calories per Day (For Those Who Surf Approximately 3 Hours a Day).

Breakfast

2 slices of whole grain bread (140 cal)
1 piece of fruit (banana) (90 cal)
1 cup of cereal (granola) (200 cal)
1 spoon of honey (20 cal)
1 cup of nonfat milk (120 calories)
2 slices of low-fat cheese (160 cal)
1 cup of orange juice 200 ml (150 cal)

Snack 10 a.m.

fruit salad (150 cal)
2 slices of whole wheat bread (140 cal)
1 tablespoon of raspberry jelly (170 cal)

Lunch 1 p.m.

1 cup of brown rice with vegetables (160 cal)
150g of skinless, grilled chicken breast (210 cal)
2 small, cooked potatoes (100 cal)
mixed salad (tomato, lettuce, cucumber, carrot) with one tablespoon of olive oil (100 cal)
1 slice of whole grain bread (70 cal)
1 cup of orange juice 200 ml (150 cal)

Snack 4 p.m.

1 banana (90 cal)
1 serving of low-fat yogurt with honey (100 cal)

Dinner 7 p.m.

2 cups of whole wheat spaghetti with tomato sauce (360 cal)
150 g of grilled fish fillet with capers (270 cal)
salad of choice with spinach (100 cal)
fruit juice: apple, grape, pear (60 cal)
herbal tea

The food suggested in this menu can be substituted according to taste, depending on the basic type of nutrition, whether vegetarian, lacto-vegetarian, ovo-lacto vegetarian or carnivore (see list of nutritional substitutes below).

List of Food Substitutes

Salads

A one cup portion has about 30 grams and an average of 10 calories: chard, watercress, lettuce, chicory, asparagus, broccoli, endive, collards, spinach, cabbage, hearts of palm, radishes, tomatoes, cucumbers and onions.

Vegetables

A 100-gram portion or about 4 tablespoons has an average of 40 calories: squash, zucchini, eggplant, beets, carrots, brussel sprouts, cauliflower, acorn squash, turnips, green peppers and string beans.

Fruits

A piece of fruit has about 60 calories
Pineapple = 1 thick slice
Avocado = two heaping tablespoons
Prunes = 3

Banana, grapefruit, persimmon, fig, guava, kiwi, orange, apple, papaya, mango, passion fruit, melon, watermelon, strawberry, nectarine, pear, peach, tangerine.

Dairy products

One 200 ml cup of milk has 120 cal and can be substituted for:
Whole yogurt = 200 ml cup
Swiss or mozzarella cheese = one medium slice
American cheese = two thin slices
Cream cheese = 2 tablespoons

Fats

One tablespoon of mayonnaise has 76 calories and can be substituted with:
Margarine = 2 level tablespoons
Vegetable oil = 1 tablespoon

Rice

One portion = 1 heaping tablespoon of rice has about 30 calories and can be substituted with: a baked or sweet potato, cooked pasta or oatmeal.

Beans

One portion = 1 ladle = 6 tablespoons, has nearly 80 calories and can be substituted with: peas, chickpeas, lentils and soybeans.

Meats

One medium portion has about 90 calories and can be either beef, chicken or fish.

Breads

One portion = 1 roll, has about 135 calories and corresponds to:
1 1/2 slices of white, rye or whole wheat bread, 3 heaping tablespoons of oatmeal.

Recommendations for an Athlete's Meal Before, During and After Surfing

Planning for the meal before a competition can be critical, and a series of factors should be taken into consideration, especially the amount of time between meals and heats.

The meal before the competition is an important source of energy. Nevertheless, the energy needed for this day is the result of the food ingested in at least the 2-3 days before the event.

Thus, in the week preceding the competition, or a highly intensive training period, the diet should be as balanced as possible. For a few days before the competition, carbohydrate intake can be increased to 65% to 70% of the daily energy intake. Preference should be given to complex carbohydrates (pastas, potatoes and grains). This will complete the energy reserves (like filling the tank). This technique, called carbohydrate loading, must be done while decreasing the amount of training during the last 3 to 5 days before competition.

This strategy can nearly double the muscular glycogen content.

Be careful with food rich in fats that accompany carbohydrates, such as stuffings, sauces and certain cheeses on pizza, which significantly increase the calories of these foods and does not change the reserves of glycogen in the muscles.

Feeling strong depends on the well-being generated by balanced meals.

407

The Competition is Tomorrow – What to Eat?

Pre-Competition Meal

The meal before a competition is very important physically and psychologically for a surfer. The content of the meal and the interval between it and the competition are very important.

It's a good idea to remember:

- Don't enter a heat on an empty stomach because you may run out of energy.

- Eat about 2-4 hours before the heat. The meal should be basically carbohydrates that are easy to absorb, such as spaghetti with tomato sauce, roasted potatoes, toast with jelly, cereal and milk or non-fat yogurt (if you have no problem digesting milk). If there are less than 2 hours between the last meal and your heat, have a fruit salad with a little granola and honey or a granola bar, a sandwich of cheese and/or turkey breast and a salad or fruit juice.

- Water complements the menu. On cold days, soup with pasta or rice is a good option. Avoid mayonnaise.

- The meal should have few proteins (meat, milk and eggs) because in addition to requiring more than 3-4 hours for their complete digestion, they overwork the kidneys, increasing the loss of water through urine.

- If you are still hungry in the 2 hours before the heat, energy bars with a mixture of carbohydrates and proteins, produced especially for athletes are an excellent option.

- In the 60 minutes before the heat, avoid eating high glycemic index food like chocolate, sugary food and sweets, which in addition to being rich in fat, can quickly elevate the amount of sugar in the blood (this response is individual), which can elevate the production of the hormone insulin, which in turn, drastically reduces the levels of blood sugar and can compromise performance. In addition, they are foods that are slow to digest and can cause an upset stomach during wipe outs or during the need for explosion in paddling and maneuvers.

- Do not change your general eating habits, that is, don't eat what you are not accustomed to.

- Do not have fatty and/or fried food because they take time to digest.

- Avoid foods that are difficult to digest and can produce gases, such as beans, soybeans, chickpeas and cauliflower, fatty foods and those that are very spicy. Foods that are rich in cellulose, fiber and seeds can cause gastric discomfort and activate the intestines.

- Drink plenty of liquids to guarantee that the body is well hydrated. In the hour before the event, drink 400-600 ml of water, in small doses (approximately 100-150 ml every 15 minutes). This quantity allows the maximum absorption of the liquid, reducing the need to urinate. After initiating exercise, the kidneys produce urine more slowly to compensate for the loss of water.

- Drink plenty of coconut juice.

Warning:
Participating in a competition with the body even slightly dehydrated reduces performance.

Yuri Sodre

Photo: James Thisted

In summary:

The best diet before exercise is something only the athlete can determine based upon experience. Here are some guidelines:

1. Have a solid meal four hours before exercise.

2. Have a snack or a high carbohydrate energy drink two to three hours before exercise.

3. Replace fluids with a sports drink 1 hour before exercise.

3 to 4 hours before competition

- fresh fruit
- fruit or vegetable juices
- bread, bagels
- pasta with tomato sauce
- baked potatoes
- energy bar
- cereal with low-fat milk
- low-fat yogurt
- toast/bread with limited peanut butter, lean meat, or low-fat cheese
- 30 oz of a sports drink

2 to 3 hours before competition

- fresh fruit
- fruit or vegetable juices
- bread, bagels
- low-fat yogurt
- sports drink

1 Hour or Less Before Competition

- fruit or vegetable juice such as orange, tomato, or V-8
- fresh fruit, such as apples, watermelon, peaches, grapes, or oranges
- energy gels
- up to 1 1/2 cups of a sports drink

Meals Between Heats

The need for liquids and nutrients between heats depends on the intensity, duration of competition and ambient temperature.

During a day of surfing or heats, a surfer should not wait until thirsty to begin drinking liquids. In addition to replacing water and electrolytes (sodium and potassium), the ingestion of carbohydrates supplies energy and improves performance.

It is an excellent idea to replace water, electrolytes and maltose (a carbohydrate) with specially formulated preparations for athletes that have from 6-8% carbohydrates, in addition to sodium and potassium (such as Gatorade).

Give preference to chilled drinks, which, in addition to being tastier, are easy to digest in the needed quantity and pass more quickly through the intestinal tract.

If an athlete has to surf one heat after another or train for more than two hours, in addition to energy drinks, carbohydrates in the form of a gel, which are easy to digest and practical to consume and transport, are a good option. There are various brands of this product on the market, with the quantity of carbohydrates varying from 20-40 grams per pack. Approximately 30 grams of carbohydrates are recommended for each hour of intense exercise. A cereal bar can be also a good option.

Meals After the Last Heat or Training for the Day

The nutritional intake after the last heat or training should focus on rehydration, the replenishment of deposits of glycogen and the restoration of the electrolytic balance.

Rehydration is very important, especially if there is considerable loss from sweating, if the ambient temperature is high and particularly if the athlete has another competition the following day. Gatorade is a good source of water, energy and electrolytes.

A surfer should begin replenishing carbohydrates as soon as the heat is over. The meal should be rich in carbohydrates (a whole grain bread sandwich of turkey or chicken breast, white cheese or tuna fish with salad, pasta with vegetables, etc.). Sodium can be replaced by adding salt or with slightly salty vegetables. Fruits and vegetables are good sources of potassium and have a moderate glycemic index. Recent investigations show that during the recovery period, ingesting carbohydrates with higher or moderate GI and a small amount of protein are effective methods of replacing muscle energy (Table1).

The optimal carbohydrate-to-protein ratio for this effect is 4:1 (four grams of carbohydrate for every one gram of protein). Eating more protein than that has a negative impact because it slows rehydration and glycogen replenishment.

Protein after exercise provides the amino acids necessary to rebuild muscle tissue that is damaged during intense, prolonged exercise.

In summary

If you are looking for the best way to refuel your body after long, strenuous endurance exercise, a 4:1 combo of carbohydrates and proteins seems to be your best choice. While solid food can work just as well as a sports drink, a drink may be easier to digest and make it easier to get the right ratio and meet the 2-hour window.

General Guidelines for Fluid Needs During Exercise

Specific fluid recommendations are very difficult due to individual differences.

However, most athletes can use these guidelines as a starting point and modify as needed.

Hydration Before Exercise

- Drink about 15-20 fl oz, 2-3 hours before exercise
- Drink 8-10 fl oz 10-15 min before exercise

Hydration During Exercise

- Drink 8-10 fl oz every 10-15 min during exercise
- If exercising longer than 90 minutes, drink 8-10 fl oz of a sports drink (with no more than 8 percent carbohydrate) every 15 - 30 minutes.

Hydration After Exercise

- Weigh yourself before and after exercise and replace fluid losses.
- Drink 20-24 fl oz water for every 1lb lost.
- Consume a carbohydrate and protein within 2 hours after exercise to replenish glycogen stores

Vegetarian Surfers

A vegetarian diet is suitable as long as the athlete pays attention to certain basic rules.

For ovo-lacto vegetarians, the ingestion of milk, cheese, eggs and yogurt supply the eight essential amino acids that the organism does not produce.

Pure vegetarians, who avoid all types of animal products (vegans), need careful planning about the ingestion of proteins, vitamin B12, calcium, iron, zinc and vitamin D. An intelligent mixture of grains, brown rice, lentils, vegetables, nuts, seeds and legumes (string beans and soybeans) guarantees the eight essential amino acids.

Vegetarian surfers need extra doses of vitamin B12, which can be taken in supplements, under the guidance of a doctor or nutritionist.

Dean Morrison
WCT surfer

Alcohol

Not represented on the pyramid, the consumption of alcohol (found in beer, vodka, whiskey, tequila etc.) should be reduced or eliminated, especially on the night before training or competition.

In addition to supplying empty calories (those without nutrients), alcohol consumption reduces the quantity of sugar in the blood and liver, lowering energy reserves. Its excess is transformed into body fat, and it induces dehydration because of its diuretic effect.

The calorie count of a drink depends on its alcohol content. Each gram of alcohol contains approximately four calories.

Herbicides and Pesticides

Herbicides and pesticides are chemical compounds used in modern agriculture to protect various crops from pests and guarantee maximum yields in harvest, transport and storage. However, many of these compounds are toxic and over the years accumulate in the body and can cause a series of diseases.

Unfortunately, food may have large quantities of herbicides and pesticides. For this reason, it is important to know where food comes from and to remove the skins of fruits and vegetables, where more of these substances accumulate, particularly in tomatoes, potatoes and grapes.

Hydroponics is a form of production that reduces the use of these chemicals. In this process, the food is produced in greenhouses in a liquid medium that has all of the nutrients needed for development, and they do not require herbicides and pesticides to guarantee their stability from production to the table.

Food free of herbicides and pesticides is known as organic food!
Go for it!

Food Additives

There are countless chemical substances – many which are not natural – used in food technology, fabrication, processing, coloring, conservation, handling, packing and shipping.

The use of these additives is regulated in most countries.

By law, all substances used in food should be indicated on the label provided by the producer. It is important to be familiar with some of these substances because in sensitive people they can cause allergies, irritate the digestive system and may be responsible for migraines and other health problems.

Fabio Gouveia

Balancing Micronutrients

Vitamins and minerals have an important role in health and exercise physiology (Table 2). The intake of vitamins and minerals is positively related to food quality and quantity.

Table 2. Principal vitamins, food sources, basic individual needs and functions. DRI – Dietary Reference Intakes. Food and Nutrition Council of the Medical Institute (USA) - Age range 14-50.

Vitamins	Food sources	Basic daily needs	Functions
B1 – Thiamine Water-soluble	Whole grain (wheat germ and brewer's yeast) seeds (sunflowers), legumes and meats.	1.2-1.5 mg	Helps to remove CO_2 – cellular metabolism
B2 – Riboflavin Water-soluble	Found in most food 1	3 mg	Involved in energy production
B3 – Niacin Water-soluble	Legumes, whole cereals and lean meats	13-19 mg	Involved in energy production
B6 – Pyrodoxine Water-soluble	Whole grains (oatmeal) vegetables, fruits, (banana) and meats (liver)	0.3-1.7 mg Needs increase after 50 years	Involved in production of energy
Pantothenic Acid Water-soluble	Found in most food	4–7 mg	Energy metabolism
Folic Acid Water-soluble	Legumes (white beans) green vegetables (spinach), whole grains, oranges and liver.	400 µg	Energy metabolism and amino acids
B12 – Cyanocobalamin Water-soluble	Dairy products, meat and eggs. Not found in vegetables	2.4 µg Needs increase after 50 years	Metabolism of amino acids

Vitamins	Food sources	Basic daily needs	Functions
Biotina Water-soluble vitamin	Legumes, vegetables (mushrooms), meats and eggs.	30 µg	Involved in the metabolism of fats, amino acids and glycogen.
C – Ascorbic acid. Water soluble	Green peppers, vegetables (asparagus, broccoli, spinach and citrus fruits (tomato, grapes, kiwi, acerola, orange, pineapple, strawberry and lemon).	60 à 120 mg	Immunological function, bones, teeth, cartilage and collagen. Antioxidant 500 mg to 1 g day
A Fat-soluble B-carotene provitamin Retinol – A	Green and yellow vegetables (papaya, carrots, squash, spinach, mango, sweet-potato and broccoli), liver, fortified milk, dairy products and fish liver oil.	5000IU/d Antioxidant dose: 25,000IU/d	Important for vision, skin protection and muscles; antioxidant.
D Fat-soluble	Dairy products, eggs, cod liver oil, wheat germ and seeds	5 µg	Growth and mineralization of bones, assists in the absorption of calcium.
E – Tocopherol Fat-soluble	Green leafy vegetables, margarine, vegetable oils, nuts, ear corn and liver. 15 mg or 11U.	Antioxidant doses run from 400 UI-800 UI/ day (280-560 mg)	Needs increase as a function of the type of animal fat consumed in the diet. Antioxidant.
K Fat-soluble	Cereals, fruits, meats and green leafy vegetables.	120 µg	Important for coagulation.

Taj Burrow
WCT top surfer

Photo: James Thisted

Principal Minerals for the Body (Food Sources, Basic Needs and Functions)

Minerals	Food	Basic needs	Main function
Calcium	Milk, cheese, dark green vegetables and dried legumes	1,000-1,200 mg	Bone and teeth formation, blood coagulation,
Phosphorus	Cereals, milk, cheese, meats and poultry salt	14-18 years 1,250 mg 18-50 years 700 mg	Bone and teeth formation and biochemical equivalents
Sodium	Salt	100-3,300 mg	Biochemical equilibrium
Magnesium	Whole grains and green leafy vegetables	400-420 mg men 320 mg women	Activates enzymes, producer of protein and muscular contraction
Iron	Whole grains, green leafy vegetables, legumes, eggs and lean meats	8 mg men 15-18mg women	Component of red blood cells and of enzymes, involved in energy production
Fluorite	Seafood and tea	2-4 mg	Maintenance of bone structure
Zinc	Widely distributed in all food, carrots, garlic, meat, seafood, poultry	11mg men 8 mg women	Involved in countless metabolic paths, digestion, immunity and part of the antioxidant enzymes

Minerals	Food	Basic needs	Main function
Copper	Seafood, meats, legumes and nuts	900 µg men and women	Assists in the metabolism of iron and some of the antioxidant enzymes
Chromium	Fats, oils vegetables and meats	35 µg men 25 µg women	Acts in the metabolism of sugar
Iodine	Saltwater fish and shellfish, dairy products and many vegetables	150 µg	Component of the thyroid hormones
Selenium	Grains, seafood and meats	55µg	Works closely with vitamin E
Molybdenum	Legumes, grains and viscera	45 µg	Component of some enzymes
Water	Solid and liquid foods	1.5-2 liters per day	Transports nutrients, regulates temperature and participates in metabolic reactions
Potassium (K+)	Leafy vegetables, cantalope, lima beans, potatoes, milk, meat	4.7 g per day	To lower blood pressure, blunt the effects of salt, and reduce the risk of kidney stones and bone loss
Sulfur (S)	Pulses, beans, eggs, peas, cabbage, pineapple, avocado, lettuce	Proteins, dried food	Acid-base, liver function

SURFING & HEALTH

Everaldo Pato Teixeira
Jaws, Hawaii

Chapter 27

Food Supplements and Ergogenic Resources

By Dr. Joel Steinman and Dr. Tania Rodrigues

The road to victory is long – very long. It involves thousands of waves, lots of workouts, plenty of healthy food and, often, some type of food supplement.

What Are Food Supplements?

Food supplements are specially prepared foods that have various purposes:

- To fulfill the increased needs for nutrients created by physical activity.
- To compensate for inadequate food habits or diets.
- To improve performance.

The growing food supplement (now considered to be nutrients with pharmacological properties) industry places countless commercial formulas on the market every day that promise everything from increased strength, explosion, stamina and muscle mass, to the loss of fat, anti-aging, increased sexual drive, disease resistance and others.

Scientific studies about some supplements have quite conflicting results. While some show benefits, others do not find improvement from the use of supplements and do not confirm the claims of the manufacturers and salespersons.

Athletes, Food Supplements and Ergogenic Resources

Winning is a primordial theme in our competitive culture, and it is clear that the pressure and even encouragement to use chemical and medicinal substances is growing and expanding in order to improve sports performance.

Coaches and athletes are always searching for an advantage in competitions and training. In most sports, including surfing, there are routine searches for ergogenic substances and procedures, or that is nutrients designed to improve performance.

Many ergogenic resources are illicit substances and prohibited in various sports (particularly Olympic sports) where blood and urine tests are conducted to detect the presence of these substances or their metabolites. The substances most often found in drug tests are anabolic steroids and amphetamines (see details in Chapter 28).

Due to the increased cases of doping in high-performance sports, the International Olympic Committee's Medical Commission analyzed 634 food supplements from 215 suppliers, from 13 countries. In 94 (14.8%) of them traces of hormones were found that were not declared on the labels. Of these, 24.5% included testosterone and 24.5% had traces of nandrolone.

Food supplements

Therefore, be careful! Surfing associations in various countries are now testing for doping.

To dictate the correct use of ergogenic resources, legislation recommends that the ergogenic substance be approved by the Olympic Committee's Medical Commission. It is fundamental to know how the substance works, if it was scientifically tested and validated, if it is a permitted substance, and if it is safe for the athlete, that is, if it does not impose a health risk.

In summary: The principal factors that influence the consumption of supplements are their nutritional characteristics, their effects on performance, their flavor, biosecurity, legality and ethics.

Surfing and Supplements

As seen in Chapter 26, surfing requires the activation of three systems of energy supply destined for explosion, muscular strength and aerobic capacity. It was also seen that in the composition of an athlete's diet, 65-70% should be composed of carbohydrates and 10-15% by proteins and 15-20% by fats. Food supplements can be used to stimulate each of the three energy supply systems, in isolation or as a group. In general, the supplements are comprised of different nutrients, particularly carbohydrates and/or proteins (amin acids), vitamins and mineral salts.

Carbohydrate Supplementation

Chapter 26 provided details about nutritional care before, during and after surfing and the importance of a diet rich in carbohydrates, the principal energy source for surfing, which is found in pasta, breads, grains and cereals.

If deposits of this energy source, accumulated in the form of muscular and hepatic glycogen, are not replenished by food before, during and after training and competition, the signs of fatigue and a consequent decline in performance become evident. Supplements are a good option for replenishment.

Supplements Before Training or Competition

If pre-competition nutritional preparation is not possible, carbohydrate-based supplements should be consumed before exercising.

1.   One Hour Before Training or Competition

When using fructose, do not exceed 50 grams. Give preference to supplements with a low glycemic index, which means, use those that do not excessively stimulate the production of insulin.

The supplements that work best include:

a.   Cereal bars, consisting only of carbohydrates, like Powerbar

b.   Energy bars, consisting of carbohydrates and small doses (less than 20%) of proteins

c.   Gels, which contain about 20 grams of carbohydrates, consumed in a pack, found commercially under the brands Squizz, Power Gel, etc.

d.   Liquids that are sold in a powder and prepared by diluting 1 cup of water with 1 heaping tablespoon of the supplement with a type of sugar called maltodextrin.

2.   Immediately Before Training or Competition

Carbohydrates should be consumed in the form of a gel or liquid, in the doses indicated above.

Supplements during training or between heats

The purpose of using supplements during training or between heats is to increase performance by maintaining or increasing the production of energy during surf and delaying fatigue.

The supplementation should be based on the following criteria:

1. The volume of the supplement

2. The composition

3. The frequency and time of consumption

4. The temperature

Sports drink formulations with 6%-8% carbohydrates have the best results, since drinks with higher concentrations can require more time to leave the stomach. They can be used in liquid or gel form.

Supplement after training or competition

(See Chapter 26)

D-ribose

D-ribose is a type of sugar essential to the structure of DNA and RNA molecules. Ribose is essential for regenerating energy in the muscles.

Research has found that ribose improves the heart's tolerance to exercise in patients with coronary heart disease (CHD). Until now, there is no evidence that ribose offers improved performance among athletes. However, there is some evidence that it improves recovery after exercise.

A dose of 10g of ribose daily has been shown to benefit high-intensity bicycle training. Use 5 grams before and 5 grams after surfing.

Hydration and temperature regulation

It is recommended that an athlete drink about 500 ml of water two hours before exercising to promote suitable hydration and provide time for the excess to be eliminated.

Recent studies confirm that the ingestion of water, combined with sodium, potassium and carbohydrates, is an excellent form of replenishment and is beneficial for hydration and as an ergogenic resource that can prolong performance. This is the base of isotonic drinks, which should be used after training and competition.

Special attention should be taken on hot days and during long periods of waiting between heats, when the need for liquids and mineral salts increases (the drink should be between 15-22°C in temperature).

Among the commercial formulations are Gatorade, Powerade, etc. Don't wait to be thirsty to begin hydration, since being thirsty is a late sign that the body lacks water.

Drink lots of coconut juice and pure water.

Protein supplements

The need for proteins among non-competitive surfers is about 1.2-1.4 grams per kilo of body weight per day, while for professional surfers this quantity can reach 2 grams per kilo of body weight per day, representing 10% of the energy consumed during exercise.

The need for proteins increases with:

1. The intensity of training

2. The duration of training per day (especially after more than one hour)

3. The period of training

4. A reduced content of carbohydrates in the diet

Thus, when the normal diet is not able to supply the quantity of proteins necessary for the amount of training or competition, protein supplements can help:

1. Muscle maintenance and growth

2. Maintenance of immune system

3. Hormonal regulation

4. Tissue recuperation

5. In athletes with normally functioning liver and kidneys, protein supplements can be used during the training or competition phase, using whey protein, in doses of 1 tablespoon mixed with fruit juice or milk, once or twice a day for a total dotal dose of 25 grams per day.

Whey protein is a component of cow's milk and an excellent source of BCAA – **branched chain amino acids**. It increases the level glutathione, a potent anti-oxidant.

Alternatively, and at a lower cost, you can have one cooked egg white per day. Egg whites are rich in albumin, which is an excellent source of protein (avoid eating raw egg whites, since they inhibit the absorption of some B complex vitamins, which are important to energy production).

WARNING

1. High protein diets increase risk of certain cancers

2. High protein diets increase risk of osteoporosis

3. High protein diets lead to a reduced intake of vitamins, minerals, fiber and phytochemicals

Amino Acid Supplements – Isolated or in Groups

Amino acids are the units that compose proteins. In addition to the acquisition of amino acids by means of diet or protein supplements, many surfers interested in developing muscle mass consume isolated amino acids for the following reasons:

1. To promote the release of hormones that are important to the increase in muscle mass (such as growth hormone and insulin).

2. To facilitate the production of certain neurotransmitters (chemical, cerebral substances).

3. To increase the intracellular level of energy (ATP).

4. To reduce fatty mass.

There are conflicting analyses of scientific studies about the effects of supplements of BCAAS, glutamina, arginina, and ortina. They should only be consumed under the guidance of a doctor or nutritionist.

Branched Chain Amino Acids – BCAAs

These include leucine, isoleucine and valine.

BCAA supplementation may delay central nervous system fatigue and enhance performance in prolonged aerobic endurance events by reducing the formation of serotonin. They are frequently used to reduce fatigue by high performance athletes in sports that require great endurance.

Their usefulness in strengthening the immune system and increasing the synthesis of growth hormones and insulin has no scientific basis.

Their use should be prescribed by a doctor or nutritionist.

Glutamine

This is a non-essential amino acid stored in the muscles that is released during exercise.

It acts as a nutrient for cells that divide rapidly, such as intestinal and immune system cells, and has been used to:

1.   Increase immunological defenses for surfers involved in intense training regimens (like a surf trip).

2.   To maintain muscle mass by preventing protein breakdown and improve glycogen synthesis, thereby increasing muscle energy reserves!

Glutamine is most abundant in high-protein foods, such as meat, fish, legumes, and dairy. Uncooked cabbage and beets are all rich sources. Start doses at 3 to 5 grams per day.

Creatine

Creatine is produced in our bodies by the liver, kidneys and pancreas from the amino acids glycine, arginine and methionine. It can also be obtained from the ingestion of such foods as meat and fish. In healthy individuals, endogenous synthesis and the diet are responsible for a production of nearly 2 grams per day.

Because creatine is involved in the re-synthesis of ATP (energy), a larger muscle stock of creatine can increase muscle strength in short duration and high intensity surfing activities, and decrease fatigue.

Supplementation with monohydrated creatine has become a popular strategy used to increase muscle phosphocreatine and make more ATP available to working muscles. This promotes gains in muscle mass and strength, permitting improved performance related to explosive movement of great intensity and short duration.

In trained athletes, creatine supplements may increase weight by 1-4 kg per month. High intensity training is needed for it to be effective. This means that supplementation is not a replacement for training. It does not increase endurance nor does not have an anabolic effect. It increases gains in muscle hypertrophy during resistance training, especially during rehabilitation. Until recently, scientific studies have not demonstrate any side effects from its use as a supplement, but prolonged supplementation in high doses causes renal overload. Supplementation with creatine no longer uses the previously recommended large dose of 20 grams a day but a daily dose of 2 grams. Cycles of 30-60 days of supplementation should be periodically interrupted.

It should be ingested with carbohydrates and water and under the supervision of a doctor or nutritionist.

Arginine

This is an amino acid that may play some role in sports performance and muscle regeneration. Arginine is a precursor of nitric oxide (NO) a potent blood vessel dilator that can increase blood flow in muscles during activity. It can also participate in the production of energy for explosive motion.

It has been used for various diseases including ischemic heart disease and impotence.

Some studies suggest it can increase levels of growth hormone.

Studies show that supplementation with arginine and ornitine can increase the loss of body fat, associated to muscular strength training, and facilitate the removal of ammonia, a sub-product of exercise, which causes muscular exhaustion.

They should be used under the supervision of a doctor or nutritionist.

Medium-Chain Triglycerides (MCTs)

MCTs are used as an energy source, because of their quick absorption.

Some athletes may notice some abdominal bloating after taking it.

A typical dose ranges from 15 to 50 grams

HMB – beta-hydroxy-methylbutyrate

Beta-hydroxy-methylbutyrate is one of the substances derived from the branched chain amino acids (BCAA). Its supplementation has been related to increased strength and muscle mass, due to its possible anticatabolic action. The effects on individuals who are not in training are more potent than among athletes with an intense training routine. It is also used to help prevent muscle damage during prolonged surfing and exercise.

A usual dosage is 3g per day.

Do not confuse the supplement of HMB with gamma hydroxybutyrate (GHB), which can have strong sedative effects.

More quality studies are needed to confirm the first scientific evaluations.

Androstenedione

Androstenedione is a natural hormone produced by the adrenal glands, ovaries and testicles.

Recently released in the form of a nasal or under-the-tongue spray, the pro-androgenic androstenedione increases levels of testosterone and perhaps estrogen, as well. It is used because of its effects on performance and muscle mass. However, it can affect hormonal balance and have unpredictable side effects.

Its use constitutes doping.

DHEA

Dehydroepiandrosterone (DHEA) is a natural hormone produced by the adrenal glands. DHEA metabolism is used to produce the sex hormones testosterone and estrogen.

Some surfers use DHEA in order to protect their bodies from cortisol, a hormone that increases with heavy exercise and causes muscle breakdown.

People use DHEA as an anti-aging hormone.

It seems to be safe when taken for short periods in therapeutic doses, under close medical supervision.

Natural Stimulants

Caffeine

Caffeine is a stimulant that occurs naturally in coffee beans, tea leaves, chocolate, cacao seeds, cola nuts and in guarana. It is regularly added to certain drinks (such as Coca-Cola), "energy" drinks (such as Red Bull) and flu medicine. Caffeine has been used by athletes for years as a way to stay alert and improve endurance. Used in moderation, it has no adverse health effects.

Research shows that caffeine acts as a central nervous system (CNS) stimulant. It increases alertness and delays fatigue. It may slightly spare muscle glycogen, allowing exercise to continue for more time.

- A nervous system stimulant, doses of 300 mg, about one hour before exercising, are capable of improving performance and decreasing fatigue. Nevertheless, these beneficial effects on performance only affect 40%-70% of all athletes, and generally those who are not accustomed to drinking coffee.

Cautions

Its collateral effects include diuresis, insomnia, gastric irritation, cardiac arrhythmia and worse, anxiety. If they occur, drink lots of fluids.

High doses of caffeine and ephedrine are the basis of supplements known as thermogenics, or those that increase body temperature. They should not be used because they frequently have negative side effects.

Keep in mind that caffeine is on the Olympic Committee's Medical Commison's substance list. Athletes in international competition would be wise to moderate its use.

Ginseng

Known as the longevity plant, ginseng root (panax ginseng) has been appreciated for centuries by the Chinese as a general tonic.

The results of scientific studies are not conclusive about its effects on athletic performance. Nevertheless, there is evidence of its assistance in restoring equilibrium to the organic and mental functions caused by the stress of training and competition. It is known as an adaptogenic substance.

Photo: Equipe 2002 Mormaii's bB wave team

Suma (Pfaffia paniculata) is an herb that is sometimes called "Brazilian Ginseng." The extract of Korean, Siberian or Chinese ginseng is recommended in doses of 1 gram per day. Excessive use can cause agitation and insomnia.

Antioxidant Food Supplements

To get an idea of the effect of oxidation on the human body, imagine an apple exposed to the air. Over time, it becomes dark, changes color, ages and spoils. This is the chemical reaction called oxidation.

Oxidative stress occurs when the body produces excessive oxidants (free radicals) and decreases their elimination.

Regular and intense exercise may result in a decrease in circulating antioxidant levels and if not corrected may lead to a chronic state of oxidative stress. Athletes suffering oxidative stress are at risk of muscle fatigue and injury.

The consequences of chronic oxidative stress may include aging, atherosclerosis, cancer, diabetes, muscular dystrophy, rheumatoid arthritis, Alzheimer's disease and Parkinson's disease.

The intake of antioxidant supplements decreases the damaging effect of free radical formation, especially during strenuous surfing sessions and may protect athletes against post-exercise infections.

Antioxidants are available in foods or are produced by the body to combat oxidative stress.

Vitamins and Minerals

Many vitamins and minerals have antioxidants, including such vitamins as alpha tocopherol (Vitamin E), beta-carotene, ascorbic acid (Vitamin C), as well as such minerals as selenium and zinc. They help neutralize the free radicals produced by stress, excessive training, improper diet and some diseases.

1. Beta-carotene: Vitamin "A" Source

The food sources for beta-carotene are: papaya, carrots, squash, spinach, mango, sweet potato, broccoli, cabbage, liver, fortified milk, dairy products and fish liver oil. They are needed for good vision, bone growth and integrity of the skin and reproductive system.

Daily, required doses are 15,000-25,000 IU per day. High doses can cause anorexia, hair loss and liver damage.

2. Vitamin C – Ascorbic Acid

Food sources for vitamin C include asparagus, broccoli, bean sprouts, cabbage, grapes, kiwi, acerola, mango, oranges, pineapple, strawberry, tomato, spinach, green pepper and others. It has multiple functions in the body, including increasing immunity.

The recommended dose is 500 mg-1,000 mg per day. Higher doses, in addition to being eliminated in the urine, can cause gastrointestinal discomfort, diarrhea, kidney stones and gout.

3. Vitamin E – Alpha-Tocopherol

The food sources for vitamin E are wheat germ, vegetable oil, nuts, spinach, fresh corn and liver. It protects the cardiovascular system.

The needs for vitamin E increase with the ingestion of animal fat consumed in the diet.

The daily, required doses are 15 units for men and 12 units for women. The recommended antioxidant dose is 100 UI-400 UI per day.

4. Selenium

Selenium is found in seafood, meat and grains.

The recommended dose is 100-150 mg per day.

5. Zinc

A source of the natural antioxidant superoxide dismutase, zinc supplements are taken in average doses of 30 mg per day. Natural sources include walnuts, Brazil nuts, green leaves and whole grains.

Other Antioxidants

1. Coenzyme Q10 – ubiquinone

Like carnitine, coenzyme Q10 plays a vital role in the production of cellular energy.

A potent antioxidant, used as a supplement it can increase stamina in aerobic and anaerobic exercise.

Its food sources are fats contained in olive oil, walnuts, Brazil nuts and whole grains.

The recommended dose is 30-100mg per day.

2. Pycnogencol (Pine bark)

This substance extracted from the bark of Pinus maritima, is considered a potent antioxidant, capable of reducing fatigue in athletes.

The recommended dose is 200 mg of extract.

3. Grape Seed Extract

Scientific studies have demonstrated that dark grape seed is a potent antioxidant, rich in bioflavonoids. It has an effect similar to wine but without the negative effects of alcohol. It impedes cholesterol from being deposited on arterial walls.

Rich in sugar (glucose and fructose), it is easily assimilated by the body and is an excellent option, along with coconut juice, for rehydration for surfers.

Indicated for liver problems along with grape leaves, it can be used in detoxification diets.

The antioxidants are found in the bark and seeds, and the darker and more vibrant the color, the greater the quantity of the antioxidant.

4. Green tea

Extracted from the same plant that is used to make black tea, Camellia sinensis, green tea helps prevent certain cancers of the mouth, lungs, stomach and breast through the action of its substances, bioflavonoids and catequins, which are capable of impeding alterations of DNA to the cells. It accelerates metabolism and helps decrease cholesterol levels.

Alpha–lipoic acid

Its food sources are potatoes, spinach, red meat, liver.

The recommended dose is 50-100mg per day.

Pomegranate (Extract of Punica Granatum)

Its food source is the pomegranate.

The recommended dose is 100 mg to 400 mg up to twice a day.

Luteina

It belongs to the carotenoid family (found in foods with yellow and orange pigments). It is important for eye health.

The recommended dose is up to 15 mg per day.

Lycopene

Lycopene is in the carotenoid family. It helps with immunological function and the prevention of heart disease and cancer.

The recommended dose is up to 10 mg per day.

Other Minerals for Performance

Chromium

Chromium participates in the efficient use of insulin and is known as a factor in glucose tolerance. It can increase muscle mass by promoting the capture of amino acids by the muscle cells and stimulating the synthesis of proteins.

Athletes in intensive training are at risk of developing chromium deficiency due to the fact that exercise increases the excretion of chromium in the urine.

Some authors maintain that chromium picolinate supplements increase lean mass and reduce body fat.

The food sources for chromium are fats, vegetable oils, whole grains, green leaves and meats.

Daily doses of 200 µg are recommended. The consumption of an excessive quantity of chromium in the form of a supplement can cause an imbalance and reduce the levels of zinc and copper in the blood.

Iron

The importance of iron in exercise is related to its role as an integral component of red blood cells that transport oxygen. A lack of iron in the diet can lead to the depletion of iron deposits in the body and, in more advanced stages, can cause anemia, the world's most common nutritional deficiency, which significantly reduces surf performance.

The need for iron is higher in growing children, in women due to their menstrual flow, during pregnancy and nursing, and when fighting infection.

Upon finding a deficiency of blood iron and its deposits, a dietary modification is recommended to increase the consumption of iron through the ingestion of lean red meat, liver, beets, beans, egg yolks and dark green vegetables.

Iron supplements are used in doses of 18-25 mg per day for a few months. Iron can be toxic in excessive doses. For better absorption, its ingestion is recommended in association with foods rich in vitamin C (orange, kiwi, lemon and pineapple juice).

**Veteran
Gary Elkerton** Photo: Roberto Price

Supplements and Foods That Help Prevent Diseases

Omega 3 acids

In addition to salmon, omega 3 acids are also found in beans, green beans, soybeans and mostly in linseed, as well as in some fish such as tuna, sardines, mackerel, shark, cod and herring.

Be sure the commercial formulation of omega 3 has a relation of 360mg of EPA to 240mg DHA per capsule.

Its effects on the body include:

1. Strengthening of the immune system

2. Reduction of cholesterol levels

3. Prevention of some types of cancer

4. Protection of brain cell membranes, decreasing the risk of Alzheimer's disease

5. Stimulation of the production of sex hormones

Nevertheless, be careful because the simple inclusion of fish in the diet does not always guarantee the presence of omega 3. The natural omega 3 acids deteriorate quickly and are removed from food in the industrialization process.

Currently, many foods are enriched with omega 3 acids. The use of a supplement of 1-2 grams per day is recommended. A salmon fillet 2-3 times a week supplies the ideal dose of these fatty acids.

Brazil nuts

A food rich in beneficial monounsaturated fats found in olive oil, and polyunsaturated fats found in fish, Brazil nuts are also a source of vitamin E and selenium. They help by:

1. Reducing the levels of bad cholesterol (LDL)

2. Increasing the levels of good cholesterol (HDL)

3. Retarding aging since

4. Preventing prostrate and breast cancer

Three nuts a day are recommended.

Garlic

Rich in alycine, the substance responsible for its strong smell, the benefits include:

1. Reduced rate of bad cholesterol (LDL)

2. Increased level of good cholesterol (HDL)

3. Regularization of blood pressure

4. Improved immunological resistance

Two cloves of garlic 3 times a week.

Oatmeal

Rich in soluble fibers, the cardiovascular benefits of oatmeal include the reduction of cholesterol levels.

The recommended dose is 4 tablespoons per day.

Soybeans

Rich in isoflavone, a chemical substance with a molecular structure similar to estrogen, the consumption of soybeans helps prevent heart disease and some kinds of cancer.

The recommended dose is 25 grams per day (one teaspoon).

Brewer's Yeast

Brewer's yeast is made from a fungus known as saccharomyces cerevisiae.

It is rich in B complex vitamins, chromium, amino acids and selenium.

Take 1 to 2 tablets per day.

Supplements for Cartilage, Muscles and Tendons

See Appendix 3

Children and Adolescents

Supplements should be avoided by children, since they give a false sense of security and encourage improper eating habits.

Children and adolescents wrongly believe that the morning dose of a supplement is capable of supplying their needs and wind up eating foods with low nutritional value.

Young and budding athletes should feel confident by having a normal and basic balanced diet to promote muscle growth and good performance.

In addition to iron and calcium, zinc, chromium and magnesium are very important minerals for growth and development.

Calcium is responsible for the development of bone mass, and a deficiency is often found if there is reduced consumption of dairy products. It is recommended that young people eat plenty of cheese, milk and milk products, soybeans and fish.

Iron deficiency causes anemia, which limits the transport of oxygen in the blood and winds up impeding growth and sports performance. Iron is found in eggs, red meat and beets, beans and lentils; children and adolescents should be encouraged to eat lots of these foods.
Zinc is found in eggs, meats, mussels and wheat germ, while chromium is found in meats, whole grains, cheese and non-refined foods.

Dehydration leads to loss of water and electrolytes in sweat, which raises body temperature and can have a negative effect on health.

Children and adolescents should be encouraged to drink large quantities of liquid, even if they are not thirsty.

The use of vitamin supplements is not considered dangerous and can be used at times when a young athlete is not eating properly. Because they are growing rapidly, an adolescent needs higher quantities of riboflavin, folic acid and vitamins B6 and B12.

**Kids should get fun
and proper food!**

Gabriel Steinman

Calunga

Chapter 28

Athletes and Illegal Substances – Doping

Free Surfers and Drug Addiction

The increase in the use of medications to improve athletic performance has triggered an intense response from some national and international surfing authorities in an effort to preserve not only the ethical quality of competition but, above all, the health of athletes.

T he International Surfing Association (ISA) and the Association of Surfing Professionals (ASP) adhere to strict World Anti-Doping Agency guidelines.

However, most professional surfers have never been tested during their professional career and only two surfers in ASP history have ever tested positive through random drug tests. No top-level surfing competition outside of France has carried out drug tests, where the government pays for tests.

Some athletes and surfing officials insist, "For surfing to be considered in the same league as other major sports, there must be regular testing."

The ISA has been testing athletes at the ISA World Surfing Games for more than a decade and so far no one has tested positive. The ISA is recognized by the International Olympic Committee.

Drugs Prohibited by the International Olympic Commitee and World Anti-Doping Agency

An increasing number of surfing competitions around the world submit athletes to drug tests. Competitive surfers, should take special care in the use of medicine for pain, colds, headaches and nasal and bronchial problems. Medications that contain only antibiotics or antihistamines (for allergies) are permitted. Combined medications that contain stimulants should be avoided, including cold medicines with caffeine, nasal decongestants that have pseudoephedrine, and phenylpropanolamine and even beta-2 agonists and medications used for asthma such as salbutamol, terbutaline, phenoterol and clembuterol, which should only be used with a medical prescription.

Be careful because a single commercial brand may include a combination of substances. For instance, some products labeled as vitamins include psychomotor stimulants and anabolic steroids.

Marijuana use is prohibited. Because it remains in fatty tissue, it can be identified in urine exams for variable periods of time, usually more than a week.

The minimum permitted limit of cannabinoids is designed to protect people exposed to passive smoke.

Due to the risk of doping, always consult a specialist before using any medication.

International Olympic Commitee Legislation

Most performance-enhancing drugs banned by the World Anti Doping Agency and the Olympic Committee are in the categories listed below.

Photo: Levy Paiva

Stimulants, analgesics, anabolic agents, diuretics and peptide hormones and their analogs, physical-chemical and pharmacological manipulation of urine and blood transfusions are prohibited. The use of any of these agents or practices is an infraction of ethical and disciplinary codes and can lead to sanctions against athletes, as well as coaches, doctors and managers.

1.   Stimulants: Amphetamines and Others

Stimulants are agents that increase activity due to their effects on the central and peripheral nervous systems. They boost alertness and physical activity by increasing heart and breathing rates, and brain functions. But some can have a negative effect on performance.

They are used to fight fatigue, increase aggressiveness and strength, accelerate reaction time or even to supress appetite and lose weight.

Amphetamines are the most common stimulants used by athletes.

There is no conclusive data that amphetamines improve performance, however, users describe an improved attitude due to increased motor activity and agility.

Nevertheless, in certain athletes, various side effects from the consumption of amphetamines can decrease performance. The most common include anxiety during use and depression when use is terminated, in addition to tremors, sleep disturbance, agitation and lack of motor coordination, gastrointestinal discomfort, high blood pressure and irregular heart beat. They can trigger psychological dependence and death.

Other drugs prohibited because of their stimulating properties, include anfepramone, amphetaminil, adrafinil, cocaine, modafinil, pemoline, selegiline.

Caffeine is permitted in concentrations up to 12 micrograms/ml (a cup of coffee has 1 microgram/ml).

Cocaine is a banned drug. It is more commonly used socially than for athletic performance.

Exceptions
Preparations with imidazole are acceptable only for topical use; vasoconstrictors such as adrenaline can be used in anaesthetics. Topical preparations (nasal and optometrical) of phenylephrine are permitted. Cathine is prohibited only when its concentration in a urine sample is greater than five micrograms per milliliter. Both ephedrine and methylephedrine are prohibited only when their concentration in a urine sample is greater than 10 micrograms per milliliter.

2.   Narcotic Analgesics

Narcotic analgesics usually take the form of painkillers that act on the brain and spinal cord to treat pain. The most common are buprenorphine, dextromoramide, heroin, morphine, pethidine.

These are substances derived from opium made from poppy seeds, which have as their principal effect the decreased perception of pain. Analgesics reduce pain and may like stimulants, allow the athlete to perform at greater intensity.

Their use is not common in surfing.

Their continuous use can lead to euphoria, mental confusion, disorientation, decreased visual sharpness, vomiting, weakness, impotence and coma.

They pose a risk of physical dependence and withdrawal symptoms.

3.   Anabolic agents

Anabolic steroids

Despite a lack of studies, it is believed that the use of steroids is not common among surfers. Considered to be doping in many sports and banned by the International Olympic Committee, anabolic steroids are the most commonly used drugs in sports that require strength, velocity and stamina.

It is estimated that illegal sales exceed $100 US million per year. The harm caused by their use among adolescents includes stunted growth. In women, there may be hair growth, growth of the clitoris and masculinization of the voice.

The serious side effects from repetitive use include: high blood pressure, increased cholesterol, thyroid dysfunction, nausea, hair loss, itching, acne, irritability, depression, decreased sexual desire, lowered immunity, gynecomastia (growth of breasts in men), sterility, liver disease, medical dependence and even death from liver cancer and leukemia.

Anabolic androgenic steroids (AAS) are synthetic versions of the hormone testosterone. Testosterone is a male sex hormone found in large quantities in most males and in some females. Anabolic androgenic steroids fall into one of two categories: 1) exogenous steroids are substances not capable of being produced by the body naturally, and 2) endogenous steroids, which are substances that are capable of being produced by the body naturally.

Exogenous steroids include drostanolone, metenolone and oxandrolone. Endogenous steroids are androstenediol (andro), dehydroepiandrosterone (DHEA) and testosterone.

Anabolic agents are prescribed for medical use only. Use of anabolic agents may enhance an athlete's performance, giving him an unfair advantage. They may also cause serious medical side effects.

Users usually begin with oral steroids that may increase self-esteem and confidence because of improved appearance and performance.

These results stimulate continued use and intra-muscular and intravenous administration.

When the athlete stops using steroids, he senses a decrease in energy levels and a reduction in euphoria. The user winds up feeling weak and small, which encourages a return to consumption.

**Derek Ho Hawaiian-Veteran,
ASP World Champion**

The hormones are used in cycles to reduce side effects and so that they can be eliminated from the body and not be detected in urine exams.

4.   Beta-2 Agonists

Beta-2 agonists are drugs used in the treatment of asthma because they relax the muscles that surround the airways and open up air passages. They are prohibited because they are stimulants that increase muscle size and reduce body fat. When taken orally or by injection, they may also have anabolic effects.

Exceptions are formoterol, salbutamol, salmeterol and terbutaline. These are permitted by inhalation only to prevent and/or treat asthma and exercise-related respiratory problems. However, athletes need to provide a medical perspcription in order to attain an exemption.

5. Diuretics

These medications cause rapid weight loss. They are not commonly used by surfers.

6. Peptide Hormones

Growth hormone is a protein produced by the pituitary gland that can also be synthesized.

It has two effects sought by athletes:

1. It stimulates synthesis of proteins in skeletal muscle

2. It increases muscle mass and decreases fat

It is not detectable in the urine by common drug-testing methods.

The possible adverse effects from the use of growth hormones include gigantism before puberty (abnormal, excessive growth) and acromegaly in adults, which is characterized by excessive bone growth most noticeable in the jaw, hands and feet.

In addition to human growth hormone, other prohibited peptidic hormones include:

a) Human chorionic gonadotropin (HCG)
It is known that the administration of human chorionic gonadotropin and related composites lead to an increase in the endogenous production of adrongenic steroids.

b) Adrenocorticotropic hormone (ACTH)
This category includes the glucocorticosteroids that are used as anti-inflammatory drugs and to relieve pain. They are commonly used to treat asthma, hay fever, tissue inflammation and rheumatoid arthritis. The most common are: dexamethasone, fluticasone, prednisone, triamcinolone acetonide and rofleponide. These hormones have been used to increase the blood levels of endogenous corticoids to obtain their euphoric effects. Athletes use it to alleviate pain felt from injury and illness.

A doctor's prescription is required to obtain a therapeutic-use exemption.

c) Erythropoietin (EPO)
EPO is used to increase red blood cell production, which improves the blood's capacity to transport oxygen and thus increase stamina.

d) Insulin type growth factor (IGF-1)

e) Insulin (except that prepared for insulin-dependent athletes)

The presence of an abnormal concentration of one of these hormones or their diagnostic markers in an athlete's urine implies doping, unless they are due to a personal condition.

7.   Cannabinoids

Cannabinoids are psychoactive chemicals derived from the cannabis plant that cause a feeling of relaxation.

The most common sources are hashish, hashish oil and marijuana. Marijuana is generally not considered performance enhancing but is banned because its use is damaging to the image of sport. There are also safety factors involved because the use of marijuana can weaken an athlete's ability to perform, thereby compromising the safety of the athlete and other competitors.

The World Anti-Doping Agency code requires each surfing authority to adopt its list of banned substances and determine for themselves whether to ban cannabinoids. Where the rules of the local drug testing authority specify, tests for the presence of cannabinoids are conducted.

Doping Methods

Other common doping methods among elite athletes are not commonly found among surfers. They include:

1. Blood doping
    This refers to a blood transfusion, which can be obtained from the same individual (auto-transfusion) or from different individuals (hetero-transfusion). It is conducted without legitimate justification of its need as a medical treatment. In auto-transfusion, 1-2 units of blood are removed from the athlete 4–8 weeks before an event and reinjected 1-7 days before competition. The goal is to increase the quantity of red blood cells that transport oxygen.

2. Pharmacological, chemical and physical manipulation or masking of urine. Masking agents are products that can potentially conceal the presence of a prohibited substance in urine or other samples. Among the substances used are epitestosterone, dextran, diuretics and probenecid.

They hide the presence of a banned substance in an athlete's urine or other sample, allowing him to cover up his use and gain an unfair competitive edge.

There are a few classes of substances subject to certain restrictions as well. They are:

1. Alcohol

2. Marijuana

3. Local anaesthetics

4. Corticoids

5. Beta-blockers

List of Permitted Pharmaceuticals

Before taking any medication, always check the World Anti Doping Agency's most recent information about permitted pharmaceuticals substances.

Free Surfing and Drug Addiction

Although surfing competitions encourage a drug-free culture, most young free surfers are highly exposed to dozens of dangerous drugs.

They run the risk of becoming addicted.

Many of us have friends who have died or suffered terribly from drugs.
Cocaine, crack, ecstasy, LSD, mushroom tea, heroin, marijuana, cigarettes, alcohol, etc . . .

There are various phases on the path to addiction. Keep a close eye to see if a good friend, son or daughter is running the risk of drug addiction.

These are the typical steps to addiction:

1. Curiosity: this leads a young person to seek information

2. Imagination: a young person begins to imagine experimenting with or using a drug

3. Questioning: what drug, with whom, when, where, what will the sensations be, etc. The more the thoughts gather in your mind, the closer you'll be to an experiment

4. Experimentation: from imagination to experimentation is a single step loaded with the anxiety and expectation that come with anything that is new and prohibited. The first time is usually with "friends"

5. Purchase of the drug

6. The act of repeating the experiment

7. Sporadic use, depending on the situation

8. Regular use; the drug becomes a habit

9. Constant and generalized use; the abuse of drugs

10. Addiction; life revolves around the drug

Just say no – go surfing instead

Photo: Flavio Vidigal

Photo: James Thisted

Kelly Slater
9 times world champion

Chapter 29

Competitive Surf and Sports Psychology for Performance and Emotional Freedom

All elements of training are essential to performance, but mental preparation is the most important form of fine-tuning to achieve good results.

Surfing champions do not sprout up overnight or appear out of luck. They are the fruit of years of development, dedication and total involvement with the sport and all its details.

The athlete should understand the principal contributions of sports medicine to the improvement in the quality of his or her surfing, including physical, nutritional, technical and tactical preparation as well as psychological training.

It is common to see surfers with good technical training and the best equipment who are really hot in free surf but perform poorly when confronting the pressure of competition because they are not sufficiently trained in the areas of concentration, decision making and self-control.

Mormaii training center, Aragua, Praia Mole, Florianopólis, Brazil

The dedicated athlete should consider each element in the construction of his or her competitive profile and should always improve habits and train weak points until they no longer interfere in the quality of performance.

The essence of sport psychology is the certainty that the most successful surfers are those who are best prepared to react professionally during competition.

Sport Psychology

In addition to establishing psycho-diagnostics, sport psychology allows identifying an athlete's personality type and analyzing his typical reactions. It can also serve as a form of mediation between the coach and the athlete, helping to resolve conflicts, and being influential in such a way that helps the athlete in the realization of his or her maximum performance potential in competition.

Psychology offers an arsenal of multiple techniques of mental control and training, which should be used during all the training phases to increase concentration and focus, thus exerting control over thoughts, emotions and competitive stress. It uses resources that stimulate the athlete train and compete, motivated by the determination to improve the quality of performance and to produce at top capacity by developing and improving self-esteem. An athlete only feels inferior to another if he or she allows this to happen.

Surfer personalities

Psychological Preparation Program for Surfing

A program for the psychological preparation for better sports performance begins with a diagnosis of the psychological profile of the athlete and of his or her personality.

Personality is the combination of all the characteristics that make each person a unique individual. It is essential to understand the psychological traits of each surfer and of the professional team involved (physical trainer, coach, manager, etc.), in order to make all of them aware of the most important qualities of the athlete, allowing an improved relationship with himself or herself, with others and the environment.

The knowledge, orientation and best utilization of individual abilities are forms of investing in one's existing potential and facilitating the route to be taken.

The Different Personality Types

Psychologist Hans Eysenck developed a widely used model based on two personality groups:

1. the introverted and the extroverted
2. the emotionally unstable and the emotionally stable

In the diagram below, the two dimensions of unstable and stable personalities, introverted and extroverted are related and compared with the four types of personality defined by the ancient Greeks: choleric, sanguine, phlegmatic and melancholy.

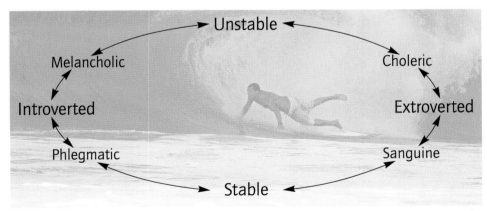

Graph 1. The stable/unstable/introverted/extroverted state of mind related to ancient Greek personality types.

455

The diagram shows that the choleric and phlegmatic, melancholic and sanguine are diametrically opposed and rarely found in the same person.

In reality, it is difficult to find individuals with characteristics only of a single psychological type.

The key to integration and equilibrium is in understanding the combination of the psychological qualities that compose the personality. Thus, the union of the traits of types sanguine-phlegmatic and melancholic-choleric suggests the route that favors equilibrium, while the union of the traits phlegmatic-melancholic and sanguine-choleric suggests probable routes for imbalance.

To try to determine your personality type, select from the list below those characteristics most similar to yours:

1.   Melancholic traits are related to the unstable and introverted types

A person with these traits tends to be inwardly focused, pessimistic, sullen, somber, nervous, distant, quiet, reserved, resigned, sad, discouraged, pensive, self-centered, demanding, vulnerable, slow, sad, intellectual, observing, ungrateful, unsatisfied, unselfish, has a good memory and is inconsolable.

2.   Phlegmatic traits are related to the stable and introverted types

A person with these traits tends to be careful, methodical, stable, passive, peaceful, pensive, calm, controlled, easy going, placid, slow, implacable, modest, tranquil, introverted, reserved, dreamy, likes routine, slow to learn, persevering, obstinate, timid, consistent, sensible, indifferent and apathetic.

3.   Sanguine traits are related to the stable and extroverted types

A person with these traits does not worry much and tends to be calm, animated, jovial, social, sympathetic, talkative, quick to act, a hard worker, persistent, talkative, eloquent, superficial, enthusiastic, friendly, intelligent, impatient, irresponsible, unreliable, rash, flexible, generous, voluble and happy.

4.   Choleric traits are related to the unstable and extroverted types

A person with these traits tends to be have lots of energy, and is ruddy, impulsive, restless, active, excitable, aggressive, angry, a leader, convincing, full of energy, extroverted, turbulent, agitated, impatient, enterprising, pioneering, loud, practical, dramatic, forgetful, competitive, resistant, dominating, intolerant, obstinate and audacious.

Occy
Veteran ASP world champion

General Characteristics of Athletic Personalities

In general, successful, high-level surfers are:

1. Motivated to perform well and have a tendency to establish realistic goals for themselves and other people

2. Organized and disciplined, with a strong disposition towards leadership and an ability to communicate

3. Highly self-confident, have strong psychological resistance, good self-control, emotional control and a tendency toward aggressive behavior

In comparison with young surfers, high level athletes have a much higher cognitive capacity (including perception, anticipation, thought process, attention and decision making). Many of these capacities are genetically inherited, but they experience strong influence from environmental factors, family support and the influence of coaches and trainers.

Many athletes, however, have neurotic traits, including anxiety, fear of failure, a tendency toward depression and an exaggerated concern with failure and outside criticism.

The contribution of psychological training in performance varies from one surfer to another and from one situation to another.

Mental Factors in Competition

Mental factors can fluctuate and vary considerably before and during competition, depending on the way that the athlete reacts to a situation. These mental variations include a lack of concentration, negative thinking, a lack of control and competitive stress. These mental factors can have a very dramatic and negative influence and can ruin an athlete's performance in that heat or competition.

Motivation for Surfing

The external motives: the pressure of competition

The incentive to compete can come from different needs:

1. To win a monetary prize
2. To beat another surfer
3. To perform well for the sponsor
4. To perform for friends, the crowd, a girlfriend and/or the family
5. To move up in the rankings
6. To win the competition

These are among the leading external reasons that push a surfer to work harder by surfing and training in all types of conditions.

There does not seem to be anything wrong with this type of motivation, however. It creates and feeds the known pressure of competition, considered one of the most important factors in a decline in performance.

Photo: Levy Paiva

Photo: Roberto Price

Competitive pressure

In reality, this type of motivation reflects the conditioning to which we are submitted by society, which teaches us to place the cart before the horse and seek the prize, and not the realization of one's best performance.

The pressure of competition has a different effect on each athlete, generating reactions of different intensities. For some it can be a stimulus to victory, while for others it can be the principal cause of a poor performance.

Internal Motives: The Ideal Performance State; Self-Control, Self-Confidence and Self-Knowledge

The quest to maintain the ideal performance state during a surfing competition is the result of internal work that reflects a combination of the athlete's physical and mental training and his ability to deal with different levels of competitive pressure.

A lapse of concentration is considered within the sports world as the most common cause of poor performance. This problem should be worked with through the athlete's principal motivation: achieving a good performance state.

To reach and maintain the ideal performance state the athlete should:

1. Adopt a preventive attitude in order to reduce the negative effects of pressure on performance

2. Train and focus concentration on the factors needed for a high quality performance

3. Focus on a motivation to perform at his or her best, blocking out and avoiding external pressure

It is very clear that poorly trained competitors spend an enormous quantity of physical and mental energy focusing on countless external reasons for better performance. They lose sight of their tasks and what is necessary to execute them. Typically they are drained by the public, special spectators and other competitors, and lose the control needed for good performance.

For a surfer to assimilate these preventive techniques, he or she should adopt and live by a single competitive philosophy, fed by the personal satisfaction achieved and experienced with high quality performance in competitive surf, in and out of the water.

The first and main compensation of the athlete should be the sensation associated with high quality performance known as the "feeling," "rhythm" or "flow."

459

This is a mental incentive that characterizes and motivates the athlete to continue to seek increasingly better performances.

It is the responsibility of the surfer to create mental conditions to achieve and develop their ideal performance state. In this way, the desired results will automatically appear.

1.   Self-Motivation Techniques

Self-motivating techniques are those measures that an athlete can use to assume control of his or her own behavior.

Wipe out

Many high-level competitors motivate themselves, even in difficult situations, by mentally reinforcing their positive capacities and concrete goals.

The most common phrases used for self-motivation are:

- I can do it.
- I am prepared.
- I trust my coach.
- I imagine a situation in which I am a winner.
- I trust my talent.

- I want to improve my physical condition.

- I imagine myself on the podium.

- I will make my best effort to win.

- I want to show my talent to other people.

- I know that intensive training will lead to good results.

- I have attainable goals.

- I have goals for the next training session.

- I can change my goals.

2.   Self-affirmation Techniques

Positive reinforcement from good results include monetary reinforcement and self-praise with typical phrases, such as:

- What I did was fantastic.

- Great move.

- I am happy with my results.

In certain problematic situations, mental anticipation through self-reinforcement includes mantras such as:

- I am happy with myself.

- I will always do something good for myself.

3.   Motor Techniques

Some athletes react to discouragement and the lack of motivation to compete by using mantras that focus on exercises and movements. The most common are:

- I am relaxed while I am surfing.

- I do certain exercises to fight discouragement.

- I train very hard.

- Running in the rain makes me feel strong.

- While running, I breathe deeply and vent my emotions by shouting.

- I train in a variety of ways.

- I participate in planning my training and this increases my motivation.

4.   Emotional Techniques

Some athletes are stimulated by positive sensations and emotions during the execution of movements, which makes them feel pleasure, and the fluidity and sensation of success. Some surfers benefit from music before or during the intervals between heats to create a positive emotional state of mind.

a.   Flow feeling – The Zone
The sensation of fluidity is related to harmony between the athlete's actions and consciousness. It is the immediate feedback information between actions and emotions.

The most common phrases used for motivation are:

• I surf like a perfect machine.

• I have total control of my surfing and the heat.

• I wait for the right wave with total concentration.

Mick Fanning
ASP World Champion 2007

b. Winning feeling

A winning feeling is the sensation of success during competition. This state is characterized by total concentration, total focus on the present moment, increased tolerance for pain and changes in perception.

The most common phrases used for motivation are:

* The next wave will be perfect.

* When I get in the water, I sense that I will win.

* I believe I can win during the entire heat.

* In difficult situations, I think only of victory.

The Competition Approaches

The Pressure of Competition

Most athletes focus too much on the external reasons for competing, consider competition as something much more important or different from training or free surf, and find themselves thinking a lot about their opponents' reputation, the public, the judges, the sponsors, the media, their family, etc. With this mindset, surfers are rarely able to perform in competition with the same quality as in free surf because they create and nurture their own pressure.

Mormaii Training Center, Aragua, Praia Mole, Florianópolis, Brazil

Mental and physical energy should be aimed carefully at controlling the ideal performance state and allowing the task to be executed in the best possible manner. Competition should be considered as an opportunity for the athlete to execute his or her best.

Developing Psychological Control

There are five necessary steps in the development of psychological control.

1.   Controlling Body and Mind Factors

One of the characteristics of the ideal performance state is the sensation that the body is working perfectly. The athlete feels comfortable with his or her breathing, heartbeat and level of muscular energy that allows quick recovery and reaction.

Outside this ideal performance state, especially under considerable pressure, tension predominates, the athlete may begin to breathe heavily or pant and the heart begins to pound and quicken. These factors reduce recovery and reaction speed.

Corporal awareness – self-perception
Work aimed at development of corporal awareness makes it possible to identify how distant one is from an ideal performance state.

The first step consists in recognizing how one feels before, during and after competitions.

Techniques for stretching, breathing control, meditation and progressive relaxation are basic tools that help to expand awareness. They facilitate learning how to recognize and adjust to negative changes in muscular energy, heartbeat and breathing. These adjustments can and should be made before a competition, before a heat, while paddling or waiting for a wave.

2.   Controlling Thoughts and Raising Confidence

In the ideal performance state, thoughts should always be positive:

*   I can do it.

*   I am a winner.

Other thoughts and mental images can be distracting, totally irrelevant and negative, leading to a lack of attention.

The capacity to improve the ability to transform negative thoughts into positive ones and control mental images and thoughts is the foundation of surfing with confidence.

3.   Controlling Emotions and Raising Self-Awareness

The emotional state of some athletes fluctuates drastically. One minute they are depressed, and another they are feeling good and positive. This fluctuation directly reflects on performance quality.

To reach and achieve the state of ideal performance, it is necessary to maintain control of the emotions, avoiding extreme variations.

With clear and realistic objectives and goals, it will be easier to pay attention to the goal.

In the quest for your best emotional state before a competition, analyze the influence of the people with whom you speak, the music you listen to and the mental images you create. Be aware of how you feel and how you would like to feel by analyzing your best previous performances.

Emotions in the Pre-Competitive Phase

There are three general pre-competitive emotional states:

1.   The feverish state

In this condition, the athlete is nervous, agitated, incapable of concentrating, lacks emotional stability and psychomotor control, and is dominated by fear of the opponent. Rapid heartbeat, body tremors and a debilitating feeling are common. In the water, the surfer looses tactical orientation, rhythm, speed and control of movement.

2.   The apathetic state

The athlete is tired and has a debilitating feeling. Concentration and perception are decreased, a bad mood and an aversion to competition set in. On the waves, the athlete is not able to tap his or her energy and lacks motivation. Reactions are slow and tiredness appears quickly.

3.   The optimum state

The athlete has excellent levels of motivation and disposition for competition, is focused on success, has self-confidence, good concentration and high psychomotor control. In the surf, the competition closely follows the tactical plan, the surfer is in control of the situation and achieves his or her expectations.

These pre-competitive emotional states are directly related to the subjective importance of the competition and its consequences.

**Neco Padaratz,
ASP elite surfer –
Former WQS Champion**

Emotions During Competition

Positive emotions during competition are related to a sense of floating, the flow, to the winning feeling and the zone described above.

Improving Concentration

A lack of concentration is the leading cause of failure by competitors.

The degree and type of concentration varies from athlete to athlete. An awareness of one's own level of concentration increases an understanding of the focus of one's attention and allows for analyzing the most common mistakes and failures made under pressure.

The surf is constantly changing, rapidly altering the need for concentration. There are basically two areas of concentration:

a.   External concentration
Some athletes are very good at concentrating and reacting to a variety of external stimuli. External concentration is divided into broad and narrow.

Surfers with broad external concentration perceive more efficiently the external stimuli, such as changes in the waves, the tide, the wind, etc., and are capable of integrating various external stimuli simultaneously.

Meanwhile, those who are deficient in external concentration may take time, for example, to perceive the movement of another competitor in the take-off area and can wind up committing an interference. In addition, they tend to react in a confused and stressful manner in the presence of various external stimuli, such as the sounds of the speakers, the siren, etc.

Those who have good, focused external concentration are very good at realizing new situations, capable of blocking out distractions for a long period and able to remain focused throughout the heat.

b.   Internal concentration

Some athletes are better at maintaining concentration through thoughts, images or sensations. This type of concentration can also be divided into broad and narrow.

Surfers with broad mental concentration are capable of analyzing and developing strategies quickly and efficiently and are called thinking surfers.

Surfers with narrow mental concentration are fast in realizing subtle changes in the degree of body tension, as well as other physiological parameters such as respiratory and cardiac frequency. They stand out for their ability to concentrate on a simple thought.

Ideally, each athlete should develop all these areas of concentration. Training should be initiated at the weakest point.

Recommendations for Training Concentration

1.   Identify and analyze the causes of disturbances to concentration. The most common are family and professional influences, illness, a vegetative psychological state, stress, fear and social conflicts.

2.   Be aware of the characteristics of your degree of concentration and of the most common types of error and lack of concentration.

3.   Get to know the special needs of concentration that exist in specific moments of your performance.

4.   Practice and perfect different techniques for focusing.

5.   Create incentives and stimuli, avoid monotony. Establish new and challenging goals.

6.   Vary the breadth of attention between different focusing techniques.

7.   Vary the concentration with the intensity of training and recovery. Initiate recovery before a drop in concentration.

8.   Concentrate in a conscious way on your focus. Avoid, ignore and block out irrelevant stimuli.

9. Improve motivation for the state of high performance and results. Perceive and analyze the experiences of success and failure and their consequences. Create stimuli for good results.

10. Use key words: I can, fight, confidence, etc.

11. Establish behavior routines.

12. Develop competition plans.

13. Practice visual control.

14. Remain concentrated in present situations.

Suggestions for Concentration Training Exercises

1. Sit in a straight-back chair, place both feet on the floor and hands relaxed on your lap. Close your eyes, breathe deeply and slowly and upon exhaling, begin to relax your head. With each breath, broaden the relaxation to other parts of the body. Continue with the eyelids, neck, shoulders, arms, hands, back, hips, knees, ankles and feet. When you feel completely relaxed, pay attention to your breath and keep focused on it for a few minutes. Progressively increase your time of observation.

2. Sit in a straight-back chair and look at an object or picture that is related to surf. Relax, but keep your eyes open. For five minutes, try to perceive all the possible qualities of the image.

Planning and Preparation

Planning should include strategies for unexpected events. For example, what do you do when you need a wave and the time of the heat is running out?

One of the main training methods for preparation is visualization.

Techniques of Visualization

Visualization exercises are basic elements in improving mental preparation for a performance. Visualization exercises should be part of the training program.

Surfing is an exciting sport!

With a command of visualization, it is possible to create mental images that are increasingly real and alive, where it is possible to see, feel, hear and smell in the same way that something happens in real life.

A relaxed state is needed to produce high-quality mental images.

You can then simulate competition, heats on small waves, large waves, in flat heats, with onshore winds, offshore winds, or surfing against particular athletes.

Bira and Jacqueline Silva (elite ASP WCT)
Coach and surfer

Persistent and dedicated training means creating images of high-quality surf, as if it were taking place (seen and being seen) in real life. Like images that can be seen on video, the athlete will be seeing himself on the screen.

These are some of the basic elements of a mental training program that can leave an athlete better prepared.

Recommendations for the Coach

1. Use intuition and sensitivity to understand the athlete's development not only in terms of physical, technical and tactical factors, but also in terms of his or her development in intellectual, motivational, emotional and social areas. For this reason, you should integrate and apply pedagogical, psychological and social measures in training.

2. A coach's behavior should be an example for the athlete, especially for youth. A coach should act in a positive, controlled and emotionally balanced manner.

3. A coach should help and support an athlete in situations of conflict, stress and failure. The coach should develop in the athlete an ability to control stress, self-motivation, concentration and an ability for social communication.

Yoga

Some athletes practice ancient techniques, such as yoga, qigong and other methods of training. They allow the development of self-control, self-confidence, self-command and self-satisfaction, facilitating the permanence of the ideal performance state for competitive surf.

YOGA

That at the depth of your being will be your desire.
Your desire will be your will.
Your will will be your acts.
Your acts will be your destiny.

Patanjali

Yoga signifies union and the road to this union.

Yoga is a tool for plunging into the ocean of consciousness, awakening it, and transforming human conscious into divine conscious.

It is learned through practice and is a path that leads to better understanding oneself.

Yoga is the art of living consciously in action!

Yoga involves:

1. Working with the body through "asanas," or positions, that allow an excellent practice of stretching and muscular strengthening.

2. Expansion of energy through breathing exercises, known as pranayama.

3. Control of emotions and retractions of the senses, known as pratyhara.

4. Concentration, or dharana.

5. Meditation, or dhyana.

6. Illumination, or samadhi.

Note:

Some yoga postures should be avoided by athletes with pre-existing ailments, particularly in the region of the neck, shoulders, wrists, backbone and knees.

Qigong

Although less popular than yoga, qigong has been used by surfers to improve the basic elements of competitive performance including persistence, motivation, discipline, purpose and willpower.

The literal translation of qigong is the art of manipulating consciousness. It originated more than 5,000 years ago in China and is linked to Taoism, a natural philosophy that seeks the equilibrium of the individual with himself or herself and the universe.

Qigong also offers a complete practice that includes exercises for stretching, strength building, breathing, concentration and meditation.

If you conquer the other, this is strength;
If you conquer yourself, this is power;
If you know the other, this is intelligence;
If you know yourself, this is wisdom.

Lao Tze

SURFING & HEALTH

Jeff Booth

Chapter 30

First Aid – Drowning, Rescue and Cardiopulmonary Resuscitation (CPR)

Drowning

Drowning is a form of asphyxia by aspiration – the inhalation of seawater into the lungs that interrupts breathing.

There are four general classifications of drowning.

First Degree

In this stage victims inhale a small quantity of water that causes coughing. Their general condition is good and they are normally lucid. They usually do not need medical attention, just rest, warmth and care so that they are comfortable and relaxed.

Second Degree

This is when victims inhale a small quantity of water, which is enough to alter the flow of air in the lungs. They are lucid, but agitated or disoriented, and may have signs of cyanosis (blueness in the lips and fingers). There may also be white or pink foam in the mouth and/or nostrils. They require oxygen but can wait to reach a hospital, while they are kept warm with clothes or blankets and calmed down.

Third Degree

In this case, victims inhale significant quantities of water and present strong indications that they are not getting enough air. They generally do not respond properly to questions. They have foamy oral and nasal secretions. Due to the severity of the condition, they should immediately have their air passages cleared and be treated with oxygen on the beach, and when possible, taken right to a hospital.

Fourth Degree A

These victims have respiratory failure but have a pulse (indicating that the heart is beating). They should be revived as quickly as possible on the beach (with mouth-to-mouth resuscitation) until they breathe normally again, and then taken to hospital (see details below).

Fourth Degree B

These are victims of cardiorespiratory attack, represented by the lack of a pulse and breathing. Resuscitation measures should be conducted on the beach, including mouth-to-mouth resuscitation and cardiac massage while waiting for an ambulance.

Rescuing a Drowning Victim

A rescue is usually conducted by lifeguards or emergency workers, but it is common for surfers to participate in saving a drowning victim. So how is this done?

What to do?

Here are the principal tips for rescue with a surfboard

When you see someone drowning, paddle as quickly as possible toward them. You may encounter two situations. One where the victim is conscious, screaming for help, falling underwater and rising to the surface, gesticulating and distressed. In the second, the victim is unconscious.

Conscious Victim

In the case of a conscious victim (who responds to questions and commands), proceed in the following manner:

Photo: Tony Fleury – Revista Fluir

1. Upon approaching the victim, maintain a certain distance and try to calm him down. Remember it is likely that he is in a panic.

2. Get off the board; keep it between you and the victim. Offer the board for a few seconds until the person feels safe. Do not let a victim in panic grab you and worsen the situation. Talk with him in an attempt to calm him down.

Photos (3): Tony Fleury – Revista Fluir

3. Place him lying down on the board toward the front, with their legs spread. Lie down with your chest between their legs so that, if possible, you can paddle.

4. Paddle to the beach. Carefully choose the location where you will get out of the water. The middle of the trough is a terrible escape route because drowning generally occurs at this point. The best area for leaving should be where the wave meets the trough, a location where the waves are usually full. If the board is small, stay off the board and tow the victim. If it is too difficult to paddle to the beach, the best option is to paddle to the outside, far away from the wave-breaking zone, and wait for help. Upon reaching the sand, remember to offer comfort and safety to the victim.

Unconscious Victim

If the victim is not responding to your call and has his face underwater, it is likely that he is unconscious. You should:

1. Approach the victim and place the board between you and the victim with the keels up.

2. Grab the victim by the hands or wrists and pull him to the board, placing the arms over the board.

3. Roll the board to the normal position, pulling the victim toward you. Be careful not to worsen the condition.

4. Place the victim on the board.

Photos (5): Tony Fleury – Revista Fluir

5. If possible, before leading the victim to a safe place, turn him chest up and begin mouth-to-mouth resuscitation while in the water, breathing two or three times. Call for help.

6. Remove the victim from the water. Upon reaching the sand, bring him to a safe place far from the water. If there is someone else to help carry the victim, use the surfboard as a stretcher.

7. If you are alone on the sand, roll the victim onto the sand, grab him by the back and drag him to a safe place, carrying him under your arms. Call for help.

Photos (5): Tony Fleury – Revista Fluir

477

On the beach, begin the basic measures of cardiopulmonary resuscitation after checking to see if the victim is conscious.

1. Check to See if the Victim is Conscious

Photos (2): Tony Fleury — Revista Fluir

Place the victim on his back and stay next to him. Ask a few questions to see if there is a response. "Can you hear me? Are you ok?" If the victim does not respond, grab him by the shoulders and shake lightly, calling once again. If there is no response, consider him unconscious.

2. Control Bleeding and Place the Victim on His Side

On the beach, if there is bleeding, apply a tourniquet with moderate pressure above the wound. Then place the victim on his side to clear the air passages.

WARNING:

If you suspect there was trauma (a fall), it is possible that there is a cervical fracture and any movement of the neck could damage the spinal cord. Immobilize the cervical region with an improvised collar (see Chapter 31). It is important to reduce neck movement to a minimum during this procedure.

3.   Clear the Air Passages

Open the victim's mouth and remove any foreign object. An unconscious person can die quickly due to an obstruction of the air passages by the tongue or a foreign object. Dentures should be removed if they are out of place or broken.

4.   Clearing the Air Passages

To open the air passages, it is essential to reposition the victim's head.

a)   Place one hand on the forehead and the other on the victim's chin.

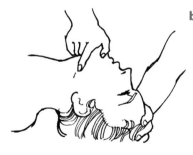

b)   Gently push the head back while raising the chin to the front and up, to see if the person is breathing. Never extend the head too far back.

5.   Check for Breathing

Check the breathing to see if there is any movement of the chest or abdomen, feeling and listening for movement of air from the mouth and/or nose.

Photos (2): Tony Fleury – Revista Fluir

479

6. If Victim is Breathing

If the victim is breathing, leave him lying on his side and keep the air passages open.

7. If the Victim is not Breathing

If he is not breathing, this means there is respiratory failure. Lie the victim on his back and clear the air passages. Place the palm of your left hand on top of the head, tipping it slightly back, while the other hand slowly raises the chin. Begin mouth-to-mouth resuscitation.

8. Mouth-To-Mouth Resuscitation

Kneel alongside the victim. Open the mouth and pinch the nose closed, keeping the air passages clear. Inhale deeply and place your mouth firmly on the victim's mouth. Blow slowly until the chest fills with air. Remove your mouth and check for the escape of air (an exhale). Blow into the mouth 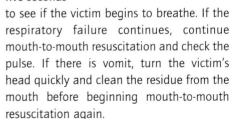 again and observe for five seconds to see if the victim begins to breathe. If the respiratory failure continues, continue mouth-to-mouth resuscitation and check the pulse. If there is vomit, turn the victim's head quickly and clean the residue from the mouth before beginning mouth-to-mouth resuscitation again.

Photos (2): Tony Fleury – Revista Fluir

9. Check the Pulse

To find the victim's pulse, place your fingers on the side of the neck under the chin. You should feel the carotid artery beating. If there is a pulse, but no breathing, continue mouth-to-mouth resuscitation with one breath every five seconds for an adult and one breath every four seconds for a child. If there is no pulse, you should suspect heart failure and immediately begin heart massage.

480

10. Cardiac Massage

Place the victim on his side. For successful heart massage, you must correctly position your hands. Locate the lowest part of the sternum with your middle finger. Place the palm of your other hand two fingers above this point.

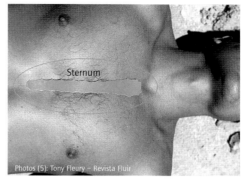

Sternum

Photos (5): Tony Fleury – Revista Fluir

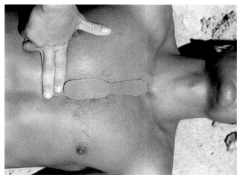

Cardiac Massage Technique

Once the region is located, place the palm of your hand in opposition and the other directly above (only the palm of one hand should be in contact with the sternum).

Cardiac Massage

a. Begin the massage by exercising pressure with the palm of your hand.

b. Be careful in the positioning of the hands because when pressure is applied improperly, there is a risk of fracturing the ribs and the sternum, in addition to injuring the liver or spleen.

c. Keep your arms stretched at an angle of 90 degrees between your body and that of the victim. Do not bend your elbows during CPR because the pressure should come from the shoulders.

d. Allow an equal rhythm for the compression and relaxation. Each application of pressure should compress the sternum about 5 centimeters. After each compression, totally relieve the weight so that the chest returns to its normal position and the blood can fill the heart. Keep contact with the hand in order not to lose the position.

If you have help, one person should conduct cardiac massage while the other keeps the air passages open and conducts mouth-to-mouth resuscitation, at a frequency of 5 pumps for each breath.

Photo: Tony Fleury – Revista Fluir

If you are alone with the victim:

• Conduct 15 compressions in 10 seconds and blow 2 times in the victim's mouth (a total of 60 compressions and 8 breaths per minute).

• Re-evaluate the pulse and breathing after 1 minute and then every 2 minutes, this will give you an idea of how the victim is reacting.

For Children Younger than 8

For children, cardiac massage should be conducted delicately and the compression of the sternum should be only about 2-3 centimeters. For each breath (mouth-to-mouth resuscitation), conduct 5 pumps.

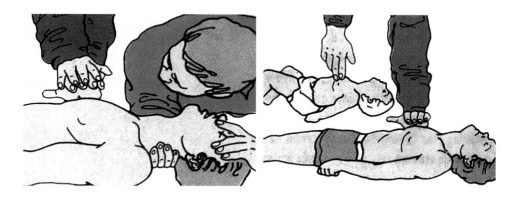

In summary, application of the rescue techniques and resuscitation maneuvers can maintain the life of a human being until he recovers sufficiently enough to be transported to a hospital or until help arrives, but **do not interrupt resuscitation**. Once beginning, you should only stop:

a. If the maneuvers are successful and the victim regains a pulse and breathing.

b. When an ambulance team arrives.

Photos (2): Tony Fleury – Revista Fluir

483

Summary of Cardiopulmonary Resuscitation

Victim with suspected spinal cord damage

(See Chapter 31)

Step-by-step

Conscious victim – Control bleeding. Check the air passages, breathing and circulation.

Unconscious victim – Place the victim on his or her side and check the breathing. Clean the air passages by clearing them (head slightly back). Check the breathing.

Victim breathing – maintain in lateral position

Victim not breathing – Place the victim on his or her back and begin mouth-to-mouth resuscitation. Check the pulse.

Pulse found – If there is a pulse, continue the mouth-to-mouth resuscitation. Check the pulse and breathing after 1 minute and then every 2 minutes.

No pulse – Begin cardiac massage and continue mouth-to-mouth resuscitation. Check the pulse and breathing after 1 minute and then every 2 minutes.

Jet Ski Rescue

Brazilian Surf Rescue Team –

Salva Surf

Heitor Alves

Photo S. Rojas

Chapter 31

Immobilizing and Transporting an Accident Victim – Techniques to Immobilize Upper and Lower Limbs

Never move an accident victim. Calm the victim down and call for help. It is essential that the victim be transported with total security.

W hat should be done in case of an accident at a remote surf peak where there is fear of head trauma or an injury to the backbone?

Fortunately, severe brain and backbone injuries are not common in surfing, but they can occur. Head and spinal injuries (see Chapters 5, 6, and 7) are risks to which surfers of all levels are subjected, especially when surfing near shallow banks of sand, stone or coral.

These grave traumas are more common as a result of a fall in skateboarding, hang gliding, paragliding, rollerblading, diving in shallow waters or in automobile or motorcycle accidents.

All traumas of this nature should be handled responsibly.

The proper care in transporting an accident victim is designed to eliminate the risks of aggravating a possible fracture or spinal cord injury.

Whenever possible, call for an emergency rescue service and wait at the location. Never handle or move a victim unless you are well trained in first aid. Calm him down while waiting for help.

If you fall, whenever possible, try to cushion the impact with your hands or arms as in judo, jiu-jitsu and other martial arts.

Transporting an Accident Victim

Step-by-step

Unconscious victim

When the victim is suspected of having a head injury or a spinal cord injury in which there is a loss of consciousness and cardiorespiratory failure, CPR measures should be started immediately (see Chapter 30) while keeping the spine totally immobilized.

If the person merely lapses into unconsciousness but is still breathing normally, CPR measures probably aren't warranted.

Conscious Victim

Traumas that involve the spine can cause local pain, as well as partial or complete loss of sensation and muscular strength below the injured area.

When approaching the victim, speak with him or her and ask: What happened? What is your name?

At the beach

1. Speak with the victim, calm him down; reassure him that help is on the way. Be encouraging. This can do a lot for an injured person's sense of survival.

2. Cover the victim with a coat or blanket to keep him warm and prevent shock.

3. Find shade from the sun or protect the victim from rain while waiting for the ambulance.

4. Do not move the victim from the location unless there is imminent danger.

5. Call for help, allowing, if possible, for transport be conducted by trained personnel.

6. Use a clean cloth as a compress to stop the flow of blood from a serious wound. In the case of head wounds, however, experts suggest you use as light pressure as possible because the skull may be fractured.

7. If a head injury is suspected, while awaiting help, place your hands on both sides of the victim's head to avoid any movement of the neck until it is immobilized.

8. Do not remove a wetsuit.

9. If possible, place or improvise a cervical collar using a towel, newspaper or magazine folded around the neck. Then, fasten it with your "leg cord," Lycra, belt or similar item.

Do this without moving the victim's head, neck or backbone.

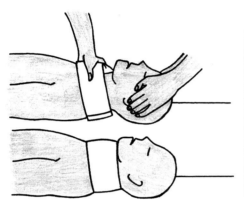
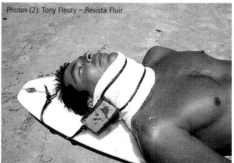

Photos (2): Tony Fleury – Revista Fluir

10. Then place the victim on a surfboard or other stiff board in a single movement.

11. Use the "leg cord," belt or straps from a car rack to secure the victim's abdomen and legs to the board.

In Automobile Accidents

Eighty percent of people injured in traffic accidents have head injuries. If a person has a head injury, you should assume he or she also has neck and back injuries.

Bandaging wounds, attempting to splint broken bones, or using CPR, especially if professional help is on the way, isn't generally recommended. If an injury is obviously life-threatening and waiting for help would endanger a life, then necessary action probably should be taken. See Chapter 30.

1. The first person to arrive should secure and hold the victim's head in place, the second should place a cervical collar or improvise one, as explained above.

2. Attach the collar with a handkerchief, belt or similar clean material.

3. With the victim inside the car, immobilize the backbone using a wooden board or something similar. The board should extend from the head to the buttocks. Then, attach it to the head and abdominal region.

In Motorcycle Accidents

1. In accidents in which the victim is using a helmet (hang gliding, skateboarding, motorcycling, etc.), the first person to arrive should secure and maintain the head in place, while the second cuts or loosens the helmet strap.

2. The person applying first aid should place their hands inside the helmet on both sides of the victim's face, immobilizing the neck and the head.

3. The second person should remove the helmet and then keep the neck immobilized until a support board is placed under the victim as described above.

4. Next, place a cervical collar and immobilize the victim on the board (as indicated above).

5. The victim is ready to be transported.

Techniques to Immobilize Upper and Lower Limbs

How to immobilize the upper or lower limbs if a fracture, contusion or sprain is suspected

It is essential to correctly immobilize the athlete for safe transport to the closest emergency medical service. The lack of immediate and proper immobilization, especially during transport, can aggravate the pain and possible injuries to bones, muscles, blood vessels and nerves.

General rules

1. Evaluate the situation.

    If the victim's life is at risk because of lack of a pulse or breathing, begin basic cardiopulmonary resuscitation (see Chapter 30).

    Fortunately, the majority of limb fractures are not immediately life-threatening, so remain calm.

2. If there is intense bleeding, staunch it with direct pressure by placing gauze or a clean cloth over the wound. If this does not work, apply a tourniquet over the injury with moderate pressure.

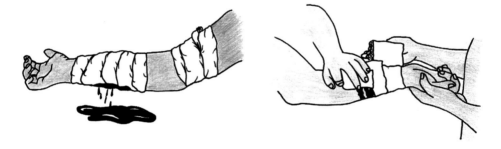

3. Do not move or manipulate the injured area.

4. Regardless of the area injured, immobilize the joint above and below the wound. For example, in case of an ankle injury, immobilize the foot and the knee. This reduces movement in the region and prevents further aggravation of the injury.

5. Special equipment is not needed to immobilize an injured or fractured limb. Improvise a splint with a wooden board, rolled-up newspaper or thick magazine, pillow, or even the victim's own body. Whenever possible, try to cushion the splint with a cotton cloth to avoid pressure or discomfort.

6. In the case of an exposed fracture (when the fractured bone passes through the skin or when a wound through the skin was the cause of the fracture), care for the wound by protecting it with gauze.

7. The bandages used in immobilizing the lower limb should be tightened appropriately without, however, blocking blood circulation. Leave the fingers or toes of the injured limb exposed to facilitate circulation.

If the extremity is becoming cold or blue, loosen the bandages because they are probably too tight and causing a dangerous loss of circulation.

How to Immobilize

Injuries and Wounds to the Thigh (Femur) and Leg

1. Improvise a well-cushioned splint and place it between the victim's legs.

2. Gently slide the non-injured leg close to the injured one.

3. Apply a bandage in a figure eight, immobilizing the feet and ankles.

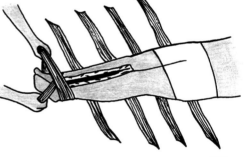

4. Delicately pass the bandages below the lower limbs and above the wound

5. Tie the bandages on the non-injured side and every 15 minutes check circulation in the limb (observe the skin color and temperature)

You are now ready to transport the athlete!

Knee, ankle and foot injuries

1. An ankle fracture can be confused with a sprain, especially if there is considerable deformity and swelling.

    It is not necessary to remove the shoe; if there are laces, open them.

    Do not place weight on the injured leg (the victim should not walk).

2. Support the injured region using a pillow, a board or even a folded blanket.

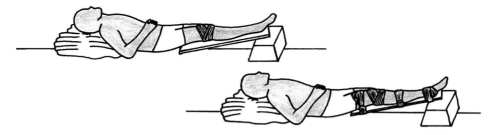

3. Immobilize the limb with bandages; initiate ice therapy.

Injuries of the Upper Limbs (Arms, Forearms and Hands)

1. Improvise a sling by wrapping a scarf or towel around the neck and under the injured arm. Keep the elbow comfortably bent and tie the sling around the neck.

2. As an alternative and with the elbow bent, place a board or piece of cardboard below the forearm and tie two scarves around the chest, immobilizing the arm and the forearm.

Fabio Gouveia

Photo: James Thisted

Chapter 32

Health and Ecological Risks in Surfboard Production

The various steps of surfboard production can create health risks for shapers and laminators.

There are two prominent dangers:

1. Inhalation of polyurethane foam dust from the shaping process can irritate the air passages, especially in people with sensitivities. Over time this can cause bronchitis and cancer.

2. Inhalation of the resin used to laminate the boards. The resin is a conglomerate of many chemical compounds. Styrene is the most dangerous of them and represents 50% of the total volume of the resin. It has a distinctive smell and causes the resin to remain strong after the addition of a catalyst. Nearly 10 % of the styrene evaporates during the hardening process, resulting in a large concentration in the air while the board is being laminated and while it is drying. It is also found in the air in high concentrations during the sanding and polishing. These are dangerous moments in board factories.

While safety regulations consider up to 50 parts per million (ppm) of styrene in the air tolerable, for exposure over an 8-hour work day, levels of 100 ppm are the maximum tolerated, however, with 15-minute intervals free of exposition for every hour of exposition. Most people can detect the odor of styrene at concentrations between 0.5-1 ppm.

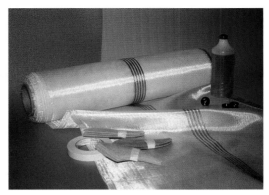

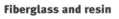
Fiberglass and resin

495

Some scientific studies demonstrate that the concentration of styrene in the air is much higher in the sanding area, reaching levels of 60-100 ppm. The levels tend to be acceptable in the laminating and glassing areas (4-30 ppm) and the polishing area (about 20 ppm).

Exposure to styrene is even higher if the laminator tends to keep his or her head close to the board while looking for uncovered areas, bubbles and locations that need correction.

Chronic exposure to styrene can cause liver illness and even lung cancer.

3. Inhalation of the catalyst and its direct contact with the skin and eyes. The most common catalyst contains methylethyl ketone peroxide, which is a powerful irritant of air passages, skin and eyes. It is a suspected carcinogen and related to some types of leukemia.

4. Inhalation of fiberglass particles and direct contact with the skin. Fiberglass can block skin pores causing a harsh, itchy rash. It is a known carcinogen.

These negative effects are caused by frequent and repeated exposure over many years.

Shaper Garry Linden

Basic Preventive Measures Related to the Health of Shapers, Laminators and Sanders in Surfboard Factories

1. Improve ventilation in workshops by maintaining good air circulation, with open windows and doors, and exhaust fans to remove air from the environment.

2. Keep the air temperature low, nearly chilly.

3. Use a respiratory mask with a carbon filter in the shaping and lamination room. This filter should be frequently changed (paper masks are not effective).

4. Use latex or rubber gloves and protective clothing when working with catalysts, resin and cloth.

5. Use protective glasses.

If one of the substances mentioned above accidently gets in contact with the eyes or skin, they should be removed by immediately rinsing the location with running water or saline solution. Do not rub the area.

If safety and health regulations and measures are carefully complied with by surfboard factories, the risks are almost eliminated.

New methods for ecologically safe shaping should be adopted.

We should soon see broad acceptance of a new kind of surfboard based on more sustainable materials. The Clark Foam company was one of the world's most famous board manufacturers, but acknowledgement by the founder that the company was using the carcinogenic toluene diisocyanate, or TDI, a highly regulated potential health hazard, was among the reasons for its closure.

A wide variety of new eco-friendly surfboard constructions have appeared on the market. Surfers, manufacturers and retailers are beginning to experience the pros and cons of the various material compositions.

SURFING & HEALTH

Fortunately, scientists and scholars are rethinking the chemistry of surfboards. Some see a promising future for epoxies extracted from sugar cane. Brazil and the United States produce millions of tons of sugar cane each year, making it a cheap, easy-to-obtain renewable resource. Lab studies indicate that sucrose-based epoxy is capable of remaining stable even when exposed to sunlight and saltwater and lacks bisphenal-A, a chemical found in petroleum-based epoxy linked to sterility in mice and humans.

In summary, a healthy and environmentally friendly surfboard will be made of plant-based foams and natural resins!

To guarantee the planet's environmental future, we have to act. Surfing Health is naturally linked to the environmental protection of our beaches, oceans and forests from pollution, contamination and destruction. Join your local environmental movement. Greenpeace, the Surfrider Foundation, and Friends of the Earth (just to name a few) are serious organizations on the frontline of the battle for a healthy planet. Do your part.

Muscular and Skeletal Problems Among Shapers, Laminators and Sanders

Fortunately computer-based shaping machines have been a great solution for muscular and skeletal problems among shapers.

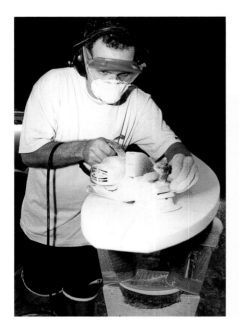

The repetitive movements made by a shaper using a plane, by a laminator in the glazing process and by sanders can cause injuries to tendons, muscles and joints in the shoulders, elbows, wrists and fingers, causing inflammations (tendonitis, synovitis, etc.) and in more chronic cases, degeneration and rupture of tissue.

Improper posture for long working hours creates tension and imbalance in the spinal column muscles, particularly in the neck and lumbar regions, which in addition to causing pain and an inability to work, aggravate problems in the upper arms and forearms.

Avelino Bastos, Tropical Brazil

The treatment for tendonitis and tendinosis (degeneration) is generally slow and should begin with the first symptoms. Rehabilitation includes rest, ice, anti-inflammatory medication, acupuncture, physiotherapy, as well as stretching exercises and muscle strengthening. Postural problems should be prevented with postural re-education and through muscular rebalancing exercises.

SURFING & HEALTH

Diego Cabral

Chapter 33

Body Boarders and Health Problems

As in surfing, studies have shown that more than 60% of body boarders complain of lower back pain and more than 30% suffer from shoulder pain.

Having originated in surfing, there are now millions of body boarders and hotly contested competitions throughout the world in male and female categories.

Using 1-meter long foam boards and fins, body boarders have explored the world's best tubes, enjoying fantastic drops, aerials, and potent, explosive and acrobatic maneuvers.

Severe Back Trauma

Fortunately, severe back injuries are not common but they can occur (see Chapter 7). Fractures and dislocations of the spinal column, in the cervical, dorsal and lumbar region are generally caused by a wipe out that causes a sharp clash of the spinal column on the water, in giant and heavy waves, or on shallow sandy, rock or coral bottoms.

These injuries can result in the permanent or temporary paralysis of the arms and or legs.

Thus, all injuries involving the vertebral column should be treated seriously. Correct transport of the victim can be a question of survival (see Chapter 31).

The most frequent health problems among body boarders involve the muscular-skeletal system and principally affect the spinal column, shoulders, knees and ankles. They are related to the specific demands that the sport imposes on an athlete's body.

The Spinal Column
Back Pain

Soraia Rocha

Causes

1. Paddling Position

The arched back position (hyperextension of the entire spinal column from the neck to the lumbar region) needed during hours of paddling and kicking is part of the biomechanics used by the athlete to gain speed, modify his or her center of gravity and reduce friction with the water.

Essential for maneuvers, this posture causes shortening and tension of the entire musculature of the back, creating muscle imbalance (see Chapter 7).

2. Maneuvers

The explosive and repeated movements cause rotation, compression and impact of the spinal column during such maneuvers as bottom turns, airs, 360-degree rolls, back flips and others that put great stress on the spinal column, including the nerves, muscles, ligaments, vertebral discs, joints, joint capsules and bones. In addition, they aggravate the shortening and tension of the lower back muscles.

Consequences

This stress initially generates progressive imbalance of the lower back muscles, which stimulates lordosis. The lumbar, gluteus and rear thigh muscles, become tense and shortened, while the abdominal muscles, if they are not well developed, become even weaker and overly stretched.

This typical muscular imbalance must be corrected through compensatory exercises, like postural re-education, and Pilates core training exercises, in order to prevent injuries, such as degeneration and herniation of the intervertebral disc, cartilage degeneration and others.

For greater details, see Chapter 6 and Chapter 7.

This situation is frequently aggravated among those athletes who do not stretch and among adolescents who have had rapid bone growth.

Mike Stuart – Pipeline

Shoulders

The injuries are due to the numerous and repeated impacts that shoulders suffer during such maneuvers as aerials and rolls.

Supported on the board, the shoulders are abruptly forced up and back upon impact with the water.

Tendonitis and injuries to the articular capsule are, common and in more serious cases, cartilage damage is found (see Chapter 8).

Ankles and Feet

Injuries to these areas are mostly related to the use of fins (often the wrong size) and kicking. There are frequent blisters, joint pain and tendonitis (see Chapter 11).

SURFING & HEALTH

Surfing Amazon pororoca Sergio Laus

Chapter 34

Surfing the Pororoca in the Brazilian Amazon

(from the Tupi word *Poro'roka, Poro'rog*, rumble)

By Serginho Laus/Surfing in the Jungle – NGO Maré Amazônia (Amazon Tide)

The word "pororoca" comes from the term "poroc poroc," meaning "destroyer, large rumble" in the indigenous dialect of the lower Amazon region. This wave phenomenon occurs at the change in phases of the moon, principally at the full and new moon close to the equinoxes. The shock of the river waters and the sea is so strong that it can down trees and change the course of the river. At times, a deafening roar is heard up to an hour ahead of the waves, which can reach up to 5 meters with a speed of 40 km/h. The pororoca occurs in Amapá, Pará and Maranhão, in northern Brazil, along the Amazon coast. An identical phenomenon is found in many rivers of the world: in France (Mascaret), England (the Severn River), Alaska (the Turnagain River) and in China, on the Quintang River (the Chinese call it the Black Dragon).

Facts About the Pororoca

Location: Amapá, Pará and Maranhão

Height: 0.5-5 meters

Speed: 25-40 km per hour

World record for the longest wave surfed: 10.1 km surfed on the Araguari River by the Brazilian Serginho Laus

Considered the Hawaii of freshwater tidal waves.

Because of its location in the Amazon forest, the pororoca presents such risks as trees in the middle of the river, trunks, plants, snakes, alligators, pumas, piranhas, candirus (tiny, bloodsucking catfish), other wild animals and the very current of the river. The strength of the waters is capable of sinking ships and forming perfect waves for the practice of surf or other board sports. An expedition on the world's greatest river phenomenon requires lots of planning, risk management and accompaniment by professionals experienced with the mysterious phenomenon of the tides.

The preparation for expeditions begins during the equinox period when the day is the same length as the night and the living tides gain magnitude and intensity. The pororoca rises for five days in each full and new moon. In Brazil, the best waves are found on the Mearim River, in Maranhão state and on the Araguari River in Amapá state. At these two locations, the adrenaline of surfers from around the world flows from February to May and in September and October.

Surfboards should be shaped especially for freshwater surfing. The water density is lower than in the ocean so the boards should be thicker and wider in the middle and at the nose and tail. Four keels are the most efficient and fastest models for surfing the different wave formations. Because of the flow and reflux of the tides, the reading of the wave is different and navigation much more dangerous. For this reason, special equipment is used for expeditions. Flex-boats with 25-40 hp motors and jet skis provide more security and agility in rescues of surfers. When the wave ends, the force of the tide continues following the riverbed and, at certain points, it is necessary to quickly grab the surfer who may be swept away by the current. A dynamic rescue allows a surfer to get back to the wave and surf longer.

The biggest difference of a tidal wave is its duration. On the ocean, one normally surfs for a few seconds and on rare occasions up to a minute. On a pororoca, the wave can last for more than two hours and each wave session can vary from three, five, 20, 30, 40 or more minutes without stopping! But this long period must be used to the maximum because the tidal wave surges only once a day, at high tide.

In 10 years of surfing the Brazilian pororoca, many stories of adventure and accidents have been told. The mythic Amazon wave has sunk large and small boats and crews from Brazil and abroad, some have also had photo and video equipment swallowed by the tides. The strength of the waters has even caused the death of ill-advised river dwellers navigating through the region. You never know what's coming and for this reason the adrenaline is always pulsing when you are in a high-risk area, where the pororoca can sweep everything away.

Motorboats and jet skis are the means of transportation and rescue! For this reason they must always be in perfect working order and well tuned. Most accidents occur due to improper equipment for the action. The Surfando na Selva staff is specialized in the process and offers expeditions that combine extreme adventure with all safety precautions.

Safety is a key word in relation to the pororoca. Some locations are isolated in the jungle, without electricity, communication or support facilities. The teams must be well prepared with fresh water, food and medication. Mosquitoes proliferate in the tropical Amazon bringing with them malaria, yellow fever and dengue. At the points where the pororoca appear, cases of these diseases have not been reported, but it is important to take preventive measures. The vaccine against yellow fever must be taken at least 10 days before traveling. A good repellent and long sleeves and pants help protect when the mosquitoes take action at day break and nightfall.

The food has a special taste in northern Brazil. Cilantro is much used in local cooking of the region's fine fish: the tucunaré, pirarucu and filhote. Wild animals rarely enter the menu. The consumption of alligators, capybaras and coatis is restricted to the subsistence diet of river dwellers, who live in harmony with nature using traditional principles of sustainable development.

Healthcare conditions are limited in the region of the pororoca. Visits by government doctors are sporadic and in case of emergency, the most isolated river dwellers need to travel along the river to seek medical help in cities with proper infrastructure. Most local adults only have a fourth grade education and for this reason they have difficulty reading, writing and even communicating verbally in Portuguese. This increases the lack of information about many issues including contraception. Birth control is lacking in much of the Amazon and the families grow quickly along the rivers. But the locals have a very healthy and peaceful life. The principal enemy of this population is the sun, which punishes them in the summer, but in the winter, the rain dominates the jungle for nearly six months.

Surfing has brought the Amazon information, which has contributed to improving the quality of life of the local people, as well as environmental awareness, reinforcing the importance of environmental protection. Surfers are true protectors of nature because they depend completely on a pure and harmonious environment for the healthy practice of the sport. The pororoca, the world's longest wave, is a reality, and no longer an unreachable phenomenon of nature that is understood and appreciated only by scientists.

Bibliographic reference: Livro Surfando na Selva – Pororoca (Surfing in the Jungle) Author: Serginho Laus. Editora: Ediouro. Site **www.surfandonaselva.com.br**

Chapter 35

Tao – The Spirit of Surfing

There is nothing that a beautiful day of surfing can't cure!

T he true spirit of surf transforms, nourishes and challenges. It is unity and totality, self-expression and exceeding oneself. It is explosion, light, renovation, creativity and love of oneself, others and nature.

The Tao of surfing explores the deep relationship between the practice of surfing with the natural, colorful and fascinating universe of waves, beaches and oceans.

Discovering the Tao of surfing involves using your intuition and sensibility to develop your mind, body and spirit in harmony with nature and thus feel connected to the universe.

The egotistical side of the surfer opens doors to the well-known feeling, this wave is mine. Violent disputes over waves usually ignore the rule of priority, generating disharmony, conflicts, accentuating regional rivalries, insensitivity, arrogance, a lack of respect, destructive anger and feelings of hostility.

Discovering the Tao of surfing helps to overcome inner obstacles, opening the door to inner peace.

Removing Obstacles

The equilibrium of surf is found in the contemplation of the wave that crosses thousands of miles of ocean and rises between the rays of sun, in harmony with the heartbeat and deep rhythmic breathing.

Tao is the Eternal, the middle path, the tube. It is the force of nature that creates waves in spirals and appears in determination, willpower, perseverance, dedication, patience and self-knowledge.

Awakening Internal Waves

Surfing stimulates the awakening to the enchantment of life, to oneself and to one's peers. It helps you discover the extraordinary force that exists within you, allowing you to feel stronger and more capable, facilitating positive transformations. Good dormant qualities flourish and inspire realizations.

Surfing is also related to confidence, faith and success. The physical challenge of surfing strengthens the mind, encouraging the visualization of a positive mental attitude.

Our society creates masks for the individual, highlighting fear, sin and the insignificance of life. It depersonalizes and destroys our sensibilities and hearts, hiding the perfection of life.

By discovering the Tao of surf, it is possible to recover the essence of divine life, opening doors to the strength that each one carries within.

Dominating Internal Waves

We are what we think.
We have to rediscover that we are strong and that in reality the only limits are those we create and instill in our mind.

The body and mind can help us surpass these boundaries. Physical training leads to mental training. You can create your ideal of success, visualizing yourself as a happy winner.

Surfing helps you develop your body and take on a new stature. This generates self-esteem and awareness of your ability to achieve and expand the possibility for achievement. Feeling stronger creates new possibilities.

Each one of us is a star with our own unique light. By integrating with a higher force that is revealed in us, it is possible to glow constantly brighter and to transmit this light to those who need it.

By dominating the internal waves, it is possible to visualize and create a virtual environment, a private, secret place that is yours, in which you can place all of the natural splendor and liberty of being completely yourself.

The Tao of surf is to reflect on the deep mechanisms of life and to realize their true meaning.

Life was offered to us in harmony with the universe. You are a unique experience that will never be repeated. Everyone has an extraordinary potential to persevere, be optimistic and to manifest the intensity of a winner. This force is the root of your existence. Search with all your energy for this true and uncontestable light of God within you.

Life is a glorious passage and a great opportunity. Aim far and high, dignify your right to live fully and completely free.

Steer your life toward truth and happiness. Use your mind at work and guide yourself with enlightened and positive thoughts. God created you to be healthy, optimistic and happy.

Feel life! Feel the surf!

Feel the present moment in your entire body and become aware of it through the fantastic experience of surfing!

Commemorate the immense gifts of health, your family and your friends.

See happiness, and you will find it within reach.

Each moment is sacred. Living each moment fully is the only way to live intensely. The past is gone and is only a reference. The future has not arrived and is unknown. If we are obsessed with it, we are not able to experience and appreciate what we have – the present.

Live and surf each moment that is offered you.

Plunge intensely into each moment, because it is the only concrete possibility that life offers.

The objective is personal enrichment. The greatest wealth is growth, self-knowledge. You reach the spirit through the body. Curiously, it is the mental side of the athlete that offers personal enrichment.

By discovering the Tao of surfing, each day will be an adventure, a challenge worth confronting.

Like the masters of medicine, qigong and yoga, my work is also inspired by the love that I see in each person that comes to me and the perception of the enormous potential for health and realization that he or she carries.

Tao is the spirit of surf.

The interior silence of the wave guides us when we surf and when we breathe. When we discover it, we discover harmony, enlightenment and health.

The true spirit of surf transforms, nourishes and challenges. It is unity and totality, self-expression and exceeding oneself. It is explosion, light, renovation, creativity and love of oneself, others and nature.

513

SURFING & HEALTH

Brothers Ho in Pipeline

Appendix 1

Surf Trip First Aid Kit

Every surfer must have a basic first aid kit, to be able to properly care for and treat his or her injuries and most frequent problems. Consider taking a first aid class, but simply having the following things can help you staunch bleeding, prevent infection and assist in decontamination. Knowing how to treat minor injuries can make a difference in an emergency.

Below we present a basic list of medicine and items. It includes some commercial names that may vary from country to country.

Never use medicine that has expired. Never use prescription medication without your doctor's instructions.

Things you should have

- Two pairs of Latex, or other sterile, gloves (if you are allergic to Latex).

- Sterilized bandages to stop bleeding.

- Cleansing agent/soap and antibiotic towelettes for disinfection.

- Antibiotic ointment to prevent infection.

- Burn ointment to prevent infection.

- Adhesive bandages in a variety of sizes.

- Eye wash (saline) solution to flush the eyes or as general decontaminant.

- A thermometer

- Prescription medications you take regularly such as insulin, heart medicine and asthma inhalers. You should periodically rotate medicines to account for expiration dates.

- Prescribed medical supplies such as glucose and blood pressure monitoring equipment.

The Kit

To clean a wound

- Toothbrush
- Saline solution
- Soap
- Hydrogen peroxide – 10 small flasks
- Povidone-Iodine
- Antibiotic ointment packets (approximately 1 gram each)
- Hydrocortisone ointment packets (approximately 1 gram each)

For dressing open wounds

- Antiseptic wipe packets
- Gauze compresses: sterile gauze pads (3 x 3 inches)/sterile gauze pads (4 x 4 inches)
- Absorbent compress dressings (5 x 9 inches)
- Adhesive cloth tape (10 yards x 1 inch)
- Impermeable adhesive tape
- Adhesive bandages (assorted sizes)
- Bandages – 1 bandage roll (3 inches wide)/1 bandage roll (4 inches wide)
- 2 triangular bandages
- Instant cold compress

For pain relief

1. Analgesics, such as aspirin, paracetamol, "Tylenol" or acetaminophen, in pills or drops.

2. Oral decongestants for sinusitis and rhinitis. Generic medication usually contains pseudoephedrine or similar medication.

3. Propolis spray for the throat.

4. Antispasmatic for intestinal colic. The generic medication is hyoscine.

5. Antacid for heartburn and digestive discomfort. The generic medication contains aluminum hydroxide. Commercial name: "Mylanta"; One tablespoon every six hours as needed.

6. Anti-inflammatory medication for traumatic pain, and sprains and strains of muscles and tendons. The generic medication contains sodium diclophenac. (One 75 mg capsule every 8 hours if necessary. Homeopathic option: Arnica C30.)

7. Gel bag to apply heat or cold.

8. Anti-inflammatory cream. Commercial name: Tiger Balm, Mineral Ice or Cataflam Gel. Massage the region in case of muscular and tendon pain.

9. Antifebriles in case of fever. The generic medication is paracetamol/ acetaminophen. Commercial name: Tylenol.

10. Calendula cream to relieve mosquito bites.

Other medication

1. Eye drops of boric acid at 3% for rinsing eyes.

2. Otological drops (for the ears). They are basically a mix of an anti-inflammatory, anti-micotic, antibiotic and an anesthetic.

3. Aloe vera gel – to relieve sunburn and other skin burns.

4. Creams based on vitamin A and zinc for skin irritations and chafing.

5. Antifungal creams for skin mycoses of the feet, groin, etc. The generic medication contains the active ingredients cetoconazol, tinadazol, etc.

6. Medication for nausea, air sickness or vomiting. Commercial name: Dramamine B6 (Warning: this medication causes sleepiness). Natural option: ginger. Homeopathic Option: Nox vomica C30.

7. Rehydration solution in case of diarrhea. Prepared with one tablespoon of sugar, one teaspoon of salt and a liter of water boiled for 10 minutes and then cooled. Drink the water after each evacuation.

8.   Anti-diarrhetic. Only to be used in desperation because diarrhea is a mechanism to defend and cleanse the body. The generic medication contains lopramide. Natural option: activated charcoal.

9.   Anti-allergic medication, pills or creams. Homeopathic option: Rhus Tox C30, Urtica dioica C30, Apis mellifica C30.

10.   Antibiotics for infections – consult your doctor.

11.   Specific medication and pump to dilate the bronchial passages for surfers with asthma.

12.   Mosquito repellent, especially in areas where malaria and dengue are common. Natural option: essence of citronella.

13.   Medication to strengthen the immune system: Vitamin C, 1 gram per day; garlic oil capsule (odorless), 300 mg once a day; Equinacea angustifolia capsules with dry extract. One 200 mg capsule 2 times a day.

14.   Sunblock with maximum protection (SPF 30).

Equipment

Scissors, tweezers, thermometer (non-glass/non-mercury), razor blade, lighter, flashlight, mirror, cotton/gauze, bandages, soap, rubber gloves and a suture kit if you have proper training.

Appendix 2

Jet Lag and Surfing

J et lag refers to the physical and mental effects of traveling quickly across a number of time zones. It has been associated with gastrointestinal problems, insomnia, depression and constipation. It can negatively affect an athlete's performance, altering his or her competitive peak. Decreased competiveness is often found after crossing 2 or 3 times zones.

Factors that Affect Jet Lag

The response is different from person to person. Some factors that determine the intensity of the symptoms of jet lag include:

1. The greater the number of time zones crossed, the more severe the disturbance to the rhythm of the body.

2. It seems to be easier to recover from trips to the west than trips to the east. Traveling from north to south does not cause jet lag, since time zones are rarely crossed.

3. Psychological factors: extroverted people tend to experience fewer problems than introverted people. Anxiety aggravates the symptoms. People in good physical condition react better than those who are out of shape.

The most effective cure for jet lag is time. The body appears to recover at a rate of 1 time zone per day. For example: if you cross three time zones, the best way to avoid problems is to travel three days before the competition.

Another strategy is to gradually pre-adjust the body clock to the time zone at your destination by changing your routine two hours per day for nearly four days. This means that your meals and bedtime should be altered until you are synchronized with the time at your destination. This strategy causes a gradual change in the circadian cycle, resulting in a smaller disturbance in your rhythm, minimizing the effects of jet lag. This can be very difficult to do in practice, since your routine may become very different than that of your family and friends.

Other Suggestions

Choose a flight that arrives at your destination closest to bedtime at the destination.

Before the Flight

On the day of departure, eat lightly, avoiding meats and fatty foods.

Increase the quantity of carbohydrates in the meals before traveling (legumes, fruits, vegetables, cereals and breads).

During the Flight

Immediately after boarding, set your clocks to the time at the place of arrival.

Drink large quantities of water to avoid dehydration, since the relative humidity of the air is extremely low inside airplanes, which increases susceptibility to dehydration. Fruit juices and water are ideal. Avoid coffee, sugar, colas and alcohol.

Small walks in flight help reduce fatigue.

Upon Arrival

Immediately after arrival, organize your time of training, eating and sleeping according to the local time.

Avoid naps until you are totally adjusted to the new time zone, because they can delay the adjustment of your biological clock. Keep active and socialize. Studies show that athletes who stay in their hotel rooms take longer to adjust to the new time zone.

It is unlikely that a competitive surfer will have a great performance soon after arrival. For this reason, do not schedule heavy training or competition for the first day or so after arrival.

Pay attention to nutrition and maintain healthy eating habits.

Appendix 3

Formulation of Vitamins and Minerals for Joint Protection

This formula is designed to provide the nutrients needed for recovery of joint tissue. You can order it from your pharmacy. It can be prepared in capsules or in a powder for consumption in a milkshake.

Glucosamine Sulphate	1500 mg
Condroitin Sulphate	500mg
Magnesium (Chelate)	150 mg
Manganese (Chelate)	3mg
Selenium (Chelate)	100mcg
Zinc (Chelate)	15 mg
Borium (Chelate)	3 mg
Silicon (Chelate)	5 mg
Copper (Chelate)	0.5 mg
Vitamin C (Coated)	300 mg
Vitamin E	100UI
Vitamin D 3	1000UI
Methyl Sulphonyl Methane	1000 mg

A daily dose is about 7 to 8 capsules.
Take 1/2 dose twice a day.

Probiotics

Probiotics are live microbial food supplements that have beneficial health effects, particularly for intestinal microbial balance. The two principal commercially used species are lactobacillus acidophilis and bifidobacterium bifidum.

Probiotics have been used to reinforce the immune systems in fatigued athletes.

Take a probiotic formula composed of

Lactobacillus Acidophilus	1 billion cells
Lactobacillus Bifidum	1 billion cells
Lactobacillous Bulgaricus	1 billion cells
Lactobacillus Casei	1 billion cells
Lactobacillus Rhamnosus	1 billion cells
Lactobacillus Streptococcus faecium	1 billion cells
Frutooligo Saccaride	300 mg

Take 1 capsule per day without food!

Digestive Enzymes

Sports injuries are often treated with protease and bromelain enzymes to reduce inflammation and speed healing.

Enzyme Formula

Protease	60 mg
Alpha-amylase	40 mg
Papain	50 mg
Bromelain	100 mg

Take 1 capsule after lunch and dinner.

Whey Protein

Protein hydrolysate supplements accelerate repair of damaged connective tissue.

Take 25 g per day mainly after training.

Phytotherapy with Anti-Inflammatory and Analgesic Properties

They can be used in capsules or as creams.

1. Harpagophytum procumbens- also called Devil's Claw

2. Uncaria tomentosa- also called Cat's Claw

3. Boswelia serrata

Anti-Inflammatory Ointment

• Tiger balm

Photo & Illustration Credits

Illustrations:	Miguel Silveira
Translation from the Portuguese:	Jeffrey Hoff

Inside Photos:

Roberto Price	Sebastian Rojas
Levy Paiva	Agobar Junior
André Larrêa	James Thisted
Aleko Stergiou	Daniel Ernst
Frank Quirate	Ricardo Werneck
Steve Ryan	Tony Fleury
Flavio Vidigal	Michele Cruz

& private archives of the author

Cover Design:	Sabine Groten
Cover Photo:	Agobar Junior @MiliN</fotolia.com;

Bibliography

Allen RJ, Eiseman B, Strackly CJ, Orloff B J. Surfing Injuries at Waikiki. *JAMA*, 1977; 237: 668-670.

Auerback PS. Hazardous marine animals. *Emerg Med Clin North Am.* 1984; 2: 531-44.

Bailey P. Surfer's rib: isolated first rib fracture secondary to indirect trauma. *Emerg Med*; 1985, 14: 246-349, 1985.

Bar-Or. *The Encyclopaedia of Sports Medicine.* The Child and Adolescent Athlete. International Olympic Commitee. London, 1996.

Barry SW, Kleinig B J, Brophy,T. Surfing injuries. *Aust J Sports Med* 14: 49-51, 1982.

Bitencourt V, Amorim S, Vigne JA, Navarro P. Surfe/Esportes radicais. In: Da Costa L. *Atlas do Esporte no Brasil.* Rio de Janeiro: Shape, 2005; 411-6.

Bennett, R., *The Surfer's Mind: The Complete, Practical Guide to Surf Psychology,* 2nd ed., 2007.

Blankenhip JR. Board Surfing. *The encyclopaedia of Sports Science and Medicine.* Mcmillian Co. New York, 1971.

Burdick C.O. Surfer's Knots (Letter to the Editor). 1981, *JAMA*; 245: 823.

Butterfield G. Amino acids and high protein diets. *Perspectives in exercises science and sports medicine.* Cooper Publishing, 2001.

Chang L A, Mcdanal C E. Boardsurfing and Bodysurfing Injuries Requiring Hospitalization in Honolulu. *Hawaii Med* 1980, 39: 117.

Cohen M, Abdalla R J. Lesões nos esportes. Diagnóstico, prevenção e tratamento. *Revinter.* Rio de Janeiro, 2003.

Cousteau J. *The Ocean World.* Harry N. Abrams. New York, 1985.

Danucalov M A D; Lauro F A A, Andrade M S, Pacheco F B M, Piçarro I C, Silva A C. Peak Oxygen Uptake in Brazilian Professional Surfers. *Med Sci Sports Exerc,* 2001; 33 (5).

Dirix A, Knuttgen H G, Tittel, K. Causes of Injuries. *The Olympic Book of Sports Medicine.* Blackwell, 1988.

Erickson J G, Gemmingen GR. Surfer's nodules and other complications of surfboarding. *JAMA,* 1967, 201: 134-136.

Finney B, Houston J DE. Surfing: *A History of Ancient Hawaii Sport.* Pomegranate Artbooks. San Francisco, 1995.

Fleck S J, Kraemer W J. *Designing resistance training programs.* Champaign, IL: Human Kinetics, 1997.

Frediani P. *Surf Flex*. Hatherleigh Press. New York. 2001.

Ferreira P H, Ferreira M L, Hodges P W. Changes in recruitment of abdominal muscles in people with low back pain: Ultrasound measurement of muscle activity. *Spine*. 2004, 29: 2560-2566.

George S. *Surfing*. Bison Books. London, 1992.

Goldberg B. Sports and Exercise for children with chronic heath condition. *Human Kinetics*, 1995.

Hall G, Benger RS. Missed diagnosis of an intraorbital foreign body of surfboard origin. *Ophthal Plast Reconstr Surg*. 2004; 20 (3): 250-2.

Hartung GH, Goebert D A, Taniguchi R M, Okamoto G A. Epidemiology of ocean sports-related injuries in Hawaii: "Akalehele O Ke Kai". *Hawaii Med J*, 1990, 49: 52-56.

Hemmings F. *Surfing,Hawaii's gift to the world of sports*. Osaka, Japan: Zokeisha, 1977.

Hides J A, Richardson C A, Jull G A. Long term effects of specific stabilizing exercises for first episode low back pain. *Spine*. 2001, 26, 243-248.

Hurst W, Bailey M, Hurst B. Prevalence of external auditory canal exostoses in Australian surfboard riders. J *Laryngol Otol*. 2004; 118 (5): 348-51.

Institute of Medicine, Food and Nutritional Board. Directory Reference Intakes (DRIs) for individuals macronutrients. National Academy Press, 2001.

Kenedy M, Vanderfield G, Huntley R. Surfcraft Injuries. *Aust J Sports Med;* 1975, 3: 53-54.

Kin JW, McDonald HR, Rubsamen PE, Luttrull JK, Drouilhet JH, Frambach DA, et al. Surfing-related ocular injuries. *Retina*. 1998; 18(5): 424-9.

Kliber W B, Hering S A, *Press J M. Functional Rehabilitation of Sports Skeletal-Muscle Injuries.* Aspen Publication, 1998.

Koury J M. Aquatic Therapy Programming: Guidelines for Orthopaedic Rehabilitation. *Human Kinetics*. Philadelphia, 1996.

Kroon DF, Lawson ML, Derkay CS, Hoffmann K, McCook J. Surfer's ear: external auditory exostoses are more prevalent in cold water surfers. *Otolaryngol Head Neck Surg*. 2002; 126: 499-504.

Lawless L, Porter W, Pountney R, Simpson M. Surfboard-related ocular injuries. *Aust N Z J Ophtalmol*. 1986; 14: 55-7.

Leslie S. Surfer's Back. *Surfers Medicine*. Spring/Summer, 1998.

Lowdon BJ. Surfing trough the aging process. *Surfing Medicine*. Winter/Spring, 1996.

Lowdon BJ, Bedi J F, Howarth S M. Specificity of aerobic fitness testing of surfers. *Aust J Science and Med*, 1989, 21(4): 7-10.

Lowdon BJ, Pateman NA. Physiological parameters of International surfers. *Aust J Sports Med.* 1980, 12 (2).

Lowdon BJ, Pateman NA, Pitman AJ. Surfboard-riding injuries. *Med J Aust.* 1983; 2 (12): 613-6.

Lowdon BJ, Pateman NA, Pitman AJ, Kenneth R. Injuries to international surfboard riders. *J Sports Med.* 1987; 27: 57-63.

Lowdon BJ, Lowdon M. Competitive Surfing, a Dedicated Approach. *Movement Publications,* Torquay, Victoria. 1988.

Mcatee R E. Facilitated Stretching: PNF Stretching Made Easy. *Human Kinetics,* 1993.

Meir RA, Lowdon BJ, Davie A J. Estimated Energy Expenditure During Recreational Surfing. *Aust J Science Med in Sport.* 1991, 23 (4): 70-74.

McGoldrick J, Marx JA. Marine envenomations. Part 2: Invertebrates. *J Emerg Med.* 1992; 10 (1): 71-7.

Nathanson A, Haynes P, Galanis D. Surfing injuries. *Am J Emerg Med.* 2002; 20: 155-60

Neer CS. Cuff tears, biceps lesions and impairment. Shoulder Reconstruction. 1990, W.B. Saunder Company.

Noll Greg, Gabbard A. Da Bul. *Live over the edge.* North Atlantic Books. California, 1989.

Paskowitz D. *Surfing and Health.* California. USA.

Petersen WL. Keeping and eye out for pterygium. *Surfer,* 26 (12) 22-23, 1985.

Rau G, Lowdon BJ. Effects of Surfing program on Primary School Asthmatics. *The Asthmatics National Journal.* 1985. 109, 67-69.

Renneker M. Skin Cancer. *Med J Aust.* 1987, 143, 433-434.

Renneker M. Surfing: The sport and the lifestyle. *Phys Sports med.* 1987. 15 (12): 96-105.

Renneker M, Starr K, Booth G. *Sick Surfers, Ask the Surf Docs and Dr. Geoff.* Palo Alto, California. 1998.

Renstron P A F H. *Clinical Practice of Sports Injury Prevention and Care.* International Olympic Committee. Balckwell Scientific Publications. Victoria, Australia. 1994.

Sapsford R R, Hodges P W. Contraction of the pelvic floor muscles during abdominal maneuvers. *Archives of Physical Medicine and Rehabilitation.* 2001, 82: 1081-1088.

Saunders S, Schache A, Rath D, Hodges PW. Changes in three dimensional trunk kinematics and muscle activity with aped and mode of locomotion. *Biomechanics*. 2005. 20 (8): 784-793.

Seftel D M. Ear hyperostosis. Surfer's Ear. *Arch Otolaryngol*, 1997. 103, 58-60.

Southdern L. *Surf's up: the girls guide to surfing*. 2005. Ballantine Books. USA.

Sunshine S. Surfing injuries. *Curr Sports Med Rep*. 2003; 2 (3): 136-41.

Steinman J, Vasconcelos EH, Ramos RM, Botelho JL, Nahas MV. Epidemiology of surfing injuries in Brazil. Rev Bras Med Esporte. 2000; 6 (1): 9-15. *Medicine & Science in Sports & Exercise*. 1998. 30 (5).

StoneD A. *Sports Injuries Mechanisms, Prevention and Treatment*. Baltimore. Willianms & Wilkins, 1994.

Surfrider Foundation. *Making Waves. Sewage in the Ocean*. June-July 1996.

Steinman J. *Surf e Saúde*. Tao Pilates Instituto de Medicina Esportiva. 2003

Taylor DM, Bennedett D, Carter M, Garewal D, Finch CF. Acute injury and chronic disability resulting from surfboard riding. *J Sci Med Sport*. 2004; 7 (4): 429-37.

Taylor DM, Bennedett D, Carter M, Garewal D, Finch CF. Perceptions of surfboard riders regarding the need for protective headgear. *Wilderness Environ Med*. 2005; 16 (2): 75-80.

Tilburg V C. Surfing Mountain Waves: Snowboarding Medicine. *Surfing Medicine*. Winter/Spring 1996.

Thompson TP, Pearce J, et al. Surfer's myelopathy. *Spine* 2004; 29 (16) E353-E356.

Young N. *Surfing Fundamentals*. Palm Beach Press. New South Wales, 1993.

Young N. *History of Surfing*. New South Wales. 1993.

Zoltan TB, Taylor KS, Achar SA. Health issues for surfers. *Am Fam Physician*. 2005; 71 (12): 2313-7.

Index

Blue ring octopus 263
Body composition 292, 306
Body fat 38, 240
Body temperature 240, 292
Bodyboard 501
Boils 233
Bone growth .206
Bosu pilates .359
    Dyna disc .364
    Facing down 360
    Facing up exercises 359
    Lunge 362
    On the side 360,361
    Side lunge 362
Bottom turn .385,
Breathing exercises 271
Broncho-dilators 271
Bronchospasm 265
Bruise 54
Bunion 172

Caffeine 431
Cancer
    Testicle 277-278
Carbohydrates 396
    Carbon dioxide elimination 387
    Complex 397
    Simple 397
    Supplementation 423, 424
Cardiopulmory resuscitation 390, 473
Cardiovascular endurance 319
Cartilage injury 111,172
Central nervous system 387
Cervical
    Chronic pain 91
    Injury 91
    Spine 89
Check-ups 27
Children 35, 400
Chiropratic maneuvers 96,

Chloroquine 255
Cholera 223
Cholesterol 23
Chrondromalacia patellae 169
Chronic back pain 106
Chronic degenerative disease 23
Closed kinetic chain exercise 180, 182
Coach 313
Cocaine 450
Coenzyme Q -10 435
Cold 230
Cold water 239
    Body adaptation 239
Common cold 227
Common infection disease 217
Competition diary 314
Competitive pressure 458
Concentration 459
Concentric contraction 331
Concussion 83
Contact lenses 210
Contrology 329
Coordination .331
Core training 74, 329
    Breathing .332
    Muscle control 93, 331
    On the ball 334
    Stability 332
Corticosteroids 114
CPR 473
Cramps 243
Creatine 428
Cut and lacerations 54, 77
Cut back 93, 107, 162

Decongestants 444
Deep walk – deep run 197
Dehydration .409
Dengue 222
Dental injuries 200

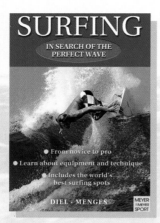